from Assassins *to* West Side Story

from Assassins to West Side Story

The Director's Guide to Musical Theatre

Scott Miller

HEINEMANN ■ Portsmouth, NH

Heinemann
A division of Reed Elsevier Inc.
361 Hanover Street
Portsmouth, NH 03801-3912

Offices and agents throughout the world

Library of Congress Cataloging-in-Publication Data

Miller, Scott, 1964–
From Assassins to West Side Story : the director's guide to
musical theatre / Scott Miller.
    p.   cm.
  ISBN 0-435-08699-5
  1. Musicals—Production and direction.   2. Musicals—History and
criticism.   I. Title.
MT955.M595   1996
792.6 '0233—dc20

                96-3248
                CIP
                MN

Editor: Lisa A. Barnett
Production: Vicki Kasabian
Book design: Jenny Jensen Greenleaf
Cover design: Tracy Collins
Author photo: Conrad Zobel
Manufacturing: Louise Richardson

Printed in the United States of America on acid-free paper

7 8 9 10 -DAP- 04 03

This book is dedicated to
Joan Zobel and Don Miller, my parents, who ignited my love for musicals;
Judy Rethwisch, my high school drama teacher, who cultivated that love;
and Anne Dhu Shapiro and Peter Lieberson at Harvard,
who taught me how to really understand musicals.

Contents

Acknowledgments

My deep thanks to my editor, Lisa A. Barnett, for being interested in this project and for being patient with me on my virgin expedition into writing a book; to Steve Spiegel at Music Theatre International and Jim Merillat at Samuel French, Inc., for their great generosity and help; and to Laura Beard Aeling, Tracy Collins, Paul Schankman, Leo and Johanna Schloss, Todd O'Bryan, Rick and Liz Miller, and many good friends on America Online, for reading my chapters and asking lots of interesting questions. Also, many thanks to all the other authors whose books about musical theatre I've read and learned from over the last twenty years—they helped me begin a journey of discovery that is only now reaching its stride.

verture

This book is not intended to tell you how to direct a musical. It's a collection of explorations, a guide into the heart of some of the most interesting works of the musical theatre. It's my hope that after reading about these sixteen musicals, it will be easier for you to analyze other shows in the same way. I had two professors in college with whom I did independent studies in musical theatre; the greatest thing they taught me was not what was happening in a particular score, but how to find the wonderful moments in other shows.

Many directors feel that it's cheating to watch the movie or video versions of a show they're about to direct, or to talk to someone who's already directed the show. I don't understand that. Are any of us so brilliant that we can't learn from those who've gone before us? And does seeing or reading about someone else's approach brainwash us, making it impossible to fashion our own vision? Much of the material in the chapters that follow is a matter of personal interpretation. It's okay to disagree with my opinions and my conclusions. Art is, by its nature, subjective. No two people will come away from a musical with the exact same response. That's part of the thrill of doing a show. You may see things in these shows that I didn't see, things that will make your *Assassins* different from my *Assassins*. This book is designed to get you started, to help you create a production that is uniquely your own. It's only a road map. Once you've found the path, the rest is up to you. Once you know what to look for, you'll make your decisions about how to communicate those ideas in your production. You have to believe in your own instincts and in your audience's intelligence and sense of adventure.

Freedom

When I directed *Assassins* not long ago, I discovered—for the first time, really—the unparalleled thrill of creating a theatre piece of genuine substance, genuine novelty, genuine relevance to that real world that we all struggle to understand every day. Working on that show was the most satisfying experience I've ever had in my almost twenty years of working in the musical theatre. It was a thrill for the cast, the technical staff, and most importantly, our audience, many of whom were astonished at the intensity and power—and hilarity—of what they saw on our stage. All of us working on the show were a little apprehensive about what our friends and family would think of this outrageous and potentially controversial work; and we were surprised at how completely audiences (even our mothers) embraced the show, its characters, and its subversive message. As the artistic director of our theatre company, it was the first time I realized that I didn't have to worry about whether or not we might offend someone. We just had to produce interesting, high quality work and audiences would thank us. *Assassins* freed me as an artistic director to follow my instincts, to do theatre I believed to be worthwhile, and to know that success will follow. Our audiences doubled that season and continue to grow.

It also freed me as a director. Because of the unusual structure of the show, the bravely nonjudgmental approach to the controversial subject matter, and the liberal amount of humor, the show made me realize how much can be accomplished by breaking the rules of conventional musical theatre. This is an art form of incredible flexibility and there's so much opportunity for exploration and discovery. Of course, it's still a major undertaking to convince some people that a musical should be afforded the same respect and contemplation as a straight play, but we have a very large, enthusiastic, and steadily growing audience staunchly behind our work.

Analyzing a Musical

Some people spend years writing dissertations about the work of a single composer or director. Some people, like me, spend a year or a semester in college studying a single work. Digging through subtext and dissecting the script and score—and in some cases, original direction—can be fascinating and can yield valuable insights into how a musical works. Many teachers and directors don't have the time to dig that deeply, yet may find themselves directing a show that merits such an analysis. It is partly for these people that I've written this book.

Why bother analyzing and dissecting a musical so intensely before directing it? The answer is complicated and hotly debated. For many people, the appeal of a musical is its simplicity, its innocence. They go to see *Hello, Dolly!* to escape the often mind-bending task of living in our increasingly complicated, politically correct mine field of a world. For others, the musical theatre is like any other narrative art form—its beauty is in its ability to make order out of chaos, to sort through the craziness of our lives and make sense of it all. We go to a Sondheim musical because we know he will say something to us that makes the world and the people around us a little easier to comprehend. We come out of *Company* understanding the complexities and compromises of marriage a little more clearly. We come out of *Follies* with a new resolve to live in the present instead of the past. We come out of *Assassins* realizing that people don't fit neatly into categories and, more specifically, that these people aren't as different from us as we'd like to believe. It may make us more tolerant of the people around us and may help us understand ourselves a little better. Best of all, while we leave the theatre with these new insights into the human condition, we may also be humming "Send in the Clowns," "You Could Drive a Person Crazy," or "Everybody's Got the Right."

The kind of analysis in this book is primarily useful for a director or performer working on a musical, although I hope the book will also be enjoyable for other people who love the musical theatre and want to explore it. Though these methods can also be used on *Bye Bye Birdie* or *42nd Street*, there is a very real danger in overanalyzing a work that was meant only to be fun. A director must decide early on what the show's creators intended. I will always remember a production I saw of *Anything Goes* while I was in college. During the show, projections were shown on the side walls of the theatre depicting the genocide and other atrocities of Nazi Germany to underline the real-world events taking place while these rich folks were cruising the Atlantic and falling in love. As much as I love a musical with guts, this production was ridiculous. *Anything Goes* is a wonderful musical (one of my favorites, actually), but it really has little or nothing to say about Life and certainly nothing to say about genocide. Trying to inject a statement into this show ended up only being pretentious and irritating.

There were several things I considered when I selected musicals to include in this book. I looked for musicals with interesting or unusual subject matter (like *Assassins*); musicals whose construction or approach is unusual (like *Company* and *Merrily We Roll Along*); musicals in which the score has a degree of sophistication and complexity (like *Carousel* and *Into the Woods*); musicals with subtext worth exploring (like *Gypsy* and *Cabaret*); and musicals with guts that are too often dismissed as being shallow (like *Pippin* and *Man of La Mancha*). Some of the shows in the book are musicals I've directed myself; others are shows I hope to work on at some point in the future. All of them are worth studying and are musicals that audiences will enjoy exploring with you.

Where Do I Start?

As you prepare to direct (or design or perform in) a musical, there are so many things to consider: textual and musical themes, subtext, character psychology, the development of a unified vision for the production, the material's relevance to the real world, the communication of central themes through sets, lights, costumes, and other physical elements.

It's important to approach every show as if it's a brand new work, *especially* the "classics." Don't have too much reverence for it; don't take the songs slow out of respect to the dead composer or make the acting extra solemn just because the show's old. So many young people hate *Show Boat* today because companies treat it like a dusty old museum piece, too fragile to touch. "Can't Help Lovin' Dat Man" and "Old Man River" are taken so slowly they sound like funeral dirges. You could go out for dinner between choruses. The acting is like something out of *King Lear*. When Jerry Zaks directed the 1992 Broadway revival of *Guys and Dolls*, he approached the material as if it had just been written for them. His cast, staff, and he looked at it fresh and ignored the fact that it was already established as one of the greatest musicals of all time. After all, they were performing the script and score, not the reputation. They did things to the interpretation of "Sue Me" and "Sit Down, You're Rockin' the Boat" that were completely unprecedented. And brilliant.

This book isn't meant to hand directors ready-made musicals. It's meant to give them a starting point, things to consider, things to discuss with their music director, choreographer, designers, and cast. As a director, the fastest way to motivate a cast is to involve them in the creation of a vision and style for your show. Talk to them about questions you have, approaches you're considering. Let them see that you're exploring the material with them. Don't pretend to know all there is to know. If given the chance, they will bring wonderful, unexpected ideas and insights to your production, and they'll feel a heightened sense of ownership in the show that will improve their performances a great deal.

But the first step is to set yourself free. Stop rejecting your ideas before you've even finished thinking them. Don't be afraid to try out some of your more outrageous ideas on your cast. Ask them for their opinion. They'll appreciate being included in the creation process and they'll respect your sense of adventure. But whatever other people think, remember that there are times when you have to trust your gut.

That said, this book is for the adventurer in all of us, the discoverer of new worlds, the seeker of new life and new civilizations, as you boldly go where you may have never gone before, taking your actors and audiences with you. The terrain may be a little difficult, but it will be worth the trip.

Scott Miller
Artistic Director, New Line Theatre

Please Note

Some chapters discuss things that have been cut or added to specific productions for various reasons. Please remember that you can't change the dialogue, lyrics, or music without permission from the licensing agent. The licensing agents are mostly very cooperative, friendly people, who genuinely want to help you make the best show you can, while doing their best to protect the artists who created these musicals. (They've helped a lot with this book.) Don't be afraid to talk to them.

Assassins

Book by John Weidman
Music and Lyrics by Stephen Sondheim
Based on an idea by Charles Gilbert, Jr.
Originally Directed in New York by Jerry Zaks
Licensed by Music Theatre International

Many people were greatly offended by the idea of a musical about presidential assassination. Stephen Sondheim was surprised by this reaction. Certainly, he argued, if *Assassins* was a nonmusical play, no one would think twice about it. Simply because it's a musical, some people thought the show would trivialize its subject. Contrary to what those people believe, an art form can't be trivial in and of itself. The ways in which people use that art form can be, but not the art form itself. The American musical theatre has proven time and again that serious subjects and stories can be treated as powerfully with music as without. Some would argue music adds *more* power. The show's creators took an unconventional and controversial approach to their subject, seeing the history of assassination in our country as a national tradition, savage though it may be. Instead of portraying the assassins as aberrations on the fringe of society, Stephen Sondheim and John Weidman saw them as *victims* of our society's high expectations and false promises, and disciples of a different American dream. Unlike the Sondheim musicals written with James Lapine, *Assassins* is a visceral, in-your-face, outrageous theatre piece, exhilarating and terrifying at the same time. From the moment we hear "Hail to the Chief" in 3/4 time—the *wrong* meter—we know things are amiss. This is not the comfortable, relatively safe America we're used to. This is an America in which we may well lose our way.

Frighteningly, this is also the *real* America, a country won with guns, a culture suffused with guns.

The most important element for a successful production of this fascinating and thought-provoking musical is a cast that is willing to take big acting risks and do research on their characters. It's difficult and scary to play a character who's genuinely insane— and *Assassins* includes several—because it only works if the actor is willing to go "over the top," go beyond what is comfortable and safe. The audience must accept that these characters' despair, rage, and feelings of impotence are extreme enough to warrant their acts of assassination. If the actors only take their characters halfway, the audience won't understand why they commit such extreme acts. Their insanity is manifested in the loss of control over their emotions. Yet, portraying a character with no control over his emotions while still maintaining control over the performance requires treading a very thin line. During "The Ballad of Guiteau," for instance, Guiteau starts off confident and cocky, becomes unsure and scared, and ends up losing it entirely, screaming and cake-walking to his death. It's the director's job to help the actors feel safe enough to take those risks and to help them shape their performances. Watching over-the-top performances by Robert DeNiro, Jack Nicholson, or Christopher Walken often helps inexperienced actors see that it's all right to go beyond the normal acting boundaries. On the other hand, some of the assassins—John Hinckley and Leon Czolgosz—have rage and madness boiling just beneath the surface, always about to explode, which can be just as hard to play. It's interesting when these two characters interact in the barroom scene, particularly since Booth encourages Czolgosz to let go and explode.

Researching the characters they play also gives the cast ownership of their roles. It gets to be a lot of fun for everyone to bring information about their characters to rehearsals. Also, they uncover fascinating information that will shape their take on these characters. For instance, the actor playing Booth will be delighted to find out that Booth's body was never positively identified and some people believe the man apprehended in the barn wasn't really Booth, that he actually escaped. When the actor playing John Hinckley finds out Hinckley's mother's nickname was Jody, that information will put a whole new slant on his lyric in "Unworthy of Your Love."

The Material

The book and score of *Assassins* are among the most interesting in all of musical theatre. The show is a revue of both songs and dialogue scenes that are connected thematically, though they do not tell a linear story. Like the Sondheim musicals *Company* and *Follies*, this is a character study, and before the show is over you realize that the assassins aren't the only characters being examined; we're also looking at the character of our country, a country in which a too-hyped American Dream and easy access to guns have provided a handful of neurotics with both the motive and means to kill a president. It is also a country in which we want everything explained in ten-second sound bites. The Balladeer wants a neat and simple motive for Booth's act. In "The Ballad of Booth" he sings:

> *Some say it was your voice had gone,*
> *Some say it was booze.*
> *They say you killed a country, John,*
> *Because of bad reviews.*
> . . . .
> *Your brother made you jealous, John,*
> *You couldn't fill his shoes.*
> *Was that the reason, tell us, John—*
> *Along with bad reviews?*

Obviously, Booth's assassination of Lincoln can't be reduced to the result of bad reviews, but the Balladeer, like the American public he represents, doesn't want to expend too much thought. He wants an easy answer. From the very beginning, *Assassins* suggests there are no easy answers.

Assassins includes some characters who represent concepts, a device found in many straight plays but rarely in musicals. Playing the Proprietor and the Balladeer may seem daunting to your actors because these characters have no three-dimensional life, no backstory. But an understanding of their purpose in the context of the show can point actors in the right direction. The Proprietor represents our country, a country run amok with violence, dissent, the refusal to understand complicated issues, and the adulation of wackos. We live in a country where the public applauds criminals whose crimes are strange enough to get them on the talk shows, where fame is happily bestowed on people who commit bizarre, violent acts against their spouses or stack up dead bodies in their cellar. The Proprietor is the personification of this upside-down world of ours, where we give disturbed individuals guns while we make sure they can't achieve the rewards we've taught them to expect. They learn that committing a crime in a very public way is an easy path to fame and fortune. In the opening scene of *Assassins*, the Proprietor preys on each character's individual insecurities, then offers them the one sure way to realize the American Dream—killing the president.

As difficult as it is to play a character who is an idea more than a person, the key to the Proprietor may be to make him a literal embodiment of the insanity of our modern world, to play him as a full blown—yet terribly seductive—psychopath. Imagine all the rage, ambition, want, and resourcefulness of America all crammed into one person. Crazed and frightening though he may be, the assassins find his message enticing and his promises impossible to ignore. Allow the Proprietor to be genuinely deranged and you will more completely communicate to your audience that these assassins are desperate enough to listen to anyone and try anything—as many people in our society today are.

The Balladeer is the other conceptual character. He represents the American public and the American storytelling tradition and so is portrayed as a folksinger, the only form of storytelling that has lasted through all the time periods represented in the show. From the beginning of our country to the present, folksingers have passed on our stories. Other forms of storytelling have emerged as well—books, radio, movies, TV, video games—but the folksinger endures. The key to playing the Balladeer lies in the fact that as stories are passed down from generation to generation, as they are turned into songs, plays, and other storytelling forms, they are, of necessity, simplified. Particularly in America, they are also infused with optimism and the inevitable triumph of good over evil. As the personification of these stories, the Balladeer embodies an intentionally shallow, oversimplified view of history. His winning smile, easygoing manner, and theme-park enthusiasm provide an important contrast to the darkness and driving intensity of the assassins, particularly in "The Ballad of Booth" and "Another National Anthem." He represents everything that the assassins hate about our country, and in "Another National Anthem," they must silence him.

To further strengthen the Balladeer's role, one production I saw set him out in the audience during the opening number; he then began "The Ballad of Booth" from out in the house, reinforcing the idea that he represents the American people. He is us. He has our many prejudices and preconceptions about America and about the assassins; he is very clearly not an objective narrator.

Weidman's book jumps madly back and forth through time, mixing people and events from different eras. The fact that many of these assassins were undoubtedly inspired by the stories of those who had killed presidents before them is dramatized by allowing the assassins themselves to stand in for those stories. John Wilkes Booth actually suggests to Zangara in 1933 and Oswald in 1963 that they kill the president. John Hinckley asks Lee Harvey Oswald for his autograph. The show's creators theorize that it was not only anger and frustration that led to these killings, but also the knowledge that it had been done before. In the climactic Texas Book Depository scene, all the assassins past and future assemble to convince Oswald to shoot Kennedy. Weidman and Sondheim aren't suggesting these ghosts actually appeared in Dallas in 1963. It is Oswald's knowledge of them and of their acts, his belief that he is carrying on their tradition, that they would approve, that motivates him. They live in him, and as a part of him, they are his accomplices.

As usual, Sondheim's score holds as much drama and subtext as the book. His period music grounds us in each time period. With one exception, the entire score is written in styles appropriate to each assassin's time and in traditional American song forms. For Sondheim, those forms include not only folksongs and cakewalks, but also John Philip Sousa marches, barbershop quartets, show tunes, even 1970s pop ballads. The exception to this is "Another National Anthem," the one song in which the overall dramatic situation of the show actually changes. Appropriately, this is the one song that is not a period piece and not a traditional American song form. It is pure Sondheim, full of rich dissonance and interesting melody. It is in "Another National Anthem" that the assassins first reject the Balladeer's American Dream and realize that there is safety—and power—in numbers.

Sondheim also combines song forms in some cases to contrast

characters and situations. In "How I Saved Roosevelt," the by-standers who claim to have saved the president sing to the tunes of John Philip Sousa marches; in the same song, the Italian immigrant Zangara sitting in the electric chair sings an Italian tarantella. The switch back and forth between the marches and the tarantella, both in 6/8 meter, differentiates the characters' backgrounds even as the lyric shows they have a common aim. As the song climaxes, Zangara's music slowly becomes a Sousa march as well, and for the first time, he sings at the same time as the bystanders, underlining their common goal—celebrity.

Bigger Isn't Better

In a production of *Assassins* I directed, we decided early on to produce the show in a small, experimental space, and for both audience and critics it increased the power of the show. Because of the small space, our assassins were pointing guns at a first row only a few feet from the stage, never allowing the audience to distance themselves from the fact that the people onstage—however funny, however charming, however pitiable—were nonetheless murderers. To underline the assassinations, we used two kinds of gunshots. When an assassin was shooting at a president, we used starter pistols, which were extremely loud in such a small space. When they shot their guns at other times, we used cap guns, which were still loud, but not as loud as the starter pistols. This aural distinction made the acts of assassination stand out even more.

Assassins is a very dense and potent show, one rooted in psychology more than in the physical world, and it's important to keep physical distractions to a minimum. So we used very minimal, often only representational sets. Three large American flags hung on the set, one up-center, and two on either side of the stage. For most scenes, one or two set pieces were brought on—a bench for Booth's barn, a small step unit and a noose for Guiteau (but no actual gallows), a few boxes and a radio for the Texas Book Depository. Several scenes, like the Pan American Exposition in "The Ballad of Czolgosz," were done with no set pieces at all. This helped the audience accept the surreal book scenes, the mixing of time periods, and the revue-like style of the show. The need for very few set changes also kept the show moving. One reviewer actually said he preferred this production to others he'd seen because of its simplicity.

The minimalism of the set and the small size of the stage also forced us to make some very interesting—and surprisingly effective—staging choices. In the opening number, instead of seeing the presidents' faces or figures in a shooting gallery on the upstage wall, we put the targets on the imaginary "fourth wall"—the audience found *themselves* in the shooting gallery. As the assassins buy and try out their guns, and also at the end of the song, the guns are all pointed out into the house, though over the audience's heads, not directly at them. Similarly, in "The Ballad of Czolgosz," the line of people waiting to shake hands with President McKinley came toward the audience, putting the audience in McKinley's place, with the first person in line shaking hands with an invisible "fourth wall" president. It kept the scene visually interesting, and when Czolgosz finally got to "the head of the line," he assassinated the audience. For the first time, the audience was actually standing in the shoes of a president as he was assassinated.

Some of the scenes, like the one in which Leon Czolgosz meets activist and anarchist Emma Goldman, can actually be stronger without set pieces. In the barroom scene, Czolgosz's anger with the plight of the working class has been established through a speech about the horror of his job in a glass factory. Two scenes later he meets Emma Goldman, whom he's been following around the country to hear speak. In the script, they meet on a street outside the house where she is staying in Chicago; but the power of her words and their impact on the young Czolgosz are the focus of the scene. It doesn't really matter if they're on a street, in a hall after a speech, or in a train station. In reality, Czolgosz had read Goldman's writings and had heard her speak. We don't know if they actually met and discussed her ideas. For the purpose of the musical, the accumulated effect of her ideas on him over a period of time is telescoped into a single meeting. For that reason, it was more effective not to set the scene in one particular physical place.

Many scenes in the show are not written to be in a specific time or place, because Sondheim and Weidman are not re-creating history; they're interpreting it. *Assassins* does not strive for historical accuracy, but instead for psychological accuracy. The original production used slides of certain locales, the real assassins, and the presidents; but in many later productions, the slides have been omitted because they are too explicit, too concrete for this very unrealistic musical. The physical look of the show can be abstract, grotesque, minimalist, even nightmarish, but the acting must be real. The actors can never step out of character or go for a laugh. They should never comment on their characters through their performance. The actresses playing Squeaky Fromme and Sara Jane Moore can't let the audience know they find their characters funny. The humor will be so much more effective if these two women deliver their lines with the utmost sincerity and passion for their beliefs. That Squeaky can't see how insane Charlie is and Sara Jane can't see how unstable she appears makes them funny. Directors, likewise, should be careful of showing their directorial touch too obviously. The show posits that this limbo land where the assassins can meet and interact across time and beyond death, is real, a parallel-dimension America. We must believe it is real. Weidman and Sondheim have painted painfully realistic portraits of these men and women and what made them tick. The power of the show—and what makes it so unsettling—is the universality of their pain and their dreams.

Just Your Average Americans

We had several of the actors playing assassins double as bystanders and fairgoers for three reasons: it helped keep the show intimate and the cast small, it reinforced the surreal quality of the show, and it reminded the audience that these assassins are in some ways just ordinary people, that they appear on the outside to be normal. In the song "How I Saved Roosevelt" this doubling reinforced the fact that the bystanders and Zangara share a common goal.

We also cast the same actor as both the Balladeer and Lee Harvey Oswald, something that the show's creators had considered in New York but ultimately decided against. The Balladeer personifies the American storytelling tradition that passes on the stories of these assassins ("Someone tell the story, someone sing the song . . .") and that in turn stimulates some of the assassins to commit their killings. Because these stories, personified by the assassins themselves, convince Oswald to kill Kennedy, we saw an interesting connection. The Balladeer actually *is* the stories passed down through the generations and then becomes the stories' receptacle in the form of Lee Harvey Oswald. Connecting these two roles created an important unity for one of the show's central themes.

The Case for Booth

The power of *Assassins* (like *1776* and other historical dramas) is its ability to make fully drawn human beings out of the one-dimensional cardboard figures in history books. In *Assassins*, John Wilkes Booth may be somewhat unbalanced, but he is a patriot. He didn't kill Lincoln for fame or glory; he killed him to save the country. Looking back, we may quarrel with Booth's assessment of the state of the union, but it's important to remember that Lincoln was a widely disliked president; he was not "the pride and joy . . . of all the U.S.A." as the Balladeer sings. Booth's indictments against him are true. Lincoln did throw political dissenters into prison without charge or trial. His decision to abolish slavery was more economic than moralistic. Booth loved his country deeply and saw quite accurately that it was on its deathbed. The issue of slavery is beside the point here. Though we can see in retrospect that slavery was unconscionable, it's easy to see how it was condoned by society and by people like Booth. (Thomas Jefferson and other very moral men owned slaves.) From our modern vantage point, we can call Booth a racist, but at the time, his view of slavery was not outside society's norm. All he could see was that Lincoln was effectively destroying the economy of the South.

The section of "The Ballad of Booth" that begins "How the country is not what it was" is profoundly moving. This is not a madman talking. This is a man who loves the U.S.A. and can't bear to see it divided and its citizens murdered in a bloody war. Many historians have commented that had Booth killed Lincoln two years earlier, he might instead have been hailed as a hero. Are Booth's concerns that different from those voiced by commentators today? Americans across our nation often feel that the president or other politicians are destroying our way of life. Booth wasn't that different from the protesters during the Vietnam war. Certainly we can't sanction his method of righting the perceived wrongs—cold-blooded murder—but we also can't ignore the despair he must've felt over the destruction of his beloved country, a destruction that was very real. "The Ballad of Booth" can be a deeply moving, impassioned plea for understanding by a man who honestly believed he was doing what had to be done. Saddest of all is Booth's hope that history (i.e., the Balladeer) will pass on the truth; it won't. Booth's motivations, passions, and beliefs will be ignored or distorted.

Anatomy of an Assassin

Like Booth, Leon Czolgosz had political motivation. The progress of Czolgosz from exploited worker to assassin is one of the fullest and most interesting sequences in the show, an anatomy of an assassin. We first see him in the barroom with John Wilkes Booth, John Hinckley, and other assassins. His monologue about the insufferable working conditions in the factory where he works paints a picture of a man filled with rage who doesn't know what to do about it. Two scenes later, he meets Emma Goldman. He tells her that if he could, he would strike down the ruling class. She tells him he can and leaves him with a pamphlet encouraging the workers to rise up against their oppressors. He realizes that he must do something.

The next scene is a barbershop quartet called "The Gun Song." In it, Czolgosz expresses his contempt for his gun and the many workers who have been exploited through its manufacture. Booth enters and tells him that "all you have to do is move your little finger and you can change the world." By the end of the song, Czolgosz realizes how he can make a difference in the world. The song ends with a list of all the men who've died for the gun—men in the mines, the steel mills, the manufacturing plants. He looks at the gun as he makes up his mind and sings, "A gun claims many men before it's done . . . just one more"—the president.

The scene changes to the 1901 Pan American Exposition and "The Ballad of Czolgosz," where Czolgosz walks up to President McKinley and shoots him. This three-scene sequence forms the centerpiece of the show and offers its most complete picture of how a man can go from desperation to rage to the act of killing the president. Frighteningly, we understand Czolgosz and some of us may even agree with his politics. His lyric at the end of "The Gun Song" makes an important point—poverty is as insidious a killer as violence—that is as true today as in 1901. Not many of us, though, are prepared to accept his actions. How uncomfortable it must make the audience to suddenly realize that, as with Booth, they *understand* why he did it. We're not supposed to understand such things. We're supposed to condemn them and try not to think about it too much, but *Assassins* doesn't let us off that easily.

Sam Byck

Of all the assassins, Sam Byck most represents the contemporary, average, working-class American. He is for some audience members the assassin easiest to identify with. He's not acting against social injustice. He doesn't have the answers, but he knows the path America is on isn't the right one. He knows that politicians lie to us, that it's impossible to really understand all the issues even if you try. All he wants is for the people with power and influence to be straight with us. He tries to enlist the aid of famous people—people who would be listened to more than Byck would—but to Leonard Bernstein and Jonas Salk he sounds crazy. Listen closely and you'll see that Byck's criticisms aren't crazy, even though his solution may be.

Byck's two monologues establish several important ideas. In the first monologue, Byck tells us that much in America is screwed up (which we know is true) and though he doesn't have the answers, he knows that honesty and genuine effort will get us further than politics as usual. We see that he's tried to enlist the aid of celebrities to get the message out, but to an avail. In the second monologue, we find out more about his view on politics and more about Byck. As Byck sees it, all the politicians are telling us that everyone else is lying, that only they are telling us the truth. It's clear, though, that none of the politicians are telling the truth. Byck astutely points out that many of the pertinent issues are too complex for the average citizen to understand. That's why we elect representatives to figure them out and come up with plans of action. Yet when our representatives disagree on how best to solve problems, they garner our support by attacking their opponents rather than by helping us understand the issues. Like the fast-food industry and other consumer businesses to which Byck refers, politics has become a matter of marketing and publicity, letting substance fall away. Byck believes that politicians—most notably the president—have sinned against the American people and must be punished. In a very basic sense, this is a view held by several of the assassins we've seen. No one else will take any action, so Byck sees himself as America's last chance. He'll kill Nixon, wiping the political slate clean so our country can start over.

The second monologue also tells us a great deal about Byck's psychology. He knows there are areas in life in which we must trust others to make decisions and act on our behalf. He's looking for someone to trust in regard to the governance of our country, but can't find anyone. But the trust issue goes further back than that. In the latter part of the monologue, Byck compares the American public to children, who need protection and guidance. This leads to a sort-of flashback for him, which graphically shows us that he's losing his mind. His obsession with his mission has taken its toll. Going back into his childhood, Byck hears his father say he loves him but his mother doesn't, hears his mother say she loves him but his father doesn't. Issues of tremendous importance to this child—caring and protection, the same issues important to the American public—are confusing instead of reassuring, contradictory instead of clear. The state of American politics forces issues for Byck that he's been grappling with all his life. He sees no answer other than assassination. Unlike many Americans who object to the state of politics, Byck cannot just stand by and watch the country he loves crumble. He has to take action. We can disapprove of his method, but he illustrates an important concept in *Assassins*. As an audience, we can sit comfortably in our theatre seats and condemn these assassins for killing, but they are Americans who care passionately about America and must take some action in its defense. Byck speaks for all the assassins and, in fact, for the entire country when he asks who we should believe and what we can do. Like those who have gone before him, he sees only one possible course of action—killing the president.

O Say, Can You See...?

Sam Byck becomes the mouthpiece for the assassins, for their frustrations and their passions. Up to this point, the Balladeer is the voice of authority in the show, but he begins to lose that position to Byck. Looking back, we can see that the Balladeer saw this possibility as early as "The Ballad of Booth." Perhaps Booth was eloquent and passionate enough that the Balladeer felt compelled to discredit him early on:

> *Listen to the stories.*
> *Hear it in the songs.*
> *Angry men*

Don't write the rules,
And guns don't right the wrongs.

Hurts a while,
But soon the country's
Back where it belongs,
And that's the truth.

But it's not the truth. The Balladeer himself has already said that Booth forever changed our country—"You left a legacy of butchery and treason we took eagerly. . . ." We don't want it to be true, but Booth very much changed the face of America by beginning a still-active tradition of political assassination in our country. Like the press and the public, the Balladeer doesn't want to assign any power to these assassins, but the truth is that though guns clearly don't right the wrongs, guns certainly can and do change the country. Oswald's assassination of Kennedy created huge changes in American politics—and by extension, in American life—that we will never be able to know completely. No matter what the Balladeer, the representative of the American public, may say or believe, these angry men and women have a very clear and profound impact on the lives of the rest of us.

In "Another National Anthem" the assassins onstage literally solicit the audience to become assassins. Led by Byck, they tell us that they've tried the traditional American Dream, the one proffered by the Balladeer, and it doesn't work. They've found a *better* American Dream, *another* national anthem. They sell it to us, asking us to pass on their message, singing over and over, "Spread the word." They know we (the audience) all have unrealized dreams just as they do; they know we all want the same thing, and they know how to get it now. In a way, it becomes the most optimistic song in the show, precisely because the assassins have found the answer. But it also must be infused with great anger, carried to enough of an extreme to justify their acts. Byck compares the fairy tale we call the American Dream to Santa Claus and we realize how meaningless the Balladeer's empty optimism is to them. For these assassins, the American Dream really is as silly as Santa Claus and the Easter Bunny. As the Balladeer spouts his homespun clichés about a country built on dreams, we see how little this means to this group of people consumed by despair, grief, rage, and feelings of abandonment. For most of us in the audience, it will be the first time we've looked at the American Dream in such a harsh light and realized how irritating it must be to the disenfranchised members of our society, who can never have what we tell them they should have.

But these people are newly empowered. They have taken over the Balladeer's role—that of passing on stories—and they literally chase the Balladeer off the stage, silencing the only voice in the show still in favor of old-fashioned American values. They become a new voice of authority and they take control of the show as they realize that they have even greater power as a group than as individuals. They see the Balladeer's and America's lie—that the mailman, the delivery boy, even the usherette, can have the American Dream if only they try hard enough. These assassins have listened to the lie for too long and have seen it for what it is. They decide it's time for them to be heard. The assassins have learned how to get their message across. The Balladeer tells them their acts have meant nothing, but it's not true. They know that:

> They may not want to hear it,
> But they listen,
> Once they think it's gonna stop the game . . .
> No, they may not understand
> All the words,
> All the same
> They hear the music . . .

The ballpark is mainstream society; the game is the American Dream. Though the assassins can't get into the ballpark, they can certainly interrupt the game. With their newfound confidence, they pick up on one of the Balladeer's themes—you have to keep on trying. Maybe they can't have the prize they were promised, but there are other prizes to be had. For those who wanted fame, they got it. For those who wanted to effect political change, they at least called attention to their cause. For those who wanted to "connect," they have done just that. They have become a new voice of America. They say late in the song, "*We're* the other national anthem . . ." (emphasis added). They realize that they really can effect change. They say, "There's another national anthem and

I think it just began. . . ." Their anthem is playing now. It's their turn.

Back to the Future

The assassins find when they come together that they have a commonality of purpose that makes them a "force of history" (in fact, only as a group are they significant enough historically to have had a musical written about them). It's this knowledge and power—and the promise of belonging to a family—that helps them persuade Oswald to kill Kennedy. Oswald can achieve lasting notoriety, as evidenced by Hinckley's intimate knowledge of Oswald's life. All the sung lines leading up to Oswald's gunshot make him feel important, significant, a man of consequence—"I envy you," "I admire you," "I respect you," "You are the future." Oswald will do what none of the others could. He will single-handedly raise presidential assassination to mythical proportions. Kennedy's death will cause worldwide grieving like no one has ever seen.

The Book Depository scene may be the most surreal scene in this surreal show. Is it all happening in Oswald's head? When Booth enters, he notices his watch isn't working. Of course it isn't—time is not right in this scene. We see in *Assassins* that Booth and Oswald live in all time periods—Booth visits other time periods and Oswald brings them all to him. But these two men are the ones we all know. Maybe we've never heard of Sam Byck or Giuseppe Zangara, but everyone knows Booth and Oswald. The show has crossed time periods before this scene, but here all periods converge on one spot at one time—the moment before Oswald shoots Kennedy. Lee has brought them together physically as well as spiritually. The mysterious way they appear and disappear and their knowledge of other time periods seem to indicate that they are really only voices in Oswald's head, telling him all the things he wants to hear, that they envy him, admire him, respect him, that they want him to be a part of their "family," that they need him to form a link between past and future. Finally, after a lifetime of not belonging—to a family, to a group of friends, to either America or Russia—Lee has found people who need him. How could this pathetic soul possibly refuse them? He has purpose for the first time in his life.

At the end of the Oswald scene in the production I directed, the assassins did not exit after Oswald's shot. They stood in a line, in chronological order, one empty space in the center. Only after Oswald shoots Kennedy and then crosses the stage to step into that space does the group become truly whole. Oswald connects past to future, creating a continuum, a perverse family tree of assassination. This is the show's obligatory moment, the moment toward which all previous action leads and from which all subsequent action follows.

A Thinking Person's Musical

Assassins is a musical about ideas. It's not a traditional romance or backstage drama; it's an often frightening psychological exploration. You have to decide if your audience will accept that. Producing this musical will be a tremendously satisfying experience for you, but it is one that demands a great deal of time and thought, as well as an audience that enjoys taking risks. It requires acting as strong as any nonmusical drama *and* singers who can handle a Sondheim score. More than anything else, you need a cast who will work together as an ensemble, for that's what ultimately makes the end of the show pay off. We have to believe that these assassins have formed a kind of family. Their unity is what wins over Oswald and what makes them a force to be reckoned with. An audience will always sense whether or not that unity is real.

To the history books, the assassins are all ultimately failures—either they failed to kill the president or they were caught and killed themselves. But from the assassins' point of view, they have succeeded by the show's end. They have found the answers, they have found a group they can belong to, they have a message to pass on. The greatest revelation for me was when I finally allowed myself to see the show from their viewpoint instead of my own—to see the Balladeer as an antagonist who distorts and oversimplifies their passions (as the stories he personifies have done) and to recognize the tremendous force of history the assassins become. By not imposing our moral point of view on the assassins, by not condemning them, by allowing them to be triumphant, the show may make many people in the audience uncomfortable. They want a final, reassuring statement: the assassins are bad. But *Assassins* isn't about good and bad. It's about hearing the other side of the story, getting closer to these assassins than we normally would, standing in their world for ninety minutes. In the finale, the assassins offer us a truly seductive opportunity—to be a part of something greater than ourselves, to belong to a family, and, in a tip of the hat to other Sondheim musicals, to connect. When the assassins repeat the word "connect," the audience should feel the power of their newly acquired/regained self-respect, building each time the word is repeated, demanding respect from the audience—the country—as well.

Be Forewarned

There are several things that make producing *Assassins* a large undertaking. First of all, depending on how you decide to design the physical production, you may have a number of sets to build. The show can be done effectively (perhaps *more* effectively, as I discussed earlier) with little or no set, but the decision is yours.

This is also a very prop-heavy show. There are a large number of props, and you will need a props master who is good at organizing and a genius at finding things, including breakaway bottles and period guns. Because the show is so unreal and because assassins from different time periods meet throughout the show, it's very important for the props and costumes to realistically establish the time period of each character.

Casting the show is not easy. Without actors that can act and sing with great skill, the show can collapse under its own weight. With strong singers who can't act, the show can become nothing more than a frightening and unintelligible revue. If, on the other hand, you cast actors who can't sing, this very interesting music can become difficult to understand and painful to hear. A performer with great acting skills but little musical background will find himself so concerned with getting the songs right that his acting will suffer during the songs, and Sondheim has packed so much drama into every musical number that you can't afford to let that happen. Even the small roles must be peopled with very strong actors and singers.

Other Resources

Music Theatre International has two valuable resources available to you when you produce this show. First, their Video Conversationpiece is an hour-long discussion with book writer John Weidman and composer Stephen Sondheim, who walk you through each scene and song, discussing their intentions, things to be careful of, and hints that will make your job easier. Second, MTI's Study Guide, designed to help teachers integrate the show's issues into their regular curriculum, is an excellent guide for the cast as well. It includes a bibliography of primary source material for research, works by and about the assassins. The original cast recording, a published version of the script, vocal selections, and the full piano/vocal score are all available if you'd like to look at the show before you decide to do it.

Cabaret

Book by Joe Masteroff
Music by John Kander
Lyrics by Fred Ebb
Originally Directed on Broadway by Harold Prince
Licensed by Tams-Witmark Music Library

The burgeoning political activism in the United States when *Cabaret* hit the stage in 1966 and its huge growth by 1972, when the film hit theatres, as well as Hal Prince's desire to break through to a new kind of socially responsible musical theatre, conspired to make *Cabaret* one of the most fascinating stage pieces of the 1960s and a show that speaks to our world in the 1990s now more than at any time since it first opened. Sally represents the people who keep their eyes shut to changes in the world around them and Cliff represents the new breed of American activist who can no longer sit by and watch the government ignore the will of the people. Today, as activism at both ends of the political spectrum has experienced a renaissance in America, *Cabaret* as a cautionary morality play has tremendous resonance.

Cabaret is a fascinating but flawed theatre piece. It was Hal Prince's first experiment in making a concept musical—a show in which the story is secondary to a central message or metaphor—a form he would later perfect with *Company*, *Follies*, *Pacific Overtures*, *Kiss of the Spider Woman*, and other musicals. Walter Kerr said in the *New York Times* that "it opens the door to a fresh notion of the bizarre, crackling, harsh and beguiling uses that can be made of song and dance." Other writers and directors further developed the concept musical in the seventies and eighties with shows like *A Chorus Line*, *Working*, *Chicago*, and *Nine*, but *Cabaret* had paved the way. *Cabaret*'s greatest flaw lies in the fact that the concept musical was still an embryo; Prince was traversing uncharted territory. The end product was groundbreaking and often shocking, but it was only half a concept musical. Believing that Broadway audiences needed a central romantic couple and a secondary comic couple (*Oklahoma*, *Brigadoon*, *The Pajama Game*, et al.), Prince and his collaborators essentially created two shows, a realistic book show with traditional musical comedy songs and a concept musical with songs that commented on the action and the central message of the show. When Bob Fosse made the film version of *Cabaret* in 1972, he jettisoned all the traditional book songs, and the piece became a full-fledged concept musical. In 1987 when Prince revived the stage version, the show's creators went back and revised the show again, returning homosexuality to the story, incorporating some improvements from the film version, and trying things audiences had not been ready for in 1966.

Deutschland

1931. Weimar Germany is in trouble. Due to sanctions imposed after World War I, the country is in economic and political ruin. There is political dissension everywhere. The people, particularly the conservative middle class, are unhappy. Adolph Hitler takes power through rhetoric and propaganda, telling the people what they want to hear. Hitler's ultraconservative Nazi party begins a propaganda war against the standing government. He promises an end to the depression, to political corruption and incompetence, to moral decay. He declares war on popular culture, which he portrays as decadent, obscene, and anti-German. He attacks Jews, homosexuals, feminists, and artists for ruining the country. He champions the family unit, traditional roles for men and women, children, and traditional values. He promises to "save" Germany from its terrible predicament. In the show, Ernst echoes the Nazi's promises when he tells Cliff that the Nazis will be the builders of a new Germany. With hindsight, it's now possible to see that he promised and attacked almost all the same things that many American politicians promise and attack today.

As I write this in 1995, politicians and religious leaders across the country are declaring that our country is in a state of moral decay and political disarray, that our culture is disintegrating, that movies, TV, and pop music are full of gratuitous sex and violence, that mainstream religion is under attack. It's not hard to see the parallels to Weimar Germany. It makes the world of 1931 Berlin that much scarier, and it makes it that much easier to see why some Germans embraced the Nazi party. They were desperate for change, for salvation from the things they perceived as deadly to their way of life.

Cabaret looks at two effects of Hitler's rhetoric. First, the decadence of the cabarets—widespread, open homosexuality; a new feminism; and other trends—gave a certain segment of the population a kind of freedom they had not experienced before. Many were so enraptured with this new world, so happily distracted, that they were unaware of what was happening politically. Some of the cabarets included biting political satire in their shows, illustrated in *Cabaret* at the beginning of Act II by the kick line—including the Emcee in drag—that segues into a Nazi goose-step (the Nazis were terrified of homosexuality within the ranks), but the cabaret owners who indulged in political satire were quickly thrown in jail. Second, many people, like Herr Schultz in *Cabaret*, simply couldn't believe that anything so terrible could happen to loyal Germans. Many never dreamed that Hitler would orchestrate the systematic extermination of millions of Jews and homosexuals. There were also those who fell into both these categories, like Sally Bowles, who simply didn't want to think about politics, believing that it had nothing to do with their lives.

It Could Happen Here

One of the show's main messages is that "It Could Happen Here." At the beginning of the show, in the original production, there was a giant mirror onstage facing the audience. The implication was that the people of Germany who allowed the Nazis to take power were very much like us, just ordinary people who found their country in trouble and looked for someone to fix things. If we had lived in 1931 Berlin, the mirror suggests, we too would have been cajoled into believing the Nazis could save the country. It also says that we—the populace—are as much to blame as politicians. Whatever happens in our country, we allow to happen.

Most of the leading characters in the show are archetypes. The Emcee is the personification of decadence, temptation, unchecked sexuality. In 1990s America, he is the movie industry, the recording industry, the television industry, and tabloid journalism. He makes immorality appealing, entertaining, and inviting. Sally Bowles is the self-involved, head-in-the-sand young person, looking only for the next party, constant gratification, and complete freedom without responsibility. She refuses to think about politics and social issues because it gets in the way of a good time. She uses sex and alcohol to hide from the real world. She represents both the decadence that the Nazis turned into successful propaganda and the passivity that allowed their meteoric rise to power. Fraulein Schneider represents those who see what's happening but believe they have no power to change anything. She doesn't like it, but resigns herself to the fact that she is powerless. Herr Schultz is foolishly optimistic. He believes so completely in the intrinsic goodness of humanity that he cannot believe that Jews will be expelled or persecuted in their own country. Cliff represents morality and social conscience. He sees what is happening and will not accept it. He says to Sally, "If you're not against all this [the Nazis], you're for it—or you might as well be." An audience wants to see themselves in Cliff, but in reality, most of us are either Fraulein Schneider or Sally.

America's political climate in 1966, when *Cabaret* opened on Broadway, was just as explosive as 1931 Berlin's. Despite the civil rights bill that Congress had passed in 1964, race riots were happening all over the country—in Harlem in July 1964, in Watts (Los Angeles) in August 1965, in Cleveland and Chicago in July 1966, as well as in Atlanta and other cities. Malcolm X was assassinated in February 1965. Martin Luther King Jr.'s first march from Selma to Montgomery, Alabama, took place in March 1965. Antiwar demonstrations began on the campus of the University of California–Berkeley in 1964, and continued throughout the sixties across the country. The first antiwar march on Washington was held in May 1965. U. S. troops launched their first full-scale combat in Vietnam in July 1965. *Hogan's Heroes*, a television sitcom about a German P.O.W. camp, debuted in 1965. The University of Mississippi's first black student was shot in June 1966, the same month that students marched on Washington again, this time for voting rights. The heavily political *Smothers Brothers Comedy Hour* debuted in September 1966 and went on to become the only television show canceled because of its subversive political content. Clearly, America was ready for a political musical. *Cabaret* opened in November 1966. While the show was running, the antiwar concept musical *Hair* opened (in

1967), as well as TV's *Laugh-In*, with its outrageous brand of social and political satire (in 1968).

A Bizarre Little Figure

Director Hal Prince saw the Emcee in *Cabaret* as a metaphor for Germany's horrible depression, which was far worse than what America was experiencing in 1931. Prince had seen a dwarf emcee at a club in Germany once and he was the inspiration for *Cabaret's* Emcee. If *Cabaret* has a central character (some would argue the concept is the central character), it would be the Emcee more than Cliff or Sally. The Emcee represents the German people, popular entertainment, the newfound decadence that the Nazis would exploit in their propaganda. He gets twice as many songs as Sally, and both opens and closes the show. When Cliff starts writing his book on the train leaving Berlin at the end of the show, the Emcee is mentioned before Sally. He is onstage during many of the book scenes, observing—a device Prince would use again in *Company* and *Sweeney Todd*. If the show's concept is the central character, the Emcee is certainly the personification of that concept. He lies constantly ("Even the orchestra is beautiful"), yet simultaneously shows us the horrible truth. He's friendly and charming but also dangerous. His behavior is completely uncontrolled. He has no boundaries, no conscience, no rules—not unlike Hitler. He shows us the total moral freedom that many Germans were enjoying but also shows us why that total freedom can be a bad thing. His welcome at the beginning is frightening precisely because it is too perky, too happy—like old-fashioned musicals. Prince used the kind of brainless happy musical comedy conventions of the twenties and thirties to illustrate the danger in ignoring the real world. Hollywood in that era put on the same happy face, asking us to forget the war, the death, the poverty. There may be some value in occasional escapism, but when does it become dangerous to escape? When do we do ourselves a disservice by "forgetting" the horrors of the world? The Emcee tells us to leave our troubles outside, but in reality, those troubles are already inside, pervading every moment of the show. He tells us the girls and the orchestra are beautiful when we can plainly see that they are garish, vulgar, scary—some of the "girls" are actually men in drag. He looks us straight in the eye and tells us to enjoy ourselves as he presents examples of immorality, prejudice, hatred, and self-delusion. When he repeats his welcoming speech at the end of the show, it is even more frightening. He's still perky even after we've watched several lives be utterly destroyed—and we know this is only the beginning of the horror for some of these characters. At the very end, the Emcee briefly reprises "Willkommen," but he doesn't finish; the song stops and he disappears. It's not over. Herr Schultz will undoubtedly be put in a concentration camp and killed, yet the Emcee is happy to have helped us forget our troubles. Is the Emcee saying goodbye to us or Cliff or both? Or is he saying goodbye to the good times in Germany?

A Perfectly Marvelous Girl

Sally Bowles connects the two worlds of *Cabaret*. She is a part of the world of the Kit Kat Klub (note the initials) and a part of the real world that includes Cliff, Fraulein Schneider, Herr Schultz, and Ernst. She is a little girl playing dress-up, making up stories, trying to be sexy and shocking, never really being too successful at it. Logically speaking, she shouldn't be too good a performer. She's supposed to be a second-rate singer who'll never make it out of the Kit Kat Klub. That's how Sally is portrayed in the stories on which *Cabaret* is based. Unfortunately, that creates a practical problem—how do you put a second-rate performer in a leading role in a musical? In the original Broadway production, Hal Prince cast Jill Haworth specifically because she wasn't a great singer, and the critics blasted him for it. In Bob Fosse's movie version, he cast Liza Minelli, who turned in an amazing performance, yet we could never believe that this astounding performer was stuck in anonymity in a seedy little night club. Sally tells Cliff in Act II that you can't really stop things from happening and that you can't really change people. She's referring to herself (she can't settle down to middle-class domesticity), but she's also talking about the German people. The Nazis will take power no matter what anyone tries to do to stop them. The tide of history can't be turned back. She is finally moving from ignorance to the beginnings of awareness, but she will end up more like Fraulein Schneider than like Cliff. She tells Cliff that he's an innocent and, in a way, she's right! He still believes that you can fight for what you believe in and make a difference in the world.

Sally's big number in Act II, "Cabaret," has become a pop standard outside the show, but in context it is a decidedly unpleasant song. She is going on stage at the club to sing about living life to the fullest, after having aborted her baby and lost the man she loves. She has decided to pursue a career that will never happen. Cliff can't stay in Germany anymore, but Sally has to stay in order to follow the dreams that will never be realized. She is a tragic character, self-deluded and self-destructive. Yet throughout the show, we repeatedly find ourselves laughing at her, believing her, getting caught up in her enthusiasm.

Gay, Straight, Bi?

Through the many incarnations of the story—Christopher Isherwood's book *Goodbye to Berlin* (1939), John Van Druten's play *I Am a Camera* (1951), Henry Cornelius' film of the same name (1955), the stage version of *Cabaret* (1966), its movie version (1972), and its revised stage version (1987)—the Isherwood character, (Cliff in *Cabaret*), has been variously straight, gay, and bisexual. Isherwood himself was gay, but because of societal restraints, some versions made the character based on him straight. The 1966 stage version of *Cabaret* made him straight; the movie made him a homosexual who decides to be straight and later ends up bisexual; the revived 1987 stage version made him mostly gay even though he sleeps with Sally. The gay subtext that underlies all these versions parallels the outsider status of Sally and everyone at the Kit Kat Klub. They live outside society's norms, outside the accepted rules. They are marginalized and they create their own insular community as homosexuals have done for decades. The Emcee in *Cabaret* reinforces this theme of any and all sexualities.

Cliff also mirrored the changing face of America in 1966. Young people were realizing for the first time that there were horrible things happening in the world and they had a responsibility to speak up and register their dissatisfaction. It was a new age of political activism. The title song's asking what the point was in sitting home doing nothing, was a question young people across America were asking themselves. Demonstrations were breaking out on college campuses everywhere. People were marching on Washington. Cliff's growing awareness of the Nazis' presence and the implications of their politics portrayed the mood of America.

Cliff begins the story no more aware than anyone else. In Act I he says everyone's having such a good time that if they were in a movie, something horrible would have to happen to them. He has no idea how right he is. He agrees to smuggle for Ernst, asking Ernst not to tell him who he's smuggling for. At the party at the end of the first act, Cliff starts to "wake up" and see what's happening. He realizes that he's been sleepwalking through life—just like Sally. Cliff eventually wakes up; Sally does not. When he demands that Sally return to America with him and leave the powder keg that Germany has become, she refuses. He orders her to pack and therein makes a fatal mistake. Sally is a woman who deeply cherishes her independence. Cliff's attempt to force her into doing as he says only makes her more resolved to stay. He forces her to choose between family life—at which she thinks she'd fail—and the exciting, dangerous nightlife of Berlin. Cliff is making a moral decision for himself, but he can't make it for Sally. He can't dictate her morality. After all, isn't that what the Nazis are trying to do? When he begins his book at the end of the show, he mentions the three main elements of the Nazis' rise to power—the Kit Kat Klub and the Emcee, examples of the decadence the Nazis will use to illustrate the downfall of Germany; Germany itself, crippled by unprecedented inflation and increasing violence; and Sally, one of the people who are unwilling to think about politics, to see what's happening, to take a moral position and stand up for what they believe. The flashbacks that end the show are Cliff's thoughts swimming around in his head, falling into a kind of logical order so that he can put them down on paper. Though he is running from the Nazis, he is making his stand by telling his story.

Fraulein Schneider and Herr Schultz

Fraulein Schneider and Herr Schultz are the traditional musical comedy couple in this very untraditional musical, yet, in keeping with the tone of the show, they are left without a happy ending. Still worried about audiences in 1966, the show's creators turned Cliff and Sally into a mostly traditional musical comedy couple (less so in the revised version), with the older lovers as the second comic couple. Fraulein Schneider is described in the stage directions as indestructible. In some ways this is true, though by the end of the show her heart, her love, has been destroyed. Her first song, "So What," shows us her ability to get past almost any obstacle, to take life as it comes, but this philosophy will turn sour by the end of the show. The older couple has two songs. "It Couldn't Please Me More" accompanies Herr Schultz's gift of a pineapple to Fraulein Schneider. They are older and wiser than Sally and Cliff, so their material needs are few, but their emotional needs are every bit as substantial as the younger couple's. Later, Herr Schultz is caught in Fraulein Schneider's room and is forced to pretend they're engaged to save her reputation—a stock comic situation right out of the Cole Porter school of musical comedy. They decide it's maybe not such a bad idea, and they sing "Married." Similar in nature to "Somewhere That's Green" from *Little Shop of Horrors*, this song is so effective because of the simplicity of their love. Merely being together is all they need to be happy. It is that simplicity that makes it so much more tragic when they are forced to cancel their engagement in the face of the prejudice sweeping through Germany. The show's creators have set up a traditional musical comedy love story, specifically to have it destroyed by the malevolence always lying just under the surface. Though Cliff can leave Germany, they can't. Fraulein Schneider's song "What Would You Do?" is a companion piece to "So What," but here her philosophy of simply surviving no longer has the appeal it did at the beginning of the show. Now that she has had love, simply surviving is no longer enough.

Comment Songs

The score to *Cabaret* has two kinds of songs—diegetic comment songs and book songs. The comment songs are those performed in the Kit Kat Klub (in the original production, sometimes in front of a light curtain). They are diegetic because the characters are conscious of the fact that they're singing. They work in a night club, so the act of singing is part of the story. The book songs are the kind of regular musical comedy numbers that you find in most traditional musicals, in which characters express their thoughts and feelings through music. These songs are not realistically motivated. If these people were real people in real life, they would not be singing; and in the world of the story, the characters aren't aware of the fact that they're singing. Traditional musicals usually use only book songs. When Curly and Laurie sing "People Will Say We're in Love" in *Oklahoma!*, the characters don't know they're singing. When Arthur sings "How to Handle a Woman" in *Camelot*, he's not aware that he's singing. In the latter case, we're hearing his thoughts; the song is an internal monologue. The film version of *Cabaret* cut all the show's book songs (unless you count "Tomorrow Belongs to Me") and only used the realistically motivated comment songs. Because of this, there is debate over whether or not it's still really a musical, technically speaking.

The first song in *Cabaret* functions as both a comment song and a book song. It welcomes us both to the Kit Kat Klub, where much of the action will take place, and also to *Cabaret*, the musical. The Emcee is addressing the audience in the Kit Kat Klub while he also addresses the real audience. Using the opening song this way prepares us for the two different uses to which songs will be put in the show. The next comment song is "Two Ladies," positioned just after Cliff has decided to let Sally move in with him. The song presents the Emcee and two female roommates, clearly illustrating the humor and immorality of cohabitation. The song works better in the film, in which it describes Sally, Brian, and Max's threesome, a situation more like the situation described in the song. The song also loses part of its punch in the 1987 revised version of the show, in which we already know Cliff is gay. Although we find out they have slept together, a woman moving in with a gay man is hardly worth commentary.

Later in the show, after Cliff accepts a job smuggling for Ernst and his unnamed political party, the scene again shifts to the Kit Kat Klub, where the Emcee begins "The Money Song." The song in this spot since the 1987 revival is actually two songs—"Sitting Pretty" from the 1966 stage version and "Money, Money" from the film. This new hybrid, "The Money Song," begins with the Emcee's telling us that though everyone else in his family is starving (as most Germans were at the time), he's got all the money he needs. The reason? He sells girls, the obvious implication being that Cliff is prostituting himself for a buck. The song then goes on to say that money makes the world go around. When you're poor, neither love nor religion makes a bit of difference. Only money can put food in your mouth and a roof over your head. If you're lonely, money can buy companionship. If you're overworked, money can buy a vacation. The message is crass but true. For the people of Germany, only money can solve their problems. For Cliff and Sally, now expecting a baby, money is more important than ever. An end to the depression was one of the Nazis' biggest promises to the German people. "The Money Song" is a testament that people will do almost anything— including abandoning their morals—for money.

Hitler Youth

"Tomorrow Belongs to Me" is used in several ways. First, it is performed by waiters in the Kit Kat Klub, whom the script describes as handsome, well-scrubbed, and idealistic. The song comes after a scene in which the romance between Fraulein Schneider and Herr Schultz is firmly established; it has also been established earlier that Herr Schultz is Jewish. Knowing what we do about 1931 Germany, we know there is trouble on the horizon. As if to reassure us of the dangers that lie ahead, "Tomorrow Belongs to Me" illustrates the sincerity and self-righteousness of the people who will follow the Nazis, the people who believe the Nazis are their only hope for saving Germany. Kander and Ebb have really stacked the deck with this song, making it sound as wholesome and healthy as possible. The first two verses are filled with lyrical themes—nature, awakenings, the future, children. Musically, the song begins with an a cappella tenor solo about the natural beauty of Germany. The other men begin a humming counterpoint against the main melody. As the second verse begins, they break into beautiful, hymnlike four-part harmony. As the lyric becomes less pastoral and more nationalistic, the orchestra joins in, the French horn and guitar prominent, adding a rustic, bucolic sound. The most frightening lyric is the second-to-last line, which promises that a time will soon come when the world will belong to the singer (Germany). On one level this can be interpreted as a deep connection to nature; on another, it refers to Hitler's deranged desire to conquer the world. The love of nature is warped into a thirst for power.

At the end of Act I, at the engagement party, Fraulein Kost sings the song again (changing it from a comment song to a book song) to liven up the party. With only an accordion accompaniment, the song still sounds pretty and innocent. Then Ernst joins her, a swastika prominent on his sleeve. If the subtext of the song wasn't obvious earlier, there can be no mistake about it now. Soon everyone at the party—except for Fraulein Schneider, Herr Schultz, Sally, and Cliff—is singing proudly about the Fatherland. Like the earlier version, this rendition moves up a key for each verse, increasing the

dramatic impact. Considering the Nazis' official position on immorality, it's ironic that the song is started by a prostitute. At the end
of the song, the Emcee appears to underline the menace of the lyric,
and as he disappears, the lights go out on Act I. Act II opens with
another rendition of this same music. Eight of the Kit Kat Klub girls
enter and do a lengthy dance number full of high kicks, all to the
music of "If You Could See Her," a song we haven't heard yet. As we
notice that one of the "girls" is the Emcee, the sound of military
drums fades in, drowning out the other music. Then, over the
drums, we hear trumpets playing the "Tomorrow Belongs to Me"
theme, and soon the orchestra joins them as the dancers' high kicks
become goose-steps. Yes, even chorus girls can become Nazis.

An important point the song makes is that the people of Germany were not rallying around a party committed to killing; they
only knew that the Nazis promised prosperity and the salvation of
Germany. In the film version, Brian and Max are sitting in a beer garden out in the country, when a young blond boy begins singing "Tomorrow Belongs to Me." Slowly the camera pans down to the
swastika on his arm band. The people in the beer garden smile at his
youth and his love for his country. Two waiters start singing with
him, then one by one the onlookers stand and join in. There is pride
in their faces, determination, fierce patriotism. As each verse moves
up a key, the crowd becomes more and more impassioned. These are
not murderers; these are patriots. They don't know the Nazis will
soon be practicing genocide. People today often ask how the German people could have been so easily seduced by Hitler. The answer
is that they loved their country as much as we love ours. At the end
of the scene in the movie, Brian and Max are getting in their car to
leave and Brian says to Max, "Do you still think you can control
them?" It is a deeply disturbing scene to watch, mainly because
these are simple, good people—patriots—who have no idea what
the future holds for Germany.

Gorilla My Dreams

In Act II, Scene 2, Fraulein Schneider, unnerved by the events at the
engagement party, comes to tell Herr Schultz she has reconsidered
and will not marry him. Though she doesn't say it outright, we
know she has a great—and legitimate—fear of anti-Semitic acts of
violence that would be perpetrated against them both. As she leaves

the stunned Herr Schultz, the scene returns to the Kit Kat Klub, where the Emcee enters with a gorilla in a dress. He sings, "If You Could See Her." The song describes the blossoming romance between the Emcee and the gorilla and the prejudice they encounter whenever they go out in public. If we only could see her through his eyes, his pleads, we would understand their love. The audience laughs along with the ridiculous premise of the song, especially during the dance break. Because of the dance that opened Act II, we already associate this music with the Nazis (though perhaps only subconsciously). At the end of the song, the Emcee stage whispers the shocker: "If you could see her through my eyes, she wouldn't look Jewish at all!" The show's writers have caught us. We easily accepted the fact that a man can't possibly fall in love with a gorilla, just as the Germans easily accepted the fact that a gentile can't possibly marry a Jew, or as many people today easily accept the fact that it's unnatural for two men or two women to fall in love. In the film version, the Emcee delivers a short speech midway through the song. He asks if it's a crime to fall in love and why the world can't live and let live. The sad truth is that sometimes in our mixed-up world, it is a crime to fall in love, and it's rare that society will ever live and let live. There will always be people who want to control other people's behavior. The song is about perception and preconceptions, and about the inherent absurdity of any kind of prejudice. It's meant to make the audience very uncomfortable and it does. It worked well enough in 1966 that the creators reluctantly softened the last line to appease the many audience members who were infuriated by it. It reinforces Prince's it-could-happen-here theme.

Like "Willkommen" and "Tomorrow Belongs to Me," "Cabaret" is used both as a comment song and a book song. It's ironic that Sally sings this song of happiness and contentedness just after Cliff has been beaten senseless by some Nazis. But soon, the song changes from a book song into commentary. This is the attitude that will allow the Nazis to win the elections. People would rather think about happy things, having fun, enjoying life. Politics, the depression, immorality, the downfall of Germany—these are not topics people like Sally want to think about. Ironically, life in Germany will soon *not* be a cabaret. Millions will be killed, war will ravage the country, Hitler will commit suicide, and Germany will surrender. To the Kit Kat Klub audience, Sally's song is delightful. To the real audience, with the knowledge of what will happen in Germany, the song is terribly disturbing. Subtextually, the lyric also describes the social activist mood of 1966 America—the refusal to sit at home doing nothing.

Designing Cabaret

The physical production is extremely important to the success of *Cabaret*. The two worlds must be firmly established visually for the audience. The show switches back and forth so often and so quickly that there can be no confusion in the audience's minds as to which world we're in at any given moment. It's almost like designing two separate shows. The easiest way to delineate the two worlds is to give them separate color palates and visual styles—the real world more realistic, dirty, dingy; the Kit Kat Klub more surrealistic, glittery, garish. In the original production, Hal Prince wanted a limbo area that was not part of either world, so scenic designer Boris Aronson created a curtain of light in front of the club. Performers could move in front of this light curtain and the club disappeared behind them. Prince wanted to distinguish between the book songs done in the club and the commentary songs; he didn't want both done in the same space. This limbo area was interesting and may have helped the audience distinguish the two kinds of songs, but the show can be done without it; it's not in the script. The Kit Kat Klub can be designed as a place that doesn't exist in real time or space. With careful staging and choreography, the surrealism of the club can be maintained at all times to make the two worlds separate. One production of the show placed the two worlds at opposite ends of the theatre and put the audience on stools. They had to physically turn around to move from one world to another.

To match the tone of the material, the choreography (with the exception of the engagement party) should be similarly vulgar and unpleasant. To emphasize the vulgarity in the film, Bob Fosse had the girls gain weight and stop shaving their armpits, and filled the choreography with lots of pelvic thrusts and strange, uncomfortable, unattractive poses. At the same time, it must be fun. We have to understand how the Germans could be charmed by the seemingly patriotic promises of the Nazis. When the show was in previews, Jerome Robbins, the noted director and choreographer of *West Side Story*, suggested to the show's creators that they eliminate all dance not in the Kit Kat Klub. They didn't follow his advice, but when Bob Fosse made the movie six years later, that's exactly what he did and it worked beautifully.

Other Resources

The script (the 1966 version), vocal selections (from the stage and film versions), and the full piano vocal score (the 1966 stage version) have all been published. The original cast recording is available, as is the film soundtrack. But remember that the show was changed in 1987. The song "Don't Go" replaced "Why Should I Wake Up." "I Don't Care" was added in the second act. "Meeskite." was cut. And "Sitting Pretty" was absorbed into the new medley, "The Money Song." References to Cliff's homosexuality were added and some things from the film script were interpolated.

The most valuable sources for background information will be history books on Weimar Germany and the rise of the Nazi party. One fascinating book that will offer great insights into the material is Linda Mizejewski's *Divine Decadence: Fascism, Female Spectacle, and the Makings of Sally Bowles* (Princeton University Press, 1992), which discusses every version of the Sally Bowles story—the short story, book, play, movie, stage musical, and movie musical.

Carousel

Book and Lyrics by Oscar Hammerstein II
Music by Richard Rodgers
Based on the play Liliom by Ferenc Molnár
Originally Directed on Broadway by Rouben Mamoulian
Licensed by the Rodgers and Hammerstein Theatre Library

arousel is often dismissed as silly sentimentality ("The vittles we et were good, you bet!"), when in fact it's Rodgers and Hammerstein's most psychological, most insightful, and most disturbing musical. It tells the tragic story of a naive young girl, a violent, sexual boy, and their doomed marriage. By the middle of the second act the girl is pregnant, and the boy has bungled a robbery attempt and committed suicide. The show is about sex, violence, spousal abuse, the indistinguishable line between good and evil, and the cruelty of fate. *The Sound of Music* it's not. Yet Richard Rodgers said on several occasions that it was his favorite of all the musicals he wrote. The score uses many of the conventions of opera, but in the vocabulary of the American musical comedy. Entire scenes are set to music. Rodgers and Hammerstein had reached the pinnacle of musical theatre writing in their ability to sustain musical and lyrical interest for such long spans of time while still maintaining musical unity and cohesion and dramatic intensity.

Unfortunately, *Carousel*'s classic status has made us so familiar with its story, its lyrics and its popular tunes that we tend to ignore the fascinating insights into human nature that lie beneath its surface. If we look at the show with a fresh eye, the lyric to "If I Loved You" isn't cliché. It's heartbreaking. Every line shows us two people very much in love who find it impossible to express that love, a problem that will plague their marriage and ruin their lives. It's tragic and touching. But we've stopped listening, and only with conscious effort can we look at the show as if for the first time—as director Nicholas Hytner did with the recent revival—and see the beauty, the subtlety, and the profound relevance to our contemporary lives.

Breaking Conventions

Rodgers and Hammerstein were known for breaking the rules when they wrote shows, both as partners and when working with others. Hammerstein wrote the lyrics to the ground-breaking, history-making *Show Boat*; Rodgers continually broke new ground with shows like *The Boys from Syracuse* (adapting Shakespeare to musical comedy), *Pal Joey* (using an antihero as a leading man), *On Your Toes* (using dance as an integral part of the story). Their first show together, *Oklahoma!*, broke additional ground. Two years later, they displayed even greater disinterest in the rules of musical comedy with *Carousel*, a morality play that sets unconquerable obstacles for its central characters and then moves unflinchingly toward tragedy. Billy Bigelow, the show's hero, is not only an antihero—arrogant, violent, inarticulate—he also commits suicide, leaving behind a pregnant wife. How did Rodgers and Hammerstein think they could get away with this in 1945? Many musical theatre audiences even today would find this story inappropriate for a musical. It's also important to keep in mind that when the show opened, women across the country had been widowed by World War II. This was a play that dealt head-on with the sorrow of real life. All the drama of the show is internal. The plot hinges on whether or not Billy and Julie will learn to express their love and heal their marriage and whether or not Billy will forsake his ego and get an honest job to support his wife and child. The conflict and resolution of the show happen entirely inside the characters' minds, again not the usual kind of story for a musical comedy.

As if that weren't enough, the show opened with a six-and-a-half-minute instrumental prologue during which the characters and relationships are introduced through *mime!* There was no traditional overture beginning the show, just this completely unprecedented wordless prologue. Throughout the show, Rodgers and Hammerstein wrote extensive musical scenes, with sung dialogue and fragments of songs, scenes in which the music would continue un-interrupted for ten minutes or more. Even today, this kind of con-struction is relatively uncommon. The show also dealt with unlikely musical comedy themes, including domestic violence, single moth-ers, suicide—themes that are still relevant to a nineties audience. Not even *Show Boat* and *Oklahoma!* were this extreme in their over-turning of the conventions of the American musical comedy. Sur-prisingly, audiences embraced the show, and it has stood the test of time; it was recently revived in both London and New York to criti-cal and popular acclaim.

You'll Never Walk Alone

One of the major textual themes in *Carousel* is that of community. The morals, opinions, and presence of the community are felt in every important event in the show. In Jeffrey Sweet's book *The Dramatist's Toolkit* (Heinemann, 1993), he talks about the nature of community in traditional musical comedy. According to Sweet, the members of the chorus represent a community, which shares words (lyrics) because it shares values; in essence the community is a char-acter in and of itself. The central character (in this case, Billy Bigelow) sings different words, and sings alone, because he does not share those values on some level; he doesn't fit in. This creates a conflict that can be resolved in one of two ways: either the two par-ties come to an accommodation whereby the hero learns to become a part of the community (as in *Brigadoon* or *Company*) or the indi-vidual is removed from the community (as in *Sweeney Todd*). They can't continue to live in conflict. In *Carousel*, Billy leaves the com-munity by committing suicide. But even after his death, the conflict is not resolved. Now, Julie and Louise are in conflict with the com-munity because of Billy's actions. With Billy's help from beyond the grave, they are brought into an accommodation with the commu-nity. The community in *Carousel* gets its own songs like any other character, including "June Is Busting Out All Over" and "This Was a Real Nice Clambake." The clambake is an important representation of this community, but Billy and Jigger use this tradition, this ritual, to commit robbery.

The song "You'll Never Walk Alone" has more than one mean-ing. On the surface, it is reassurance to Julie that she will not have to bear the grief of Billy's death and the raising of his child alone, that

Nettie (and God?) will be there for her. It's this reassuring message that has made the song so popular over the years. But it also has a deeper meaning. Like *Into the Woods*, *Carousel* makes it clear that it's not possible to act without regard for others. Every action has repercussions, and every individual has responsibility to the community. Billy doesn't learn this until after he's died. Nearly forty years after Oscar Hammerstein wrote the lyric for "You'll Never Walk Alone," his protégé Stephen Sondheim wrote a related lyric for "No One Is Alone" that includes the lines "No one acts alone. Careful, no one is alone." In any story, the main character has to learn something before the story ends. Billy's lesson is responsibility. When Julie tells him she's pregnant, he feels a certain responsibility, expressed in the last few lines of "Soliloquy," but he sees it more as a financial duty. He doesn't understand the full nature of responsibility until the end of the show.

Another prominent theme in the show is God. The most obvious example is in Act II when Billy goes to heaven and meets the Heavenly Friend and the Starkeeper, who may or may not be God. The Starkeeper shows up again in the last scene as Dr. Seldon. If we see the Starkeeper as God, then when he becomes Dr. Seldon, God is truly among us. As the doctor, he comments on having brought most of the graduating kids into the world. He can see Billy even though no one else can. He begins "You'll Never Walk Alone," which is more hymn than traditional finale. The lyric promises that if you have hope in your heart, you will never have to face your problems alone. On one level this refers to the friends that Julie and Louise have, but it also clearly refers to God. At the end of the scene, the Heavenly Friend escorts Billy back to heaven and as they pass Dr. Seldon/God, the stage direction says he "watches and smiles wisely." The Starkeeper has given Billy a chance at redemption, a chance to right his wrongs against his loved ones.

Sex and Violence

Throughout the first two-thirds of the show, Billy can express himself only two ways—through sex and violence. From the first moments of the prologue, we see that Billy has learned how to use his good looks, his sex appeal, for various means. He uses it to keep his job with Mrs. Mullin and to attract female customers to the carousel. He uses it to charm Julie. But sex gets him in trouble. Julie gets pregnant, which is Billy's primary motivation for agreeing to the robbery. When he can't express his emotions adequately, he gets frustrated and he resorts to violence. He hits Julie in Act I and Louise in Act II. He uses the threat of violence to scare away Mrs. Mullin on two different occasions. Julie knows he has this problem, but she thinks loving him is enough to get past this obstacle, as she sings in "What's the Use of Wonderin'." In contrast to Billy, Mr. Snow is also abusive to his wife, but on a verbal, emotional level, a kind of abuse frequently seen as more acceptable.

Billy the Kid

Billy Bigelow is not an evil man; he's screwed up. There is a constant internal struggle between his good side and his bad side. His fatal flaw is that he's still a kid. Though the roles of Billy and Julie have often been played by older adults, it's clear from their dialogue and their emotional immaturity that they are kids. Julie is probably still in her teens and Billy isn't much older. The recent revival of *Carousel* worked so well in large part due to the youth of the two leads. Billy is stubborn, selfish, arrogant, tempestuous. He experiences feelings of responsibility toward Julie and the new baby that he's never experienced before, and they lead him to profound panic. He doesn't know how to be a parent. He knows he has to support his new family, but doesn't know how. He is fiercely independent and proud of the fact that he doesn't have to rely on anyone else; so when he finds that he *needs* Julie and her love, it scares him. He has worked all his life at being his own man, at not bending to society's expectations. Now, suddenly, he finds himself on the road to conformity and respectability. He doesn't want that, yet he knows that refusing it will probably mean losing Julie. So he tries to accept the conventionality he's fought for so long, but ultimately he can't. Billy is charismatic and charming, and he knows how to woo the ladies. On the other hand, he's also a misogynist. Until he falls in love with Julie, women are only playthings to him; that he has such profound feelings for Julie is a big shock. Even though he loves her, he still orders her around, treats her like a child and servant, and even hits her. In "Soliloquy" he sings, "You can have fun with a son, but you gotta be a father to a girl" as if females are somehow innately weaker, more fragile, more needy. It's this unconscious sexism that prevents him from making Julie an equal partner in their marriage, which might've allowed him to communicate better with her. Because of his nearly paralyzing fear of how deeply he loves and needs Julie, it's impossible for him to ever discuss these feelings. It's not until after his death that he finally has the courage and self-knowledge to be able to articulate what he feels.

In the Act II ballet, Billy is forced to watch as a young man like him breaks the heart of his daughter, in much the same way that he broke Julie's heart. Louise is playing on the beach when a carnival arrives to the strains of the "Carousel Waltz," which accompanied the prologue. One of the boys in the carnival fascinates Louise; he is a carbon copy of Billy. He flirts with her and eventually makes love to her—her first time. When he begins his flirtation, it is to a musical motif that is an alteration of the first few notes of Billy's "Soliloquy." As they get more involved, the music changes to a pure quotation of "My Boy Bill." This boy is what Billy believed himself to be and what he hoped his son would be—a lady-killer. Remember that Billy had planned to teach his son "the way to get 'round any girl." Louise has, unfortunately, fallen in love with the young man, who, when he realizes this, is scared by her intensity and leaves her abruptly (as Billy did to Julie when he killed himself) as the music turns to the melody that accompanied "I wonder what he'll think of me. . . ." Now what does Billy think of himself and the macho persona he tried so hard to develop? He has had demonstrated for him how his attitude about women was hurtful and dangerous. Louise is devastated. The very qualities Billy once prized in himself and other men are the ones that have broken his daughter's (and his wife's) heart. Other children enter to play, and when Louise tries to join them, she is ostracized—as Julie and Louise have been by the rest of the town since Billy's suicide. Like her father before her, she lashes out at "polite" society. Billy finally begins to see the impact he has had on the lives of his loved ones.

In the following scene he sees Julie, though she can't see him. He sings a partial reprise of "If I Loved You," almost exactly the same as the original rendition except for minor lyric changes. Instead of singing "Soon, you'd leave me," he now sings "Now, I've lost you." Instead of the *possibility* of love lost expressed in the first version of the song, the lyric of this reprise recognizes that loss as an established fact. At the end he sings "And you never will know how I loved you." He understands fully the consequences of his actions.

It's interesting that Rodgers and Hammerstein chose to have Billy start singing halfway through the verse of the song. He doesn't have to sing the beginning, because he and Julie both know that he does in fact love her. This is the moment in which Billy has learned the lesson he must learn before the show can end, a moment set to the same music and (almost) the same lyrics that introduced his problem to us in Act I. In fact, the whole scene is underscored by "If I Loved You," music that represents both Billy's love for Julie and his inability to tell her, the two things that he finally reconciles in the scene. Now Julie must learn her lesson as well. As Billy decides to attend Louise's graduation, the underscoring appropriately changes to "My Little Girl."

A Queer One—Julie Jordan

Though Billy is the character that must change the most, Julie also has lessons to learn and demons to exorcise. As already mentioned, she is terribly young, probably still in her teens. She's probably never been in love before. During the Act I bench scene, it's pretty obvious that as she talks about being in love, it's a topic she knows nothing about. Her pronouncements about never getting married come from a girl who knows about love only in the abstract; she's never been there. She is dazzled and charmed by Billy. To her, he's a grown man, though he's not much older than she is. It's important to remember her background—she works in a mill and lives in a boardinghouse with other young girls. She obviously has no parents. She has no life experience. She's attracted to the bad boy in Billy. He's exciting, rebellious, and completely indifferent to the rules of polite society. He's all the things she'd like to be if she weren't afraid of the consequences. He also has an incredible air of self-confidence, which can be very sexy. Why does she stay with him, later, even though he hits her? Because she has fallen in love with him. She thinks she understands him and that her love can change/save him. Julie is what we call a "rescuer" today. The appeal of seeing herself as his only salvation is too strong to resist. She loves him unconditionally, but like him, she is unable to express her love and this undoubtedly makes it even harder for him to express his. Her song "What's the Use of Wonderin'" speaks volumes about the way she sees love and marriage—and it isn't healthy. Julie must learn to express her love and to look at love (Billy) realistically. Billy is neither God nor devil. Like most men, he's somewhere in between.

Breaking New Ground

Carousel has a number of extended musical scenes in which the music does as much to advance the plot and characterizations as the words do. Rodgers and Hammerstein elected to completely skip the traditional overture as well as the opening number and conventional character exposition. In their place, they created a six-and-a-half-minute mimed prologue to Rodgers's now famous "Carousel Waltz." The strangely dissonant music establishes the tone of the entire show within the first few moments. As the curtain rises on the carousel and townspeople, conflicts already exist between Billy and Mrs. Mullin, between the upper and lower classes, between the girls vying for Billy's attentions. Before a single word of dialogue, we've met the three main characters (Billy, Julie, and Carrie), we've established the nature of Billy and Julie's relationship, and even some of Billy's personality flaws that will haunt their marriage.

The first of the integrated musical scenes is between Julie and Carrie. Rodgers and Hammerstein smooth the often bumpy transition from spoken word to singing by beginning with rhythmic spoken dialogue over music, as Carrie quizzes Julie on whether or not she's fallen for Billy (of course, we know she has). Carrie then sings "You're a Queer One, Julie Jordan," introducing the concept that Julie doesn't talk about her feelings—an important issue later in the show. This section includes a bridge about how spaced-out Julie is when she is weaving in Bascombe's mill; the music plays a repetitive rhythmic pattern over and over, illustrating the monotony of their work. Then Carrie reveals to Julie, in dialogue over underscoring, that she has a man as well. She sings "His Name is Mister Snow," which segues directly into "When I Marry Mister Snow." Yet even after she sings of how much she loves him and how happy they'll be, she describes him as overbearing in the last line of the song. Earlier, she has discussed the fact that he smells profoundly of fish. Hammerstein is introducing the concept of marriage as an imperfect thing, not the ideal institution old-fashioned musical comedies had painted it to be.

Two Pair

Later in the same book scene, the show's most famous extended musical scene, which lasts for more than twelve minutes, begins between Julie and Billy. Again, the transition from spoken word to song is smoothed by beginning underscoring beneath spoken dialogue. The music is "You're a Queer One, Julie Jordan," the song that described Julie's inability to express herself. Billy himself sings a verse of the song. After a short bridge sung by Julie, the two move into a musical dialogue about whether Julie has had any other boyfriends. Julie sings "I'm Never Goin' to Marry" and we see how naive and immature she really is about love and marriage. Over more instrumental music, they both cautiously drop hints about their feelings. The music returns to the "weaving" music from Julie and Carrie's earlier conversation, and Julie describes how it would be if she were in love with Billy, using the conditional "if" to protect herself. This leads into the central ballad of the show, "If I Loved You." The lyric to this song fully and richly characterizes both Julie and Billy, two kids who have never learned to trust anyone enough to allow them to express their feelings. As the music continues underneath, they make small talk. Billy talks about the world around them, as usual seeing his own characteristics reflected there. He sings, "The tide's creepin' up on the beach like a thief, afraid to be caught stealin' the land." This is how he always feels, afraid that he will be "caught" for refusing to live by society's rules. He goes on to comment on the enormity of the stars and the sky (a reference that foreshadows his trip to heaven in Act II) and that in the grand scheme of things, he and Julie don't really matter. After some more dialogue over music, Billy sings a variation on Julie's "weaving" music, describing how being in love would affect him. As it did with Julie, this music leads him directly into "If I Loved You." His rendition is exactly like Julie's, even in the same key; however, it's interesting that though they sing the same material, they never sing *together*, as Carrie and Mr. Snow will. Though they share feelings, they don't really fit together. The scene closes with a short bit of dialogue that sums up their conversation. Billy says, "I'm not a feller to marry anybody," and the truth is, he's not. Julie says, "You're right about there bein' no wind. The blossoms are jest comin' down by themselves. Jest their time, I reckon." Things just happen sometimes because it's their time to happen, and Julie believes that's why she and Billy have found each other. As the music climaxes, Billy leans over and kisses Julie.

The next extended musical scene is between Mr. Snow and Carrie. Snow is portrayed as the exact opposite of the unpredictable, unreliable Billy. The scene begins with Snow outlining how he's going to build a fleet of fishing boats and become a respectable businessman. After a short dialogue scene over music he describes, to the same music, how he'll build a family of children in much the same way. This leads into "When the Children Are Asleep," Carrie and Snow's anthem of peaceful domesticity. The first verse is Snow's, the second is Carrie's. In the third verse, Carrie sings the melody, while Mr. Snow sings a countermelody between her lines. As the song builds to its finish, they finally sing at the same time. Unlike Billy and Julie, these two don't just sing the same things, they sing together. Not only are their dreams similar, but they belong together, as the music illustrates. In most musical comedies, the second couple are comic characters whose relationship mirrors the romantic leads in a comedic way, like Ado Annie and Will Parker in *Oklahoma!* But again, Rodgers and Hammerstein broke the rules with *Carousel* (and would do the same in *The King and I, South Pacific, The Sound of Music*). Here, Mr. Snow and Carrie represent everything Julie and Billy want but will never have—a quiet, respectable life, a big family, and financial security. Here, the second couple is what the leading couple would be if not for their fatal flaws.

Flying Solo

Billy's "Soliloquy" is one of the most impressive and often studied songs in the musical theatre. It lasts more than seven minutes, yet never gets boring and maintains a sense of unity by using two main musical themes—one for Billy's dreams of a baby boy and one for his fantasies of a baby girl. The piece starts with Billy's revelation that he's going to be a father and how fun it's going to be to raise a son. He decides he'll teach his son to be exactly like him. When Billy launches into the first musical theme, "My Boy Bill," he is describing his son but we soon see that he's really describing himself. More so here than at any other moment in the show, we get tremendous insights into how Billy's mind works, his values, his self-knowledge (which is minimal at this point), and his feelings about himself. The characteristics he catalogs for "Bill" are strength, independence, and attractiveness, all of which he sees as his own best qualities. As the song continues, he sees "Bill" in various situations that illustrate these qualities. It's terribly important to Billy that his boy not be a sissy, which is how Billy sees Mr. Snow, Bascombe, and the other upper-middle-class people in the town. Billy's son will work with his hands. Billy will teach him "the way to get 'round any girl," tricks Billy has learned to get and keep girlfriends. Midway through the song, it suddenly occurs to Billy that his child might be a girl. The idea is shocking to him. After all, how can a girl be a carbon copy of Billy? He says, "Bill . . . oh, Bill!" as if his son has let him down by becoming a daughter. The second major theme of the song, "My Little Girl," takes over as the main theme as Billy considers this second possibility. Again, he imagines her being charming and attractive to the opposite sex. Even though he sees her looking like Julie, he tries again to imbue her with his own characteristics. The difference here is that Billy is terribly sexist and misogynistic. "Bill" will be tough, tall, strong, maybe even the President; but the daughter will be "pink and white" as well as "half again as bright as girls are meant to be" and, of course, totally dependent on her father for her happiness and her survival. Though he will undoubtedly love his daughter, she will be weak and needy; sadly, this is the way Billy sees Julie. Of course in Act II, Julie will prove that she's strong enough to raise a child by herself, a task forced upon her because her screwed-up husband killed himself. Billy ends the piece vowing that one way or another he'll support his child, even if it means stealing money. It's sad that he thinks stealing will make him a good father.

It's important to notice that Billy starts "Soliloquy" by speculating on what his child will think of him. As always, Billy only perceives the world in terms of how it affects him. The first line of the piece is "I wonder what he'll think of me!" Even though he's just found out he's going to be a father, his first thoughts are still of himself, of his image. Throughout the song, Billy invests so much of his personality in his child that his song of pride over his new son or daughter is largely a self-congratulatory valentine to Billy. The song ends as it began—with Billy talking about himself.

To Wed or Not To Wed

The last of the extended musical scenes begins with a new conflict. Mr. Snow has caught Jigger carrying Carrie over his shoulder. Though Jigger's intentions were to seduce her, nothing has happened yet; but Mr. Snow believes something has, and he breaks the engagement. Mr. Snow begins singing "Geraniums in the Winder," describing the perfect domestic life he had planned, which now can never be; Carrie whimpers continuously in the background. This is followed by Jigger's "Stonecutters Cut It on Stone," in which he declares that there's nothing worse for a woman than a man who believes that he's a good man (like Mr. Snow). The chorus joins Jigger's song, and when it's done Mr. Snow and his supporters start a shouting match with Jigger and his supporters. There is some brief dialogue without music. Then one of the women in the crowd starts "Stonecutters" again and she's quickly joined by the other women. Arminy, a married woman, supports the argument with her own firsthand experience. Carrie has serious doubts about men by now, so Julie sings "What's the Use of Wonderin'." On the surface, this song sounds like a lot of old-fashioned love songs, the main point of which is that all that really matters is love. But this lyric is undercut with some very disturbing lines. She sings, "Common sense may tell you the endin' will be sad, and now's the time to break and run away." The line that offers us the most insight into Julie is "And something gave him the things that are his. One of those things is you." The music continues underneath as Billy and Jigger reenter. Julie tries to keep Billy from going with Jigger. She finds the knife he's carrying and asks him to give it to her, but he refuses. She has no control over him. How could she when she sees herself as one of his possessions? The scene ends with Julie worried, Billy going off to his death, and the women reprising "What's the Use of Wonderin'," though now, the lyric's fatalistic attitude is a good deal grimmer.

A Few Words of Warning

After discussing the incredible power and subtlety of *Carousel* and its relevance to our contemporary world, I must also offer some words of warning to anyone planning to do the show. First, some audiences demand a happy ending, and despite the last song, this show doesn't really have one. Julie and Billy have finally expressed their love on some level, but Julie is still raising a daughter on her own, Billy is still dead, Billy and Julie will never be together again. The ending will leave audiences with a mixed reaction, which is the idea, but don't think this is *Brigadoon*. (Rodgers and Hammerstein liked to write about death. Just look at *Carousel*, *South Pacific*, and *The King and I*.) And the hymnlike "You'll Never Walk Alone" is ridiculed nowadays as often as it's praised. Upon close inspection, it's exactly what was required, but can you get a contemporary audience to take it seriously, to really listen to its lyric? The other song that poses a problem is "The Highest Judge of All," reportedly written just to cover a scene change and cut from the recent revival (remember, you can't cut songs without permission). Another problem the show suffers from is its movie version. *Carousel* on film is extraordinarily bad (for dozens of reasons not interesting enough to go into here), and people who only know the show through the film will come in (*if* they come in) daring you to make them like it.

The most important thing for the people working on the show is not to be too reverent. Yes, *Carousel* is a classic, but it doesn't have to be a museum piece. Don't take the songs extra slow because you think that'll make them more dramatic; it will only bore your audience. And remember that the show is a fable, a morality play. Though the emotions are real, the story is not realistic. You don't need realistic sets. Let the show be as fantastical as it is. It's also important not to be too extreme with characterizations. Despite the hocus-pocus of the plot, the things these people are feeling are real, and the more real they appear, the easier it will be for the audience to relate to them. Jigger will seem to be more of a threat if he's a real person instead of a cartoon villain. He's not evil; he's just amoral. If he's played more subtly, allowed to be more smartass than Snidely Whiplash, the audience will be constantly wondering when he's going to strike out and really cause trouble, thus raising the tension level considerably. It will also be more disconcerting if Mr. Snow is more real than cartoon, with his very real kinds of prejudice, snobbery, and manipulation. The more real the people, the more deeply audiences will be moved. Most significant, Billy and Julie's star-crossed love will be all the more tragic (and easier to empathize with) if they are played as the mixed-up kids they were intended to be. It's not their actions that ruin their marriage nearly as much as their profound immaturity and naïveté. Neither of them are really ready for the things they have to face, and we've all been in that situation at some point in our lives. Be true to the emotion of the piece and you can't go wrong.

The World of *Carousel*

Why is *Carousel* considered such a classic? Why is it so powerful, more so than any other Rodgers and Hammerstein show, more so than all but a handful of musicals? It's because Rodgers and Hammerstein acknowledge the evil and danger in the world—death, despair, loss, loneliness—without sugarcoating it and yet at the same time imply that there is a goodness that can overcome the bad. Certainly, today as much as in 1945 postwar America, this is a message we need to hear. Stephen Sondheim once compared Rodgers and Hammerstein's first two shows very succinctly, and his statement is frequently quoted: "*Oklahoma!* is about a picnic; *Carousel* is about life and death." Hammerstein believed that though there is pain in the world, there is also healing. Especially in the current atmosphere of politicians lashing out against the entertainment industry for destroying the moral fabric of our country, *Carousel* has become an interesting example of an unflinching look at what's wrong with our society but also what's *right*.

Other Resources

The script, the score, and vocal selections have all been published. The movie version is on videotape, but it's pretty bad and takes a lot of liberties with the stage script. Watching it may be more of a hindrance than a help. There are many recordings of the score. The original Broadway cast recording is interesting because this is presumably the way Rodgers and Hammerstein wanted their songs performed. Unfortunately, most of the extended musical scenes were mercilessly cut down to fit on the record. The 1987 studio recording is well sung, but slow and tedious. The most exciting, most interesting recording is the 1994 Broadway revival cast recording.

Company

Book by George Furth
Music and Lyrics by Stephen Sondheim
Originally Directed on Broadway by Harold Prince
Licensed by Music Theatre International

When *Company* opened on Broadway in 1970, audiences were not accustomed to concept musicals—this was the first that was a success—or to shows that dealt with the warts-and-all reality of love and marriage. John Lahr wrote in the *Village Voice*, "In *Company*, no one dreams, only survives." Audiences were generally used to shows about ideal love and happy endings. *Company* thumbed its nose at this shallow view of life. The show presented five different kinds of couples—Harry and Sarah, who constantly ridicule each other; Susan and Peter, who are getting divorced, discarding legal marriage, in order to maintain a happy and close relationship; David, a control freak, and Jenny, his submissive wife; Amy and Paul, who've been living together for years and are finally getting married; and Joanne and Larry, each married several times. The unmarried Robert observes and interacts with his married friends over the course of the show and must come to some conclusion about whether or not he wants to be married himself. Each couple teaches Robert a different lesson about commitment.

If some people think the end of the show is ambiguous, it's because it is. Sondheim wrote four different climactic songs for the show, each a different decision for Robert; but even "Being Alive," the one that survived, doesn't completely resolve Robert's ambivalence. Rebelling against musical theatre's traditional oversimplification of the human condition, Sondheim, Prince, and Furth were determined to make a theatre piece about the real world. Not everyone loved *Company*, but everyone agreed it was something new and courageous. Even today, it is remarkable in its form and ambition.

The Concept Musical

Company established the concept musical as a new kind of show that contains snapshots, ideas, questions, presented without linear logic or plot. In fact, even the vignettes within the show don't have traditional beginnings, middles, and ends. *Company* comprises a series of impressions that the audience—and Robert—must use to form conclusions about love and marriage. Most of the songs in the show are commentary songs, often sung by characters not involved in the scene, addressing the audience directly. Only occasionally ("Barcelona" for example) does a song grow organically out of the scene as in traditional musicals.

But *Company* isn't about marriage as most of us usually think of it. It's about marriage in its most basic, purest sense—the union of two people. This show isn't about four-tiered wedding cakes, marriage licenses, and joint tax returns. It's about emotional commitment, sharing lives, loving unconditionally, surviving the tough times together. Robert doesn't realize during "Being Alive" that he wants to get a marriage license and have a nice wedding ceremony; he realizes that he wants to share his life with someone. In fact, the show makes a strong argument that legal marriage and commitment are not necessarily one and the same. Susan and Peter are getting divorced, rejecting traditional, legal marriage, so that they can be happy together. Amy and Paul have been happy together, and committed, for years without legal marriage. When the couples sing about how important marriage is to them, they're talking about emotional issues, not legal ones. *Company* is about the basic, universal, human need for love and companionship.

A close reading of the script suggests that perhaps what we're seeing onstage is actually a collection of Robert's memories or impressions. If indeed we're swimming around inside Robert's head, reading his thoughts about his friends and therefore about marriage, this explains a great deal. It provides a rationale for the episodic, seemingly random nature of the scenes, as well as the fact that we seem to be seeing everyone and everything through Robert's cynical eyes. If this is true, then as Robert slowly forms a more mature understanding of relationships, so must the characterizations of the married people get deeper and more complete; the more Robert understands them, the more fully they are portrayed in his mind. Since the show is about Robert's mental journey and transformation, it makes sense that we take that journey inside his mind. There is nothing concrete in the text to suggest that this is the only way to interpret the show, but it's consistent with the show's structure and presentation and it opens up lots of interesting possibilities in regard to staging, characterization, and design.

Sondheim's score is perfectly integrated into George Furth's book, yet, contrary to all the rules of musical theatre, the show would work without the score. This anomoly exists because the characters step outside of scenes with most of the songs, offering a Brechtian commentary on the action that has preceded. The scenes could exist without the commentary, but the show is much richer because it's there. The deeper motivations, fears, and joys of these characters are subtext in the dialogue scenes and are more fully explored in the songs. The book presents us with situations and problems; the score provides analysis and understanding. As in Sondheim's later shows, characters often end their songs in a different place emotionally or intellectually from where they started. Unlike most musicals that had gone before, *Company* was driven by character not plot. The primary concern is who Robert is and who he becomes (or is about to become).

Staging

Because *Company* is a concept musical and because the book and score are so dense, it's important to be very careful with staging. There are two primary concerns. First, the show is about Robert's isolation and disconnection from the rest of the world. Aside from the scenes in which he is an integral part of the action, Robert should be kept visibly separate from the other people onstage. The audience has to be able to *see* his detachment. This can be accomplished with lighting, leaving dark areas between him and other playing areas, or by having a separate platform or stage that is Robert's personal space throughout the show.

Second, it's important not to overstage the more densely written songs. "The Little Things You Do Together," "The Ladies Who Lunch," and the other songs that impart a great deal of information and subtext must be staged minimally so as not to distract the audience from concentrating on the lyrics. Movement on stage always overshadows words. When words or subtext are the primary concern in a song (and it's largely a judgment call for the director to decide which songs fall into this category), the blocking can't be allowed to pull the focus. Many songs, like "The Ladies Who Lunch" (or "Somewhere That's Green" in *Little Shop of Horrors*, "Send in the Clowns" in *A Little Night Music*) are far more powerful when the singer doesn't move.

Bobby Buby

Though Robert is the main character, the show is just as much about marriage, as personified by the five couples. He is an instrument through which we view the others. He is the audience's surrogate, observing and occasionally commenting on the couples and the love and marriage they illustrate. This was a new way to use the main character in a musical when *Company* opened in 1970, but the concept musical was a new kind of musical. Five years later, *A Chorus Line* would use Zach as a similar device. In 1978, Stephen Schwartz tried this device in *Working* but couldn't get it to work and abandoned the idea. Much later with *Assassins*, Sondheim and John Weidman used the Balladeer both to view the characters for us, as Robert did, and to represent the American storytelling tradition, which motivated several of the assassins' acts. Long after *Company*, this kind of character study developed to a point at which the show no longer needed a "viewer" character, in musicals like *March of the Falsettos*, *Falsettoland*, *Nine*, *Sunday in the Park with George*, and others.

At times, Robert functions as a kind of narrator, yet a very biased one. We see the five marriages through his eyes, the faults and shallowness intensified and the genuine emotion underneath all but ignored. This of course poses a problem for the actors playing the married couples. They have to find the real love in the songs and the subtext of the dialogue and play it despite Robert's refusal to see it.

Robert is the most difficult character to play, though, because he is in many ways a blank page with no observable emotions, no admitted conflicts to resolve. He's okay where he is. Yet he is the most troubled and the most in need of change. Because we don't see him through someone else's eyes, he must also be the most real. More than anyone else on stage Robert must create a full and complete life with very little help from the text. The actor must be aware of the arc of Robert's change throughout the show and help us see him move slowly toward the revelations of "Being Alive."

Audiences and critics have speculated about Robert's sexuality. Is he gay? Is that why he won't get close to women? There's nothing in the book or score to suggest that and pursuing it would only muddy an already complex show.

Looking Back

It is interesting that the couples also provide a lens through which we see Robert. Hundreds of little details in the couples' attitudes toward Robert characterize him for us. The most significant of these is the nicknames they call him in the opening number and throughout the show. Each married person has a different nickname for Robert, and these nicknames tells us a lot about how that person feels about Robert. They also tell us a great deal about the couples. Robert is passive throughout the entire show until the last song. It's hard for the audience to develop any real feelings for him, since he has no goal, no desires; he is essentially content where he is. In a normal musical, this would mean stagnation. But in this case, the five couples around Robert want a relationship for him so much that *their* desires *for* him become what moves the show along. They take action in his place—fixing him up with girls, etc.—in order to achieve what they want him to have.

Joanne is the real commentator in the show. She sees the truth more clearly and more unsentimentally than any other character. She is a very real woman who sees faults in herself as readily as in others (as in "The Ladies Who Lunch"). She understands the joys and pains of marriage better than anyone else, because she's been married more than anyone else. She also understands Robert. She says to him just before the finale, "You were outside looking in the window while everybody was inside dancing at the party." She sees what it's taken us a full evening to figure out—that Robert keeps the world at arm's length. He observes but never participates for fear of the inevitable pain and failure that comes with pursuing relationships. Most important, it is Joanne, armed with her unique knowledge and insight, who finally pushes Robert toward the revelations of "Being Alive" at the end of the show. Her character is summed up in one of her lines in the Act II opening: "Sometimes I catch him looking and looking. I just look right back."

New York, New York

Company is about the chic, intellectual, spiritually empty people living in the Big Apple. More so than Sondheim's earlier scores (*A Funny Thing Happened on the Way to the Forum* and *Anyone Can Whistle*), the music is driving and pulsing, the lyrics sophisticated and cynical. "Another Hundred People," a song about New York, is often criticized as not belonging in the *Company* score, but the people who criticize it are overlooking its central theme. The song is about the inability of people in New York City to connect to each other. New York is an exciting city, and Robert certainly wants excitement, which is part of what his male married friends envy about him. But it is a "city of strangers," a comment on both the city itself and on Robert's relationships. The trumpets even quote the "Bobby Buby" motif in the last verse to remind us that Robert is one of the disconnected strangers Marta is describing.

This is not the New York City we see in musicals like *On the Town* and *Annie*, but it is a *real* New York. All the physical descriptions of the city are unpleasant—graffiti, battered trees, "crowded streets," "guarded parks." People in New York (according to the song) meet at parties filled with people they don't know. They leave each other messages through answering services. The unrelenting pulse of the music characterizes both the city and Robert's life. The accompaniment figure is busy, hurried, seemingly chaotic. It consists of four separate voices, all running against each other—the regular, minimalist 4/4 bass line; a tenor line that sounds like a 6/8 rhythm with one extra eighth note every other measure; an alto line that also sounds like a 6/8 rhythm, but displaced by one eighth note from the tenor line; and a top line of displaced half notes that doesn't line up with any of the other voices. Four separate voices come together in controlled chaos underneath a vocal part that is firmly in a regular 4/4 meter, lining up with only the bottom of the four accompaniment voices. In the bridge before the final verse, Jonathan Tunick's orchestrations even add to the fray with the "Bobby Buby" motif in the trumpets. Like the people described in the song's lyric, the several musical voices never quite come together, leaving the listener intentionally unsettled.

Words and Music

Because *Company* was conceived as a show about contemporary urban life, the score employs many of the conventions of rock, pop, and folk-rock music: an often slow or stagnant harmonic line, a rock bass line mostly on the root of each chord, repeated notes and chords, heavy percussion, and electrics (both electric keyboards and electric guitars). Much of this is in the basic construction of Sondheim's songs, but it's also enhanced greatly by Tunick's orchestrations. Though some of these instruments may make the score sound unnecessarily dated today (the sound is firmly rooted in the early 1970s), careful substitution of the electric sounds with more contemporary sounds will eliminate that problem. Because of the nature of the subject matter, the show can be played as a period piece set in 1970 or as a contemporary show set today. Either way, the music can work effectively.

Sondheim has often said that rhyme in lyrics equates with a character's intelligence and presence of mind and that expressions of intellectual ideas contain more rhyme than expressions of emotion. So, the clever commentary songs that cover up the characters' emotions ("The Little Things You Do Together," "The Ladies Who Lunch") are filled with internal rhymes. The songs of genuine emotion and less forethought ("Sorry-Grateful," "Someone Is Waiting," "Being Alive") have far less rhyme. A song like "Getting Married Today" has virtually no rhyme in its verses because Amy is in a panic and not at all in control of her faculties.

Like many of Sondheim's later scores, *Company* is filled with commentary songs. In more traditional musicals, songs grow naturally out of dialogue, and characters aren't aware of the fact that they're singing. In many of the songs in *Company* (and in *Follies, Into the Woods, Assassins,* and other Sondheim shows), the characters step out of the scene and address the audience directly. Bertolt Brecht called this theatrical device the "alienation effect," intended to make the audience step back and *think* about what's happening rather than just feeling all warm and fuzzy. The use of pastiche sprinkled throughout the evening contributes to this alienation effect. Both the close-harmony Andrews Sisters style of

"You Could Drive a Person Crazy" and the frenetic vaudeville flavor of "What Would We Do Without You" are so different from the rock/pop-inspired rhythms of the rest of the score that the audience is jarred by the change and forced to step back from the action.

Company's score was also unusual in its extensive use of musical motifs to connect characters and events, something that Sondheim would develop more and more throughout his career. The "Bobby Buby" motif used throughout the show focuses our attention on the married couples in opposition to Robert. Both "Tick Tock" and "Being Alive" make interesting use of motifs from earlier in the show (as discussed later in this chapter).

In Comes Company

It has been said that you can do anything you want in a musical as long as you do it within the first ten minutes. In other words, audiences will accept any style of music, any unusual structural devices (the reversed time sequence of *Merrily We Roll Along*, for example), any subject matter (*Little Shop of Horrors*, *Assassins*), anything at all, as long as the show's particular ground rules are established in the first ten minutes. And that's exactly what the opening of *Company* does.

The opening bars of the song "Company" instantly establish the frenetic, pulsing rhythm of the score with the telephone busy signal followed by opening chords that continue the pulse (it's interesting that the first words heard over this pulse are "Phone rings"). The busy signal immediately suggests the difficulty of connecting and communicating in the crazy world of modern city life. When the voices enter, the couples and their almost smothering attention to Robert are established as the focus of the show. They begin with their various nicknames for him, which recur throughout the score. This quickly segues into a succession of short phrases ("We've been trying to call you," "I've got something to tell you," "We've been trying to reach you all day") that illustrate how hard it is to communicate with Robert.

We hear the voices through Robert's ears, overlapping, overwhelming. It is the constant noise of New York, literally "filling the days" as the lyric says. The couples give Robert too much attention to keep straight. It is emotional and literal chaos. Robert sees them as "good and crazy people." Toward the end of the song, the couples sing "We love you," holding the note on "love" for a full twenty measures. In the original production, this was partly to accommodate the movement of the elevators used in the set. It also emphasizes to an almost ridiculous degree that this is a show about love; but the length of this note makes it an unnatural, uncomfortable (try holding a note for twenty measures) kind of love. The last full sentence in the opening song is "Love is company!" The title of the show is equated with the concept of love and, by implication, both are equated with marriage. Before the first song is over, Sondheim has established the style and energy of the show, the brittle cleverness of the lyrics, the relationships between Robert and his married friends, and the show's major themes.

Marriage May Be Where It's Been, But It's Not Where It's At

The show now gets underway and we meet the first of Robert's friends, Sarah and Harry. As we will throughout the show, we see them through Robert's eyes, at their worst. Their conversation is full of humiliating barbs, put-downs, contradictions, jokes that aren't just jokes. The verbal abuse soon becomes physical as Sarah demonstrates her karate on Harry—repeatedly. Joanne enters, the scene freezes, and the show's first commentary song, "The Little Things You Do Together," begins. Before the song is over, the other couples have all joined Joanne, all of them watching Sarah and Harry. Like the scene, the song is full of unpleasant references ("children you destroy together," "shouting 'til you're hoarse together, getting a divorce together"). The list of "little things" that "make perfect relationships" is full of negative connotations. The irony of how "perfect" marriage is in their eyes gets thicker and thicker as the song progresses. The sharp edge of *Company's* take on marriage was hinted at in the opening number, but here it is explicit. At the same time, though, the married couples know something Robert has yet to learn: even unpleasant situations are easier to endure when you're not alone. Marriage is about shared experience.

At the end of the scene, after Robert has left, Sarah says, "I love you" to Harry as she leaves, and despite the scene we've just witnessed, we know she means it. From across the stage, outside the scene—looking in from the outside as always—Robert asks Harry if he's ever sorry he got married. Harry sings the song "Sorry-Grateful," which encapsulates the main point of the show—that marriage is difficult, sometimes lonely, sometimes oppressive, but ultimately worth it. This is something Robert doesn't yet understand, but all the married men do (they join Harry in the song). This is the principal lesson Robert will learn by the end of the show. Once this song is done, *Company* has made a sharp departure from most of the musical theatre that came before it. This realistic, eyes-open depiction of love and marriage is rarely found in musicals. Consistent with Sondheim's theories about rhyming, "Sorry-Grateful" has very little internal rhyming. This is a song about genuine feeling, devoid of the clever, intellectual banter of "The Little Things You Do Together."

In "Have I Got a Girl for You" the husbands express an envy of Robert's free, single life. Yet we (and Robert, too, probably) remember "Sorry-Grateful" and know that despite their envy, they don't wake up alone in the morning. All the girls the husbands describe for Robert are one-nighters. They slam the institution of marriag again, but their actions belie their words. None of them are looking for another girl. They can enjoy the safety and companionship of marriage while vicariously enjoying the freedom and adventure— but not the anxiety—of Robert's bachelorhood. "Call me tomorrow, I want the details," Larry sings.

In "Someone Is Waiting," Robert comments for the first time on his situation. With very little rhyme, the lyric is one of genuine emotion. We believe what Robert is singing. But he doesn't want a real woman. He wants a fantasy composite of the married women he knows. He wants all the good and none of the bad, and he only wants women he already knows, so that there are no surprises. At the end of the song he sings, "I'm ready now," yet he isn't. He's only ready for an artificial, carefully constructed, completely safe relationship. He is not ready for the reality of marriage.

Crazy Amy

The last scene of the first act is particularly interesting because Amy "becomes" Robert for a moment. She and Paul have been living together for many years, but are finally getting married. Her song, "Getting Married Today," is an anguished (though very funny) cry of terror. Amy sings terribly fast patter verses that have no rhyme because Amy is not thinking rationally. At the end of each verse, she slows down slightly for a break, which does have minimal rhyming. In between her verses, a soprano and Paul have slower verses of their own. Though much slower, Paul's verses also have very little rhyme, because they are full of genuine emotion. When Paul's and Amy's vocal lines come together in counterpoint at the end of the song, it's the first time in the show that two people have sung a duet. In a show about marriage, you'd expect love duets, but only this song and "Barcelona" involve a couple singing to each other; and these are no ordinary love duets. In "Getting Marred Today," one of them doesn't want to get married and the other does. In "Barcelona," the two are having an uncomfortable conversation after a one-night stand. After "Getting Married Today," Amy tells Paul she won't marry him and he leaves distraught.

Now that Amy feels the same way about marriage that Robert does, he asks her to marry him, though not for the right reasons. He says to her, "Marry me! And everybody'll leave us alone!" Robert's lack of understanding about marriage—about the love involved— jolts Amy back to reality. She will marry Paul. The act ends with a silent return to the birthday party the show began with, the symbol of Robert's growing up.

Three Is Company

The second act opening contrasts Robert with his married friends. Even the title of "Side by Side by Side" hints that something is not right. The twist of the third "side" added to this very common phrase catches our attention. The audience knows that people don't go through life in threes. Robert's idea of heaven is being with a pair of his married friends, who dote on him nonstop. He sings, "Three is company, safe and cheery." Again, his problem is right there—that he only feels safe with his married friends—but it's camouflaged by the charming music.

The song segues into the more raucous vaudeville number "What Would We Do Without You?"—a tribute by the couples to the value of Robert's friendship. The most chilling moment comes when the couples sing, "What would we do without you?" Robert answers, "Just what you usually do," and they all yell, "Right!" The truth is that they *don't* need him; they have each other. Despite what the lyrics of these two songs may say, it is clear that Robert is an unnecessary though pleasant addition to their lives. No one needs him. In a stroke of choreographic genius, each couple gets a tap break during the last section of the song. The couples sing the words "side by side" before each break, but there is no third "by side" anymore. The third "side," which represented Robert, has been dropped from the lyric. In each tap break, one spouse does a step, then the other mirrors it. Robert gets his break last; he does his step, *but no one is there to mirror it.*

A City of Strangers

Next, the five wives sing the blues-inspired "Poor Baby," in which we see that they like Robert's tremendous reliance on them and that they find something wrong with every girl he dates. In some ways, they don't really want him to find someone, because then they will lose him. *They* want to be the women in his life. The unfairness of their criticisms is driven home very powerfully with Joanne's wonderfully absurd comment, "She's tall enough to be your mother."

Robert brings home a stewardess named April. The scene that follows between them is almost painful to watch. They relate only on a physical level, and their effort to have a conversation before sex is ridiculous. They go to bed, and Kathy does a "sex" dance to the sound of their thoughts during sex. The stage direction in the script says, "Kathy's dance expresses the difference between having sex and making love." If that seems like too daunting a task, remember that it was originally staged by the brilliant Michael Bennett.

This dance, called "Tick Tock," has an interesting background. When Michael Bennett choreographed *Promises, Promises* (also orchestrated by Jonathan Tunick) in 1968, the show contained a song called "Tick Tock" sung by a group of women that included Donna McKechnie. The song was cut during the Boston tryout. Two years later, with Bennett, McKechnie, and Tunick all working on *Company*, a dance number emerged also called "Tick Tock."

Constructed by David Shire, this is a musical sequence worth dissecting, both to understand its place in the show and to help the choreographer structure the dance. It starts with dissonant chords like those in the opening number, characterizing the tension between Robert and April. The music changes to a fast, pulsing musical vamp very like "Another Hundred People," implying that Robert and April represent the thousands in the city who can't connect to each other. The music then changes to "Poor Baby," reminding us of the wives' conviction that this girl isn't right for Robert. The pulse of "Another Hundred People" then combines with the melodic material from "Poor Baby." At measure 113 in the published score, the *Twilight Zone* theme makes a funny and telling appearance over the melody of "Someone Is Waiting." The music stops when April says, "I love you." Robert panics and we hear the "Bobby Buby" motif, the musical signature of his married friends, the only people with whom he feels safe. He can't say "I love you," but the couples can, and they do, as the music quotes two important phrases from the opening number: "love filling our days" and "to Bobby with love." These married friends are the only people for whom Robert feels real love. The music returns to "Someone Is Waiting," the song of Robert's desperate quest for the prefect woman, which April clearly is not. The sequence ends as it began, with chords like those accompanying the lines "phone rings, door chimes" in the opening number. The "Tick Tock" sequence is fascinating because it follows Robert's thoughts using musical motifs we've heard earlier in the show, capitalizing on the associations the audience has with those pieces of music.

"Tick Tock" moves directly into "the morning after" and perhaps the funniest song in the score, "Barcelona." This song shows Robert and April trying to have a conversation after a night of meaningless sex. With short, intentionally banal lyrics and a minimal harmonic vocabulary, the song is completely stagnant, like their conversation. There's nothing to talk about, but they try anyway. The music alternates, seemingly endlessly, between only two chords for much of the song. This limited musical vocabulary not only reinforces the feeling of stagnation, but it also literally represents the two-person back and forth between Robert and April. When acted well, the song is hilarious in its inanity and uncomfortableness. In the final analysis, the wives are right—Robert is not happy.

The Ladies Who Lunch

"The Ladies Who Lunch" is *Company's* Act II showstopper. In contrast to "Another Hundred People," this is the song that seems possibly out of place in this show. Sung by the archetypically cynical Joanne, the song catalogues the various kinds of modern women who lead boring, artificially filled lives. Perhaps this song shows, as a companion piece to "Have I Got a Girl for You," that marriage is not a cure-all for women any more than it is for men. But it doesn't really deal with relationships and has very little to do with Robert's journey to maturity and self-understanding. On the other hand, it contains a brilliant, biting, bitchy lyric full of multiple internal rhymes and insightful observations about various types of women. After the song's break, Joanne nails *herself* ("the girls who just watch") just as accurately and coldly as she has nailed other women. She knows what she is, and this strengthens her credibility as commentator. After the song, Joanne propositions Robert, offering to take care of him, and shocks him into an important realization. He asks, "But who will I take care of?" The stage is set for the finale.

Too Many Endings

Four separate endings were written for *Company*. All of them can now be heard, on recordings of *Marry Me a Little*, *The Unsung Sondheim*, and of course, the *Company* cast album. The first one, "Marry Me a Little," is a proposal to Amy (who didn't end up getting married to Paul in early drafts of the show). In it, Robert is lying to himself, believing that he can be *sort of* married, having the advantages without the disadvantages. But the creators felt the audience might not pick up on the self-deception. The second finale, "Multitudes of Amys," followed "Someone Is Waiting" in one version of the show. This straight-out love song shows Robert convincing himself that he really is in love with Amy when in fact it is only infatuation. After the song, Robert proposed to Amy (who had not married Paul in Act I). The show was then to end with a final reprise of some sort. But "Multitudes of Amys" offers no resolution to the many problems and obstacles established throughout the show. The third finale, "Happily Ever After," is a bitter and angry song, the first verse of which ends with "happily ever after . . . in hell." Audiences were much too disturbed by it, and it offered no resolution either. If "Happily Ever After" were to end the show, then Robert would have learned nothing. He would've ended the show exactly where he began it. This character-driven musical would have had no dramatic arc.

The finale the show ended up with is "Being Alive." This ending has been criticized for being too easy, too pat, too instantly self-knowing, but there is evidence to the contrary. Robert has been slowly realizing throughout the show that his ideal woman (and relationship) can never be, that he can't have the good without the bad. In the first half of "Being Alive," Robert reviews what he's observed about marriage—its impossibly difficult problems and contradictions. In between lines of the lyric, his friends push him to see beneath the surface. The bridge to the second half of the song is provided by two of the husbands. Harry says, "It's much better living it than looking at it." Peter says, "Add 'em up, Bobby, add 'em up." Their point is that Robert can *look* all he wants, but he can only know what commitment is really about by being married. Despite how awful it has appeared all evening, the compensations are to be found underneath. If we assume that this is all in Robert's mind, then he is finally understanding that it's a risk he has to take in order to find the truth. Robert "adds up" everything he's seen and experienced over the course of the show and makes a reluctant decision.

At this point, halfway through the song, the music changes keys (Robert and the song both move into a new place), and the lyric is subtly but profoundly changed. "Someone to hold you too close" becomes "Somebody, hold me too close." The lyric switches from passive observation to active decision as Robert decides to accept the imperfections of reality over his unattainable fantasy and look for a wife. He has learned the lesson first articulated in "Sorry-Grateful," that being married may be hell, but it's better than being alone. He has finally grown up. In the first half of "Being Alive," the orchestration quotes "Someone Is Waiting" (beginning in measure 60), Robert's unrealistic plea for the perfect marriage. After he finally hears what his friends have been telling him all along, the trumpets quote the "Bobby Buby" motif (measures 104–5), the music associated with his married friends. And the strings quote the "Company" motif (starting at measure 118) as Robert finally comes around to his friends' way of thinking. After all, as his friends sing in the opening number, "Love is company." Finally, Robert wants company, a partner. He finally understands that "alone is alone, not alive."

Critics of the song contend that it's too happy, that after an evening like this one, a happy ending is a cop-out. "Being Alive" isn't a happy ending, though; it's a song of compromise. Robert knows marriage will not be what he wants it to be. He has given up his dreams of a perfect marriage. By the end of the show, Robert finally has a *realistic*, though far from complete, understanding of marriage. Like the rest of the show, "Being Alive" describes quite eloquently and realistically what marriage is about. It is also more interesting dramatically than the earlier finales. As the song begins, Robert has watched his married friends all night and has seen only the difficult side of marriage. He hasn't seen what it is that keeps them together. He knows (or hopes) that this isn't all there is and he's asking them to help him find the *whole* truth. His "What do you get?" isn't an accusation; it's a genuine question. He doesn't know the answer. Everything he talks about in the first half of "Being Alive" is true. He's seen all of it over the course of the show. His lyric is in some sense a summary of the show, but it's only a superficial description, without real understanding. After the key change, Robert finally *understands* what he has seen. He looks around the stage and sees five couples still together despite all the hardships, dealing the best way they can with the obstacles of marriage, facing those obstacles because they love each other deeply and they know it's worth it.

After "Being Alive," *Company* ends with a final birthday party tableau, this time without Robert. He's not coming. After a moment, the couples realize that they shouldn't wait for him. They are no longer the focus of his life and they have to leave him to his new journey.

Putting It Together

Company is a seminal piece of the American musical theatre and an interesting, meaty show to share with your audience. It was created to disturb, to provoke thought and discussion. It will be unnerving to audiences used to traditional plot-driven musicals with an easy resolution by the finale. There are no cheap thrills here—a minimalistic unit set, very little dancing, not much ensemble singing. The show requires serious, in-depth understanding of the characters and themes by the director and actors, and a solid communication of the same to the audience. We must see the genuine love between the husbands and wives even though that love is often not articulated or demonstrated. On the surface, the couples are combative, competitive, insulting, but there's more under the surface. Robert sees complex, realistic behavior and only later comes to understand it. We must see Robert's transformation not as sudden or magical, but as believable steps toward this understanding.

In casting, it's important to create an ensemble in which every actor is a strong and definable character. There is no room in the show for dead weight. Robert has to have a strong upper register, Joanne has to be a really low alto, and Amy has to be able to handle one of the musical theatre's more difficult patter songs.

When directing *Company*, the first decision should be whether to play the show as a 1970 period piece or to set it in the present. Surprisingly, most of the dialogue doesn't seem dated despite its age, and the situations don't seem dated either. Divorce is even more commonplace now than it was then. People still smoke pot, go to dance clubs (we just don't call them discos anymore), learn karate. Some things, like Harry's being a recovering alcoholic, seem even more relevant today. Robert's reluctance to meet women could easily be connected to anxiety over AIDS. Perhaps putting the show in a contemporary setting could include making one of the married couples gay or lesbian. Sondheim has said he thinks making one of the couples gay would be a cliché, but in contemporary New York society, a group of five educated, cultured couples could quite easily include a gay couple. Far from being a cliché, nontraditional families are now a very visible part of the American social fabric. After all, changing a character from straight to gay shouldn't be any different from changing a character from white to black, a widely accepted practice. It's a fair assumption that a gay couple can have the same difficulties and can desire a lifelong commitment as deeply as a straight couple.

Remember that like most Sondheim shows, *Company* is about relationships and personal journeys. Don't let the physical production overpower the material. The original Broadway production used a unit set and very few pieces of furniture. It was important to director Hal Prince to keep the show moving without lengthy blackouts and scene changes. He also intentionally kept the playing areas small and somewhat claustrophobic to suggest the crowded, cramped feel of New York City.

Other Resources

The script and score to *Company* have both been published and the original cast album is available on tape and CD. There is a documentary available on video about the recording session for the cast album called *Original Cast Album: Company*. While it doesn't show any of the staging, it shows the performers singing their songs, Sondheim making adjustments and corrections, and director Hal Prince giving the performers acting notes. It's worth watching.

Godspell

Book by John-Michael Tebelek
Music and Lyrics by Stephen Schwartz
Conceived and Originally Directed by John-Michael Tebelek
Licensed by Theatre Maximus (New York)

Godspell is the musical theatre's equivalent of ABC's animated *School House Rock*—a thoroughly entertaining way to approach serious subject matter. Though the show is often dismissed as "empty calories," it has a lot going on under the surface, much like Stephen Schwartz's *Pippin*. John-Michael Tebelek, who conceived and wrote *Godspell*, spoke about the impetus for the show in an interview in *America* in 1971. He had attended an Easter Vigil service and was greatly disturbed by what he experienced: the congregation seemed bored and the priest seemed to be in a hurry to finish. Tebelek wanted to make the religious experience accessible once again to the masses. He saw that a religious service is theatre—the text/script, structure, use of ritual, and to a degree, standardized blocking and gestures (especially in the Catholic church). But making the religious experience into a play or musical isn't easy. There's a big difference between dramatizing a religious story or event (*Jesus Christ Superstar*, *Two by Two*, *Joseph and the Amazing Technicolor Dreamcoat*, *Children of Eden*) and dramatizing the actual experience of formalized worship. When you attend a church service, there is no dramatic action, no conflict and resolution. You have already been converted to a set of beliefs. The religious ceremony is an expression of an already achieved goal—religious faith. *Godspell* does dramatize the conversion leading up to the ceremony, but this is ultimately its greatest structural flaw. The conversion is complete in Act I, and consequently, there is little left to dramatize in Act II. But despite its flaws, it can genuinely move an audience—Christians and non-Christians alike.

In 1970 Tebelek assembled a cast of college friends and mounted the first production of *Godspell* at Carnegie Tech School of Drama. Members of the cast set hymn texts to their own original pop music. Tebelek's script was taken almost entirely from the Gospel of Matthew. The show was a success and moved to Cafe La Mama in New York, where the New York producers decided they needed a full, unified score. Another Carnegie Tech grad, Stephen Schwartz, was shopping his idea for a musical called *Pippin Pippin* around town and was invited to write the new score. Completed in five weeks, his soft rock score, with lyrics from hymns, psalms, and other religious sources, was interpolated into the already running Off-Broadway show. It moved uptown to Broadway in 1976. Much more accessible to the adult ticket-buying public than the harder rock of *Hair's* score, Schwartz's songs became immediately popular. *Godspell* ran in New York for six years, was made into a movie, revived Off-Broadway in 1988, and still has road companies touring the world.

Bringing God to the People

Tebelek's intention was to recreate the situation of Jesus and his disciples in contemporary terms. Like the disciples in the Bible, the twelve followers in the show are average people. Jesus teaches them through stories and, in this modern context, through other contemporary forms of storytelling, including puppetry, mime, improvisation, and sketch comedy. The main point of the biblical parables is to translate complex philosophical ideas into terms easily understood by lay persons. In the Bible, Jesus uses everyday situations familiar to the disciples to create stories that illustrate his lessons. In *Godspell*, he does the same thing, but because *Godspell* is set two thousand years later, the details of the stories are modernized. In both cases, he makes religious philosophy easy to grasp. People today can't relate to masters and slaves, innkeepers and silver pieces, Pharisees and tax gatherers; but they can relate to contemporary pop culture references, pop music, and modern slang.

The most important point for anyone mounting a production of *Godspell* is that it's not a revue or a variety show. It is literally a religious experience. In far too many productions, the spiritual side of the material is flatly ignored in favor of flashy song and dance. These productions are still entertaining, but not moving. The Last Supper and Crucifixion are not powerful moments because there has been no emotional base created on stage. Those of us familiar with Christianity know that we *should* be moved, but we aren't. For the show to succeed, the audience must be converted along with the cast.

The experience must be genuine in every sense. The skits, puppets, and ad libs are a way into the material for the audience; they are not ends unto themselves. Though the show is a lot of fun on its surface, the text is taken almost entirely from the Bible, and the parables are attempting to define a moral code. The purpose of the show is not merely to be cute, but to communicate serious philosophical and moral concepts in a user-friendly context. Even the structure is like a mass—readings and lessons alternating with songs/psalms. The point of the show is that religion should be fun, accessible, joyful, but should not be supplanted by razzle-dazzle.

Developing a Concept for the Show

John-Michael Tebelek wrote *Godspell* in order to give people a "way in" to religion in general and the teachings of Christ specifically. The physical production must work toward that end as well through the sets, costumes, staging, and acting style. The show's original concept was based on Harvey Cox's 1969 book *Feast of Fools*, which argued that for religion to once again reach the people, it had to reclaim its festivity and fantasy. Much of organized religion had become so somber, so serious, that the joy had gone out of it. Tebelek seized on the idea of using clowns to recapture that lost feeling of celebration and revelry. The cast put on clown makeup and wild, colorful costumes after being drawn together by Jesus. This concept was based not only on Cox's work, but also on the joy and freedom of the youth movement of the 1960s and early 1970s. The cast as ordinary people becoming clowns illustrated a dramatic change, a very visible kind of conversion. This hybrid of clowns and flower children was a familiar image to audiences of the early seventies. It is not, however, to audiences of the nineties.

In the years since *Godspell* premiered, thousands of productions have been mounted. Many directors have looked for ways to make the show fresh again, to remove it from the confines and perceived shallowness of the 1970s and update it. The sixties youth movement is no longer familiar to most people, and as a society we're getting used to more and more realism on television and in the movies. The fantasy world of the original *Godspell* may seem too naive, too innocent for those of us brought up on *Hill Street Blues* and CNN. The purpose of *Godspell* is to use what is familiar to the audience to help them connect with the material. It's considered common practice to insert your own jokes and pop culture references into the script, and this helps update the material to an extent; but fundamental elements of the show must be reexamined. To reflect a society that is no longer controlled completely by white males, many productions of *Godspell* cast women, blacks, or Asians as Jesus, which gives the show a strongly contemporary feel. I've seen productions that portrayed the twelve disciples as painters or construction workers in an empty building, young people on a playground, or street people in a junkyard or vacant lot. The only flaw in these conceptions is that they have Jesus coming to an already assembled group of people, instead of drawing average people from the general populace as he did in the Bible. It is the diversity of the disciples that makes them an interesting group, capable of going back to various parts of society to spread the word after Jesus is gone.

A production I directed set the action in a diner. A group of twelve very different people assembled in the diner where they encounter Jesus. The twelve included the diner's owner, two waitresses, the cook, a businessman, a businesswoman, a dance teacher, a cop, a married woman on her way to tennis, a salesman (John the Baptist/Judas), and a hooker. They came from all parts of society, yet they found common ground in the diner. They were dressed in street clothes and they applied no clown makeup; their conversion was a gradual one, conveyed through their acting. As might be expected in real life, some of them immediately accepted Jesus as teacher, others did not. The clown costumes in the original production signified dramatic change, but was that change too instant, too easy? We have become a skeptical, cynical nation. If someone came up to one of us and told us he was Christ, we would naturally assume he was delusional. Though any musical requires a certain suspension of disbelief, there are limits to an audience's cooperation. Depending on the personality of each character in our production, some of them became involved in the stories more quickly than others. Eventually, they had all accepted Jesus as teacher and as the son of God. The disciples are the audience's surrogates, their representatives, and the audience must be able to see themselves in the situation on stage. Like we would, the people in the diner had to consider what Jesus was saying, had to doubt him, weigh the risk of trusting him, and finally decide to let their guard down. The dramatic action of the first act is almost entirely in the conversion of the twelve, so letting it happen more slowly provides that much more of a dramatic arc. Because this more contemporary, realistic group of people represents the audience, the opportunity for nontraditional casting among the disciples is perhaps even greater than with the original concept.

Right from the Start

Godspell is incomplete without the Prologue, yet the majority of productions eliminate this opening musical number (perhaps because it's not on the recording). *Godspell* is about reconciling God and the Bible with our modern world. Yet, how can we do that if we don't put both in their proper context? The subject of God and organized religion has dominated philosophical discussions for centuries; at this time in history, when organized religion is frequently under fire, how can we examine where we are morally and intellectually without looking at how we got here? The Prologue, a fascinating survey of some of the greatest minds of the western world—Socrates, Thomas Aquinas, Martin Luther, Leonardo Da Vinci, Edward Gibbon, F. W. Nietzsche, Jean-Paul Sartre, and R. Buckminster Fuller—accomplishes this. Each philosopher has a verse (each with a different melody) in which to expound upon God and religion and their impact on society. Some of the philosophers believe in God; others do not. Yet even the atheists among them admit the profound force of the *concept* of God. Because the philosophers are presented in (mostly) chronological order, the audience can see the evolution of religious thought over time. The lyrics of the Prologue give the audience a more solid base on which to understand the whole show in philosophical terms. Also, having the actors research these men will give them a stronger base upon which to build this religious experience.

The Prologue segues directly into "Tower of Babble," in which the philosophers come together in unison to tell us that they are indeed the greatest minds of history and that we should listen to what they have to say. They then proceed to sing their verses again, this time all at once, creating a carefully constructed mosaic of conflicting philosophies. The point is that all these views have combined (as their melodies now have) over time to create the basis for contemporary religious thought. Though many of the ideas are conflicting, they still work together to form a solid foundation on which to build. The Prologue and "Tower of Babble" place both Christ and us, the audience, in historical context.

With the Prologue in place, the need for the clown costumes is not as great because now we can see a different conversion—the cast changes from philosophers to "believers" before our eyes. We see the dramatic difference between philosophy, something complex that is forged in the brain, and faith, something very simple that resides in the heart. This difference is underscored by the transition from the intricate counterpoint of "Tower of Babble" to the extreme simplicity of "Prepare Ye the Way of the Lord," a song with an unadorned melody over a very basic chord progression and a one-sentence lyric. As the cast has been transformed, so has the score. Jesus enters and we see the last element of the transformation, from the philosophers' complicated discourse to the intentionally unpretentious words of Jesus Christ.

Losing Your Religion

The broad appeal of *Godspell* lies in its pop/rock score and its cheerful approach to the Gospel. People like to direct and perform in *Godspell* for the same reasons they like to see it—it's fun and it makes you feel good. But the show isn't just about doing funny skits. It's about the teachings of Christ. This is serious fun. The jokes, skits, and other shtick must *support* the parables, not overwhelm them. We must see the disciples learning what Jesus is teaching them, and we must learn along with them. The most important element of the show is the relationship between Jesus and the twelve disciples. Their relationship with Jesus is really *our* relationship with him. This relationship must be explored and developed throughout the first act. Each actor must be aware of how his relationship with Jesus grows and changes. We need to understand that Jesus sees them as his friends, his students, and his children, and loves them deeply in all these ways. Whether the last half hour of the show is as moving as it can be depends entirely on these relationships. During the Last Supper, the knowledge of their impending separation should be utterly gut-wrenching to everyone in the cast, especially Judas; and it can be equally so to the audience if we've seen the love and trust between them all grow over the course of the first act. If you wait to focus on this until the Last Supper, there will be no emotional basis established for the grief the audience should be feeling. Everything in Act I leads to the Last Supper and Crucifixion, so everything must be staged and acted with that in mind. Act I not only teaches the parables, but also sets the audience up for the tragedy of Act II.

Words and Music

Though Stephen Schwartz's score was interpolated into the show after it had already been running for a while, it is well integrated and functional, but in different ways from an ordinary musical theatre score. There are two kinds of songs in the score: book songs and diegetic songs. Book songs are those that grow out of the action, in which the characters are saying something in the context of the situation on stage. These songs are more like traditional musical comedy songs. They function like speeches and the characters aren't aware that they're singing. They're not singing to the audience; they're "talking" to Jesus, to each other, or to themselves. For instance, in "Save the People," Jesus is talking to God. In "Day by Day" and "By My Side," the cast is telling Jesus what he means to them. In "On the Willows," the cast (or band) is expressing their feelings as they say goodbye to Jesus. In "Alas for You," Jesus is talking to the Pharisees.

Diegetic songs are those in which the *act* of singing is part of the story (like when a character in a musical sings in a nightclub), and the characters are aware that they're singing. The songs would still be there even if it weren't a musical. Diegetic songs in other musicals include "Willkommen" and "Cabaret" in *Cabaret*, "Dames" and "We're in the Money" in *42nd Street*, "Parlor Songs" in *Sweeney Todd*, "Honey Bun" in *South Pacific*, and the title song in *La Cage aux Folles*. In *Godspell*, the diegetic songs are mostly the songs in which the lessons are summarized or the cast is just having fun, including "All for the Best," "Turn Back O Man," and "We Beseech Thee." These two different kinds of songs should be staged and acted differently to help the audience see the distinct function of each.

There are four basic kinds of prayers: those in which we ask for physical or emotional help, those in which we ask for forgiveness, those in which we ask for help in becoming better people, and those in which we give thanks. Because the lyrics in *Godspell* are largely taken from the Bible, many of the songs in the show fit into these four categories, thereby reinforcing the parallel between *Godspell* and an actual religious service. "God Save the People" asks for help; "We Beseech Thee" asks for forgiveness; "Day by Day" asks for help in becoming better people; and "All Good Gifts" and "Bless the Lord" give thanks. The most important thing about the score is to understand how each song works and why it's in the show. The actors should read the lyrics as text and make sure they understand the message of each song so they can successfully communicate it to the audience. Because the songs will invariably be staged as one showstopper after another, it's important to help the audience see beyond the visual razzle-dazzle to the meaning underneath.

Act II Trouble

It's interesting that so many musicals have trouble with the second act when they're in previews. In fact, a number of wonderful musicals still have Act II trouble even after they open. Most of us don't think of *Godspell* as having a problematic second act, but if you're not careful with it, it can. As mentioned before, a great deal of the success of Act II depends on how well the emotional ties between Jesus and the disciples are established in Act I. Without a solid base already set, the drama of the second act will fall flat. The narrative Act II has an entirely different tone from the more presentational Act I. In Act II, we're actually observing a series of events that follow logically toward a climax and resolution. The only action in the first act is the growth of the relationships. The encounter with the Pharisees early in Act II is the first time there is an extended dramatic conflict. It's the first time Jesus encounters a serious antagonist. It is significant that though Jesus knows this is coming, the disciples don't. They are completely stunned by this sudden confrontation. This should be dramatized in the different ways Jesus and the disciples react to the Pharisees. To avoid the evening feeling like two separate musicals, "We Beseech Thee" has been saved for Act II in order to use fun and frolic as a connection between the two acts. But despite this brief respite, it has become a very different show and, in many ways, a more traditional plot-driven musical by this point.

The Last Supper is the first of the two major events in Act II. The scene opens with "By My Side." The cast knows Jesus will be leaving them, but they don't know if he'll be back. They're scared and they don't want to lose him. Jesus wonders whether he has prepared them sufficiently to go on without him and to pass on what he has taught them. The Last Supper is their last time together; if the audience has been properly prepared emotionally, this scene will be devastating to watch. Perhaps Judas is the most upset of all because he knows he must betray Jesus. In some productions, when he leaves to go to the priests, he physicalizes the fact that he's been trapped by fate through mime or other abstract staging. This can be very interesting, but not if it's the only instance of this style of acting in the show. An abstract moment can't be randomly thrown into an otherwise realistic show. The entire Last Supper scene must radiate tremendous tension, for slightly different reasons in each character. The audience should feel the loss and fear the disciples are experiencing and the fear that Jesus is feeling as well.

The Crucifixion is the climax of the show. Jesus has to be put up on the cross and you can be creative about this, depending on the set you've designed. In our diner set, the front door of the diner, up-center, became his cross, his "doorway" to heaven. The finale must be extreme, uncontrolled, anguished, completely over the top. These twelve people are watching their friend, teacher, father, and God nailed to a cross to die. It's a frightening thing for an inexperienced actor to portray extreme emotion, but the power of the scene depends on it. In the production I directed, the disciples tore apart the diner during the instrumental sequences in the finale, throwing chairs and tables across the stage, ripping down signs. Their grief was so extreme, so consuming that it couldn't be expressed just through the voice. The anger and rebellion associated with hard-rock music, the distortion of the electric guitar, the driving beat of the drums, the flashing lights, all contributed to the intensity of the moment. During these sections, the actors writhed in agony on the floor, beat their fists on the stage, screamed, and moaned. The sudden silence after Jesus had died, as the music paused before going on to "Long live God," was deafening. The silent theatre, filled only with the quiet sobbing of audience members (this usually hits them

pretty hard), was a powerful illustration of the emptiness and alone-
ness of the disciples. But the disciples know they must go on, must
pass on what they've been taught

One by one—the women first—they rise as they sing "Long Live
God." Soon the men begin "Prepare Ye" in counterpoint. They will
now prepare the way for the teachings of Christ. In this way, "Prepare Ye" bookends the action, each rendition a reminder of one of
the show's central themes—the passing on of the teachings of Christ.
As the counterpoint continues, the disciples take Jesus down from
the cross and carry him off (in our production, out through the audience). Some productions end the show there, where the script
ends, but most use the curtain call (a reprise of "Day by Day") as the
Resurrection, and Jesus returns to the stage with the cast. If you've
done it right, your audience will be instantly on its feet, clapping,
singing along, and probably sobbing. As long as you don't forget the
spiritual and emotional underpinnings of the material, *Godspell* can
be a unique theatre experience for both the cast and audience.

Other Resources

Vocal selections from and the full piano score for *Godspell* are published. There are a number of cast recordings, including the original
Off-Broadway cast, the film cast, and several foreign cast recordings.
The movie version, with several members of the original New York
company, is on video. It's not that great, but it's worth seeing if
you're not at all familiar with the unusual style and structure of the
show.

6   Gypsy

Book by Arthur Laurents
Music by Jule Styne
Lyrics by Stephen Sondheim
Originally Directed on Broadway by Jerome Robbins
Licensed by Tams-Witmark Music Library

Gypsy's lyricist, Stephen Sondheim, paid its book writer, Arthur Laurents, a high compliment once by telling him the book was so strong it could survive without the score—something most musicals' books could not do. Laurents disagreed. He believed that the characters, particularly Rose, were so big, so overblown, that they could never live in a nonmusical play. Laurents was probably right. Though Rose is a very real and believable character (I've known at least one real-life Rose), she is truly Bigger Than Life. It is her grotesque yet captivating personality that drives this "musical fable." This is certainly the most sophisticated and electric music ever written by composer Jule Styne, and with Sondheim's hilarious, subtextually loaded lyrics and a first-rate book, Gypsy elevated the musical comedy antihero to a new level. Rose is a monster of mythic proportions who exploits and torments everyone around her, yet we actually *like* her for some reason. It is the role of a lifetime for actresses, and the show is one of the juiciest projects a director can find. The actress playing Rose must be willing to give a no-holds-barred, over-the-top, utterly outrageous performance.

The Act

The central focus of the characters in Gypsy is the Act. Like Rose herself, it must be too big, too loud, too tacky, and impossible to ignore. It can't just be bad; the audience must know it's *intentionally* bad and in very specific ways. Because the Act is Rose's creation, it reflects aspects of Rose's personality. It is an act that Rose thinks people will like because it is overflowing with the kind of excesses that Rose likes. Throughout the show, the Act must seem old-fashioned—it's important to establish the world of vaudeville that is the backdrop to the story—but it is only the representation of vaudeville in a musical that is decidedly not old-fashioned.

When designing and staging the various incarnations of the Act, approach it as if Rose is putting it together. There is one song, "Let Me Entertain You," that shows up in every variation because Rose isn't going to spend the extra money to have another song written and orchestrated when she's got one that she likes. The first version we hear does have a slightly different lyric, but when Rose decides to get the kids into professional vaudeville, it's important enough to justify the expense of having the song revised and reorchestrated and the "Extra, Extra" opening written, all paid for with her father's gold plaque. The third version, "Dainty June and Her Farmboys," is even funnier because it starts with farm sets and costumes, yet still uses the "Extra, Extra" intro even though it's completely inappropriate and incongruous. The four versions of the Act all perfectly capture the empty banality of mediocre vaudeville. The genius of Sondheim's lyric lies in its adaptability to Louise's strip in Act II. The double entendres, which are so funny in the strip number, are completely hidden in the early kiddie versions.

Everything's Coming Up Rose

The first scene of the show presents brilliantly the outrageous excesses that will characterize every move Rose will make throughout the show. When she makes her entrance down the aisle of the theatre as June and Louise perform onstage for Uncle Jocko, Rose disrupts both the action on stage and the expectations of *Gypsy's* audience. All the other mothers at Uncle Jocko's audition have been banned from the house, but Rose never plays by other people's rules. She is tellingly separate from the other mothers. She is not an ordinary mother in any sense of the word. Rose interrupts not just the audition in general, but specifically her own daughters' audition. It doesn't occur to her that she may be ruining their chance of winning. She only knows that she must control everything. At the same time, she's not like any other character in the show and so is not bound to the same conventions. She can break the fourth wall. This is partly because the first scene is set on a stage in a theatre, but it's also because she adheres to no rules, including those of the theatre genre in which she lives. Usually, a show either breaks the fourth wall often or not at all; yet here, Rose is allowed to do it just once. Though Louise talks to the audience later in the show, the fourth wall remains intact: she isn't talking to the *Gypsy* audience, she's talking to the audiences of the burlesque halls she's working.

Rose has never grown up. She is an adolescent in three major ways: she is foolishly optimistic, she has a fiery temper, and she has a deep but well-hidden vulnerability. She lives through her dreams even when they don't come true. She always believes vaudeville's coming back when everyone else knows it isn't. She knows June will be a star even though there's no reason to believe it. The song that best illustrates her irrationality is "Mr. Goldstone, I Love You." As usual, Rose goes too far. Her gratitude and enthusiasm are borderline scary, excessive to the point of being inappropriate. The second verse of the song, in which she begins to mix up her words ("Have a gold-stone, Mr. Eggroll"), reveals Rose's state of mind. Her volume and intensity, her piling food on Goldstone, her near canonization of Goldstone, her confused vocabulary, all point to the fact that she is genuinely unbalanced. She has finally realized her dream—playing the Orpheum circuit—but it's not going to be enough.

The next time her girls have a chance at greater success, Rose's emotional instability destroys their opportunity. Her explosion at Mr. Grantziger's assistant demonstrates once again that Rose is not dealing on the same plane of reality as the rest of us. This very influential theatre producer wants to book the Act, but only if he can send June to acting school and groom her to be a serious actress. Though Rose claims always to be doing everything for June (and later Louise), here we see proof that it's not true. June wants the acting lessons; she wants to be an actress. But Grantziger's proposition cuts Rose out of the loop. The thought of being left behind and, more significant, the thought of June succeeding without Rose's intervention terrify her and she erupts in a fury of selfishness and self-pity. She refuses the offer despite June's pleas. This is the first time we see that Rose will reject success if it isn't on her terms. It's also the first time that June knows positively that her mother doesn't care about her success or her happiness. The wedge has now been irrevocably driven between Rose and June.

Throughout Rose's yelling, manipulating, and pushing there is a vulnerability that she keeps hidden from the other characters but not from the audience. She has convinced herself that her motives are noble ones. When that illusion is finally shattered at the end of the show, it is devastating. Each time someone leaves her—first the boys in the Act, then June, then Herbie, and finally Louise—we must see the heartbreak that she covers up with the bravado of her next big triumph, always designed specifically to prove that she never really needed whoever has just left. When Rose has her breakdown at the end of the show in "Rose's Turn," it should not come as a complete surprise. Her fragile grasp on reality and her feeble self-image are battered down time and time again, and when the last of her loved ones, Louise, turns her back on her, Rose's mind crumbles.

The World According to Rose

Rose's first song, "Some People," puts forth Rose's philosophy of life, which essentially boils down to fame at any price. She is not a rational person. She is a person of extreme moods, ambitions, and needs. She could never be happy with a normal domestic life. This last detail is important because later we'll see that Herbie and Louise both want a domestic life more than anything. These fundamentally incompatible wants will forever keep Rose and Herbie apart. Rose has only one purpose in this song—to get money from her father. Everything she tells him is designed to convince him that she knows what she's doing and his money will be well spent. Of course he doesn't believe her any more now than he has all the other times. After he refuses to give her any money and leaves, her determination is so great that she steals his gold retirement plaque as the song climaxes. We see that Rose will go to absolutely any lengths to get what she wants. This song also introduces Rose's dreams, a recurring theme. These dreams are not only an expression of Rose's unrealistic view of life, but also function as her way of telling Herbie and the kids when she has a new idea for the Act. She thinks presenting her ideas as dreams lends them some kind of credibility. The phrase that introduces the dream motif, "I had a dream, a wonderful dream, Poppa," is the phrase that will open the song "Everything's Coming Up Roses" at the end of the first act. The concept this represents—Rose's dreams at any cost—is so important and so central that this musical phrase both begins the overture and is the last thing heard at the end of the show. Her dreams are the motivation behind every move she makes.

"Everything's Coming Up Roses" is *really* "Everything's Coming Up Rose's." While she's trying to convince Louise and Herbie that she will still realize success for them, she's also convincing herself that she will get everything *she* wants. The verse starts with two huge blasting notes at the top of the song's range—a choice made to show off Ethel Merman's famous belting voice, but one that also adds to the chilling effect of the song. This number should be frightening to watch. If there was any doubt before that Rose was out of her mind, here is conclusive proof. Herbie and Louise are both stunned and a bit scared. The stage direction in the script says that Herbie and Louise stand silently by as Rose explodes in manic optimism. Neither they nor the audience know if Rose is having the nervous breakdown she always seems on the verge of. This is one of many moments in which the actress playing Rose must literally assault the audience with her Dr. Frankenstein-like passion. After the opening dream image, the rest of the lyric is filled primarily with images of traveling, show business, and children. That's all that's on her mind now—taking her daughter down the path to stardom in the theatre—and it's all she's ever known. Setting the scene at a railroad station further reinforces the image of moving on instead of standing still to mourn June's desertion.

Above all, Rose is a con artist of the first degree. She threatens to reveal that Uncle Jocko's competition is rigged unless June and Louise win—in other words, unless he rigs it in *her* favor instead. The Act is not good—and each new Act is really only a barely altered version of the old one—yet she manages to get it booked in progressively better and better venues. She keeps Herbie in tow by keeping alive his hope that she will one day marry him. She has no intention of marrying him, of course, and she knows that if he ever finds that out, he's gone (whatever happened to June and Louise's father, and does it have something to do with Rose's hesitance to marry?). But she sees none of her enterprises as dishonest. To her, it is merely survival.

The Girls

Like Rose, the girls have a song that characterizes their dreams as well as their feelings about their mother, "If Momma Was Married." This song, late in Act I, is about their dreams, which are in sharp contrast to Rose's dreams "for" them. June's dream is to get as far away as possible from Rose. She believes that Rose only cares for her because of her talent and her potential for getting them all to the Big Time. She'd like Rose to marry Herbie because that would mean June would finally be rid of her. Louise still believes in Rose's dreams. Her dream is a life of domesticity for her, Rose, and Herbie. Louise wants to be part of a real family. Louise thinks this kind of life would change Rose and end the insanity. It's interesting that the same event would provide both girls with their very different dreams. It's a funny song, but it's also disturbing in its depiction of the girls' feelings for Rose.

June resents Rose on so many levels. Rose won't let June grow up. June is "Baby June" for years, then only when she's already a young woman does she graduate to "Dainty June." June has learned that Rose's dreams are not real and that Rose is doing everything for herself. June is just waiting for an escape and she finds it in Tulsa. Rose's dream must always by necessity supersede anyone else's dreams, so June's dream of being a serious actress and Tulsa's dream of having his own vaudeville act are both impossible as long as the two of them are with Rose. Tulsa needs June to make his act work, so the two of them elope. It's interesting that again, someone else is using June to achieve his dream. She has gone from one user to another, though we can assume Tulsa won't be nearly as emotionally abusive as Rose. June's sudden abandonment of Rose and the Act shatters Rose. She has finally pushed someone far enough to leave her. June's leaving is hard for Herbie and Louise, but it presents the opportunity for what they both have always wanted—the end of the Act in favor of a normal home life. It seems now that everyone will get what they want, except Rose. They think Rose will admit defeat, but they are wrong. Rose's mind works at the speed of light and she immediately formulates an alternate plan for their climb to stardom. She still has one daughter left.

"Rose Louise"

As long as June is around, Louise is ignored. She is just one of the backup boys for the Act. She's not talented, not pretty, not worth attention. Rose's neglect and Louise's lack of a sane female role model force her to grow up faster; in some ways she becomes a mother to

Rose. On Louise's birthday, Rose gives her a baby lamb as her present, but only because they need it for the new Act. Louise sings to her lamb, "I wonder how old I am." She is an adult and a child all at once, the wisdom and responsibility of an adult, mixed with the emotional needs and innocence of a child. She needs to believe in Rose's dreams, even though part of her knows they're not going to be realized. In "Little Lamb" she sings, "Do you think I will get my wish?" What is her wish? To be June.

Louise finds her first love in Tulsa, but loses him—like everything else—to June. Initially, she tries to use Rose's tactics to win him. As she saw Rose do with Herbie, Louise points out to Tulsa the things they have in common (being secretive, having dreams), but Louise lacks Rose's incredible confidence and astounding chutzpah. She doesn't have the disregard for other people's feelings that allows Rose to railroad everyone in her life. Louise even offers to make the costumes for Tulsa's act, anything to be a part of his life. With Tulsa's song, "All I Need Is the Girl," we see again that Rose isn't the only one with dreams. While Tulsa spins his fantasy, Louise puts herself into his scenario. As he mimes dancing with a girl, Louise closes her eyes and mimes along with him. He doesn't notice her, doesn't know she is visualizing herself in his arms. Louise can't be a part of Rose's dream (not yet, anyway), so she tries to be a part of Tulsa's dream instead. She has no dream for herself. But in this story, the dreams don't come true. Tulsa elopes with June.

Once June is gone, Rose has no choice but to make Louise the star instead. She immediately tells Herbie and Louise that she had a dream that Louise was the star. Now we *know* the dreams are fabrications. If she already had the dream about Louise, why wait until now to tell her? The truth is that it doesn't matter who's the star. It's all about Rose anyway. Despite Rose's claims, June wasn't very good, so it won't really matter if Louise isn't either. Rose will now focus on Louise. But as June learned the hard way, this won't mean that Rose actually cares about her, only that Louise is her last option. Rose tries to make Louise into June, even going so far as to put her in a blonde wig. But once Rose has done that, she has started down the irreversible path of creating another June, one who will leave her just like the first one. Even Louise buys into Rose's perception of beauty. Louise tells Rose that the girls should wear blonde wigs because it will make them pretty. She thinks they won't be pretty until they're blonde and, of course, she can't be pretty because she's a brunette.

Eventually Rose finds that vaudeville is dying and she doesn't have enough time to make Louise into a new June. After all, she had years to make June into a saleable commodity. With no other options, Rose leaps at the opportunity for Louise to take over the star stripper's spot at the burlesque house. Even though Rose herself has expressed disgust at burlesque and at stripping, at least it's a chance for them to achieve some kind of stardom. Rose says, "I always promised my daughter *we'd* be a star."

A Man Who Likes Children

Herbie is a real, honest, genuine person, in pointed contrast to Rose. He is a man of moderation, at least on the surface—underneath his frustration and anger are building. He knows that if he ever lets his anger loose, he'll leave, and he says so in Act I, Scene 7. Rose keeps putting off Herbie and his proposals, assuming he'll wait forever. Herbie, meanwhile, thinks he can get her to settle down and change. Eventually, he will see that he's wrong. Herbie loves her, but that's not enough to build a life on. When he meets Rose, he knows she's conning him with "Small World," but he doesn't mind. But can a relationship built on manipulation—even if Herbie willingly allows it—possibly last? Does Rose genuinely love him or is he just useful? Can we ever know if Rose genuinely loves anyone? Has her mother's abandonment when she was a child made Rose a woman who won't allow herself to love or be loved?

Herbie's threat of leaving is a real one. He is serious, but Rose dismisses it quickly with "You'll Never Get Away from Me." She knows she can charm him out of his anger. Though she may diffuse that anger for the moment, his threat is based on real uneasiness with their relationship. The issues that Rose refuses to discuss will not evaporate and her avoidance will be a contributing factor to Herbie's eventual departure. She knows what buttons to push (as evidenced in the dreams of familial life in "Together Wherever We Go"), but with each transgression against her loved ones, her grip on Herbie slips. When the chips are down, smartass answers won't cut it:

ROSE: I need you.
HERBIE: For what?
ROSE: A million things!
HERBIE: One would be better. Goodbye, honey. (*He leaves.*)

All You Need to Have Is No Talent

Louise's transformation into a stripper should elicit mixed emotions. On the one hand, we're disturbed to see her thrust into stripping by her monstrous mother and humiliated in front of an audience of horny old men. On the other hand, it provides Louise with her much needed escape from Rose's control. It's easier for us to swallow if we like Tessie Tura, Mazeppa, and Electra. "You Gotta Get a Gimmick" has to be cheap, vulgar, tacky, really funny, and *true*. First, the song shows us the generosity of the strippers. They're more than happy to offer Louise professional tips. Though she doesn't know it yet, this lesson will be important for her later. The most important point of the song is that you don't need talent to be a successful stripper, and this humility endears the strippers to us. This also reminds us that our heroes have in fact landed in the armpit of show business, a theatre where talent is decidedly optional. It also tells us that if Louise ever wants to be a stripper, she doesn't need talent, which is good, since she doesn't have any. All she needs is a gimmick. When she finally takes the stage, her gimmick will be her inexperience, her innocence, and her naïveté. It is ironic that she shares some of that innocence and naïveté with Rose, though in Rose these qualities have been seriously twisted. In this sense, Rose does contribute to Louise's success.

Once Louise becomes a success as Gypsy Rose Lee, we see a montage sequence of strip routines in theatres across the country. It's important that Louise's "gimmick" works beautifully. Her act must be classy, clever, sophisticated, and ultimately self-mocking. Louise, the only one of the women in the family who *didn't* want to be a star, has achieved stardom, and she has done it without Rose's orchestrating it, which drives Rose crazy. Louise has not only grown up, but has successfully severed her emotional ties to Rose, though there are still some unresolved issues.

Rose's Turn

The finale is an all-out musical nervous breakdown, one of the greatest "mad scenes" of the musical theatre, perhaps equalled only by Ben Stone's breakdown at the end of *Follies* (it's no coincidence both lyrics are written by Sondheim). Rose must exhibit bona fide insanity in this number. The defeats and indignities are more than she can bear and her mind literally snaps. As the song progresses, her sanity slips further and further away. Her dream has come true—her daughter is a star—but it's not on her terms, so it doesn't count. Laurents has said that "Rose's Turn" happens in Rose's mind. It is a review of Rose's life, music and words from her past, colliding in an explosion of anger and hurt. A new song wouldn't have the impact of this maniacal musical tour of Rose's memories and mistakes. It must be a medley of other songs, but all in dissonant, scary variations.

The finale starts with Rose's own strip routine. Before the song, she says, "I could've been better than ANY OF YOU!" She does a bump and grind for us and, in her dementia, she even hears the "boys" in the orchestra responding to her. In a parody of both June and Louise she shouts, "Hello, everybody! My name's Rose. What's yours?" She launches into a list of phrases all starting with "Momma" (in imitation of a song that was cut from the show, in which June and Louise comment on Rose's con artist seduction of Herbie). When she says "Momma's lettin' go," the words stop her cold. She stutters over the word "Momma." The enormity of her mistakes is hitting her. She remembers the mother that left her as well as the daughters she's now driven away. The section ends with "Momma's gotta let go!"—not because it's best for her daughters, but because Rose feels betrayed by them and can't let herself be hurt by them anymore. She knows she's losing her mind. She goes back over her life, her mistakes, her excesses. Unfortunately, she doesn't see how wrong she was. She only sees how much she did for others and that she got in return what she perceives as unprovoked anger and abandonment. So she resolves that from now on she'll live her life for herself, not realizing that she's always done that. Her life, her family, and now her mind have all disintegrated. The song ends with her anthem of optimism and survival, "Everything's Coming Up Roses." But before she sings the title phrase, she first sings a variant of it: "Everything's coming up Rose."

She stands alone on the empty stage, looking small and isolated. She is truly alone for the first time in her life. There is no one to believe in her dreams, no one for her to manipulate, no one to love her. At the end of the song, Rose bows grandly to her hallucinated audience. When staging the number in London, Arthur Laurents created a chilling moment by having Rose continue to bow after the real audience had stopped clapping. The applause was over but Rose still heard it. This reinforces the idea that it's all in her head and that she really is crazy.

Louise comes out on stage and Rose snaps out of her dream. They talk briefly and affect a temporary, somewhat uneasy truce. Louise, in the mother role again, comforts Rose. Laurents' stage direction reads:

> [LOUISE] holds out her arms to Rose, who hesitates, then comes running to Louise like a child. Louise pats her, kisses her hair . . .

As they leave together, Rose looks back at the runway and the lights go out. It's over. The dreams are dead.

Other Resources

The script for *Gypsy* has been published in a collection called *Ten Great Musicals of the American Theatre*, edited by Stanley Richards (Chilton Book Co., 1973), and the score has also been published. There is a tolerable movie version with Rosiland Russell and Natalie Wood and an outstanding television version starring Bette Midler. The television version is remarkably faithful to the stage version, with almost no changes. Midler's Rose is a little tame for my taste, but she is electrifying nonetheless. Cast recordings are available of the original Broadway cast starring Ethel Merman, the London cast starring Angela Lansbury, the film cast, the Broadway revival cast starring Tyne Daly, and the television cast (my personal favorite).

7 How to Succeed in Business Without Really Trying

Book by Abe Burrows, Jack Weinstock, and Willie Gilbert
Based on the novel by Shepherd Mead
Music and Lyrics by Frank Loesser
Originally Directed on Broadway by Abe Burrows
Licensed by Music Theatre International

The director Antonin Artaud once said that the theatre "causes the mask to fall, reveals the lie, the slackness, baseness, and hypocrisy of our world." The American musical theatre braved the waters of satire for the first time in 1931 with the Pulitzer prize–winning *Of Thee I Sing*. Only a few musicals since then have successfully tread those dangerous waters. It took thirty years for another to equal the biting wit of *Of Thee I Sing*. It was called *How to Succeed in Business Without Really Trying* (from here on to be referred to as just *How to Succeed*), and it took on one of America's great icons, Big Business.

Shepherd Mead published the book on which the show is based in 1952 and it became a huge bestseller. Jack Weinstock and Willie Gilbert wrote a stage version of the book, but according to most sources it was truly awful. The producers brought in Abe Burrows to fix the book, and apparently almost none of the original version survives. It is claimed that satire is never commercially viable. *How to Succeed* is one of the exceptions—a searing satire that was also a big popular success. It's a bigger-than-life, wacky musical that's intentionally artificial, using freezes and other theatrical devices (Finch breaks the fourth wall from time to time) and casting the same actor as Mr. Twimble and Wally Womper (representing the bottom and top of the corporate ladder, as well as our hero's humble beginnings and outrageous final success). The show dishes out a savage satire of the world of Big Business complete with the grumbling boss, lecherous executives, secretaries that really run the company, and a generous dose of lying, cheating, and stealing. Like *Of Thee I Sing*, it was one of only a very few musicals to win the Pulitzer prize for drama.

In the Beginning

The central premise involves J. Pierrepont Finch (Ponty), a window washer who has a book called *How to Succeed in Business Without Really Trying*. The book offers a simple step-by-step process for moving up the corporate ladder without any genuine effort or talent. The book's introduction (dramatized by an offstage voice) says: "If you have education and intelligence and ability, so much the better. But remember that thousands have reached the top without any of these qualities." And from that point until the final curtain, we see a parade of executives who don't, in fact, have any of those qualities. The show sets up a corporate structure so complicated and so large that it's possible to lie and cheat people without ever getting caught. It's this detail that makes the story of *How to Succeed* possible. Finch learns from the book that his greatest advantage is the knowledge of what a lumbering giant the modern corporation is. Everyone at World Wide Wickets, the company Finch infiltrates, is a monster, an incompetent, or both, all of them trying to get what they want no matter how much they step on others in the process. Finch is in many ways just as big a monster as the executives he tramples, but because those he dupes are unprincipled jerks, we enjoy seeing them get what we think they deserve. Finch is amoral and unethical, but we still love watching his triumphs.

One of the things that makes the show such fun is that it skewers all the things that people take so seriously. World Wide Wickets makes wickets, though none of the executives apparently knows what a wicket is. From the first dialogue scene on, the show systematically deflates the corporate ego, suggesting that perhaps corporate America is too self-important. The song "The Company Way" explodes all myths about climbing the corporate ladder. Finch's presentation at the board meeting is so elaborate, yet so lacking in any substance, once again suggesting that Big Business takes itself too seriously.

Inside jokes abound, including college ties, slams against the advertising department, and digs at human resource departments (at the end of the show, Bratt is promoted to Vice President in Charge of Employee Morale and Psychological Adjustment). *How to Succeed* was way ahead of its time in portraying coffee as an addictive drug, in the wild over-the-top song "Coffee Break," which describes the "one chemical substance" that can jump-start a tired executive. The name of the new Vice President of Advertising—Benjamin Burton Daniel Ovington—is even a joke. His initials are the initials of a famous advertising firm in New York.

How to Succeed trades on dozens of Big Business stereotypes. The appropriately named J. B. Biggley is the traditionally vague but demanding boss, complete with incompetent nephew (Bud Frump) and a buxom bimbo for a mistress (Hedy LaRue). The other executives are all overeager sycophants who truly have no minds of their own. Despite the promise of Finch's book to reveal the "science" of getting ahead, it's clear to the naked eye that the only real requirement for advancement is serious butt-kissing. The executives have an exclusive boys' club not open to women or to new arrivals like Finch. The corporate world Finch finds is a corrupt backbiting playground where only the slimiest survive. These are stereotypes that many people outside the corporate world believe are real and that those inside the corporate world *know* are real.

A Secretary Is Not a Toy

One of the major themes of the show is the unofficial power that the women of the company wield. True to the stereotypes, it is really the secretaries who run the company. The men are all idiots and the women are all patient, slightly amused, and far more intelligent. Finch sees this immediately and goes about making friends with the women who can help him, including Miss Jones, Biggley's secretary and Hedy, Biggley's girlfriend (and Achilles' heel), as well as Rosemary, Smitty, and the other executive secretaries. The women all know that Finch is manipulating the men, but they figure they deserve it, so they let Finch do his stuff. There is a great gap—and liberal humor—between perceived power (the executives) and actual power (the women, especially Hedy). Like Dolly Levi, Desirée Armfeldt in *A Little Night Music*, and Golde in *Fiddler on the Roof*, these women have a far-reaching unofficial kind of power. Because Hedy is so dumb and so ingenuous, she's both powerful and the only one in the show who doesn't play games. She's completely honest at all times. She says what she means and asks for what she wants. For that reason, she also frequently stumbles upon Great Truths about Big Business. On the subject of power, she says to Biggley in Act II, "You didn't keep your part of my bargain!" And that pretty much sums it all up. We know instantly in the second-to-last scene, when Wally Womper says he intends to talk to Hedy, that she'll charm the pants off him (literally, maybe). Sure enough, by the finale, Womper and Hedy are married.

The men's attitude toward women is pretty Neanderthal and this just adds to our desire to see them get their comeuppance. The executives make jokes about their wives and their secretaries, Gatch comes on to Rosemary, and the executives nearly go berserk when Hedy comes into the office. In Act II, Hedy threatens to quit and go back to the nightclub where she used to work. Biggley, not wanting her to leave, reminds her that the men at the club were always making advances. She replies, "It's no different around here in Big Business. At least at the Copa, when I got pinched, I got tipped." It's this attitude toward women that Rosemary plans to exploit when she sings, "Happy to Keep His Dinner Warm." She knows if she's going to snare her man, she's going to have to pretend to play the game.

J. Pierrepont Finch

We know the show is a satire from the first time we hear Finch's full name, modeled comically on J. P. (Pierpont) Morgan, the ruthless American financier. What's so funny about the story this musical tells is that Finch just *can't* lose. No matter how far he pushes his luck, no matter how ruthless he is, no matter how little he deserves to win, it is utterly impossible for him to fail. Of course, that's one of the points of the show—fairness and rules have absolutely nothing to do with Big Business. Part of our desire to see him triumph is that the odds are so against him. The script contains a lengthy description of the Finch Smile in a stage direction in Act I, Scene 2. The Finch Smile is an integral part of his character and of the style of the show. The Smile is between Finch and the audience. We see it, but the other characters on stage don't. It's the only time the fourth wall is broken, and it's important to avoid breaking the fourth wall at any other time, in order to give the Smile special status. The songs can be played forward, but should not be played "to" the audience. Only the Smile—and only at special moments—can break the fourth wall. The Smile tells us that Finch has once again successfully scammed someone else. It's not a smile of happiness as much as one of false modesty, of mischievous achievement, as if to say, "You didn't think I'd pull that one off, but I did." It's important not to overuse the Smile. The script is very specific about when to use it. Do it more often and it loses its punch. The biggest Smile of all comes at the end: just as Finch is about to accept defeat and sign the letter of resignation, he finds out that Wally Womper was also once a window washer. Finch sees his opening; he smiles at us and goes for the touchdown. There was no way Finch could've won the game until that moment, but by a perverse twist of fate, even though all his scheming couldn't save him, his past as a window washer could.

Finch wins in the end for two main reasons. First, he watches and learns before he acts. Frump just acts, without any thought, and therefore loses every time. Second, Finch lies and cheats. At everything. The moral of this story is actually that in America lying and cheating are the way to get what you want. It's a warped moral, but it's funny because we know that sometimes it's true. Finch learns quickly who his enemies are and who he can use as a step up the ladder. Miss Jones, Biggley's secretary, feeds him valuable information (about the opening in Gatch's department, about Biggley's college, his knitting) that he uses later on. He makes friends with Hedy and uses her to get rid of unwanted executives who are in his way. When Finch finds Ovington in his way, he reads up on him and finds out he went to the college that always beats Biggley's college at football. And Finch gets to be buddies with several of the top executive secretaries, both for insider information and favors. Knowledge is power. At first, this is the only reason he stays close to Rosemary.

Finch manipulates every character in the show, from Twimble all the way up to Biggley and Wally Womper. They are all chess pieces, easily moved, easily sacrificed. He says to Bratt early in the show, "Glad to be playing with you, sir," and he means it. Finch's presentation at the board meeting is nothing but slick manipulation. He tells them exactly what they want to hear about how business will turn around without actually mentioning what his brilliant idea is, and at first they accept that. Chiefly for Biggley's benefit, who's having trouble with Hedy, Finch builds some thinly veiled sexual innuendo into his presentation, his point being that if Biggley goes with ·Finch's idea, he can save his disintegrating relationship with Hedy. To guarantee Biggley's cooperation Finch even uses Hedy in the presentation, dressed in a skimpy pirate costume. It works. The treasure hunt show provides Finch with an idea and Biggley with a job offer for Hedy—Treasure Girl. The problem is, the idea isn't Finch's. It's Frump's. And this will cause his downfall. As long as he follows the book, he's fine. But Frump is a loser. Using his idea can only cause difficulties. Everything that goes wrong comes from the treasure hunt idea. Only because he's J. Pierrepont Finch and because this show is such an outrageous farce can Finch turn his misfortune around and end up on top (literally).

Why do we like Finch? Why do we want him to get away with all his lying, cheating, and maneuvering? Because the people he's beating are bigger jerks than he is, and because we'd love to be able to get away with the outrageous stuff he can. He's so gleeful, so childlike about his triumphs that it's hard sometimes to remember how ruthless he is. "Brotherhood of Man" gets us caught up in the excitement as much as Womper and the other executives. Despite his methods, he's just another ambitious hard-working young man chasing that American Dream. Of course, *How to Succeed* suggests that the American Dream isn't quite as squeaky clean—or as difficult to achieve—as we'd like to think.

Rosemary

The character of Rosemary produces an interesting problem for both director and actress. Is she to be played in period style, like a young June Cleaver? Is she to be played sincerely or with tongue planted firmly in cheek? Rosemary is smart, resourceful, attractive, and occasionally manipulative, with a good job. Why would she be "happy to keep his dinner warm"? Contemporary audiences often have a problem with that song and with "Cinderella Darling." The 1995 Broadway revival cut "Cinderella Darling" and the 1967 movie version cut both songs (remember, you can't cut songs without permission from the licensing agent). In many ways, Rosemary is a lot like Finch, so we can understand their attraction. He's not just another smarmy skirt-chasing executive. In Act I, Scene 2, they both say the same line: "I'm prepared for exactly that [this] sort of thing." They belong together. But why is Rosemary, a successful working woman, so eager to be a housewife? Even if you play the show in period 1961 style, it's still hard for contemporary audiences to swallow. One option is to play Rosemary as a cartoon, like the executives. But since she's the romantic lead, this will water down the love story considerably. And maybe that's okay. The show isn't about the romance; it's about Finch's rise up the corporate ladder. The other option is to play Rosemary as a sixties Dolly Levi, a strong woman who knows she's in control, secure enough with herself and the man she loves to accept playing the traditional role on the surface. In this case, Rosemary would sing "Happy to Keep His Dinner Warm" with an amused detachment. A close reading of the lyric can support this interpretation. Either way probably works, but keep in mind your audience's reaction as you decide.

Rosemary is at times just as manipulative as Finch. Though she is treated as a serious character, she's also very funny. Even her name, Pilkington, after the well-known girls' finishing school, is funny. She knows how to play the game as well as Finch does. She cleverly tricks him into asking her out to lunch the first day. She helps him at several points along the way. First, she gives him the flower that he then uses to charm Miss Jones (of course, she only helps him here by accident). She also helps keep Hedy hidden and lies to Biggley when Frump tries to get Finch caught with Hedy in Biggley's office. The romance between Finch and Rosemary happens so fast, as fast as his climb to the top of World Wide Wickets, that it makes us wonder if it's really love. But again, maybe in a show this crazy, it doesn't really matter. In most musicals (and plays and movies), the main character learns something important about himself before the story ends, but Finch doesn't. He's just as manipulative and sneaky at the final curtain as he was when the curtain went up. In the same way that Finch tramples the rules of Big Business, so *How to Succeed* tramples many of the rules of musical comedy. Perhaps we're not meant to care as much about the romance as we usually would. After all, in another break with traditional musicals, the romance is the secondary plot here.

The Company Man

Bud Frump is the stereotypical antagonist. He's cowardly, incompetent, funny-looking, and usually gets his way by cheating. But in

How to Succeed, the hero *also* gets his way by cheating. Frump tries to double-cross Finch by offering him the treasure hunt idea, knowing full well that Biggley already hates it. But Finch manages to double-double-cross Frump by first getting Biggley to accept the idea anyway and by then pinning it on Frump (and Biggley) when it all explodes in his face. As an audience, we actually feel sorry for Frump at the end when he is reduced to washing windows. Finch won, but *not* fair and square. Good did not triumph over Evil. Instead, Sneaky was beaten by Sneakier. Frump acts as Finch's exact opposite. He's cowardly; Finch is absurdly brave. Frump runs to his mother to get things his way; Finch makes everything happen himself. Frump goes from World Wide Wickets employee with a lot of clout to window washer; Finch goes from window washer to chairman of the board. Frump represents corporate karma—one man can only move up if another moves down. Finch can't have success unless Frump suffers failure. Frump realizes this early in the show and it only makes his campaign against Finch that much more intense; ultimately, however, Finch is smarter and sneakier.

What a Crescendo

How to Succeed has one of the most kinetic, most jazz-inspired scores written for the stage. From the opening bars of the overture through the end of the show, the music jumps with a kind of intensity seldom heard in mainstream Broadway musicals. Harmonically, the score is full of chords and melodies straight out of the jazz idiom, including lots of minor seventh, diminished seventh, and half-diminished seventh chords, as well as interesting, jarring syncopations. The instrumentation of the orchestra contributes to the jazz feel, with a vibraphone, lots of saxophone, and heavy percussion. Composer/lyricist Frank Loesser is constantly switching meter, shifting the downbeat, playfully not meeting our musical expectations, thereby keeping the music exciting and full of unexpected jokes and surprises. He peppers the score with musical jokes—the quotation of the Grieg piano concerto in Finch's lavish love song "Rosemary," which pushes the piece over the edge of absurdity; the solemn funereal organ music before the board meeting; the musicalization of "Brotherhood of Man," the moment of confession and ethical rebirth for these crooked businessmen, as a musical revival meeting complete with hand-clapping and tambourines. As is evident from his daughter's biography of him, *A Most Remarkable Fella*, Frank Loesser was a very funny man, and his off-center sense of humor pervades every note of the score. Even the more traditional songs like "Happy to Keep His Dinner Warm" find themselves barrelling through hilariously bizarre chord progressions. Loesser wrote the score for *How to Succeed* in only four-and-a-half months, and though it wasn't his favorite of the theatre scores he wrote, it is clearly the best integrated. More so than even *Guys and Dolls* or *The Most Happy Fella*, this score was matched perfectly to the style and tone of the book. The sense of satire was consistent from beginning to end, seamlessly moving from dialogue to song and back again. Loesser employed parodies of various musical styles to match the sparkling wit of his lyrics and Abe Burrows's razor-sharp script. He wrote a dissonant cha-cha for "Coffee Break," an absurdist soft-shoe number for "A Secretary Is Not a Toy" (complete with manual typewriter added to the percussion instruments), a manic football fight song for "Grand Old Ivy," and a shouting, hand-clapping, foot-stomping revival meeting spiritual for "Brotherhood of Man," underlining not just the charade of the sleazy executives pretending to confess their sins and to be born again but also the devoutly practiced religion *of* business. In addition to writing a terribly fun and hummable score, he also wrote a very sophisticated one.

There are a number of musical motifs weaving in and out of the score, pointing up dramatic moments and making important connections between characters. The motif we hear the most is from "The Company Way." This is Finch's theme song, the music that charts his progress up the corporate ladder. Appropriately this melody begins the overture, letting us know that this is an important motif and that the concept it represents is central to the show's story and message. It moves into a jazzy, syncopated vamp in the lower register that is also a fragment of the melody from "The Company Way." The vamp then segues into "Happy to Keep His Dinner Warm," Rosemary's main theme. Later in the overture, the vamp comes back, this time faster and more driving. On top of it, the flutes and piccolo come in with the melody to "Brotherhood of Man," but in a completely different key (the vamp is in C major and the melody is in G major). After a move into "Brotherhood" all in the same key, the overture ends with a short quote from "Rosemary" underneath the last chord. The overture introduces Finch and Rosemary, Finch's corporate ladder motif, and their love theme, essentially setting up the entire score. Though overtures are not usually constructed carefully enough that you can analyze them this closely, this one is exceptional. It sets up the important musical themes and motifs in the score, it establishes the musical style for the evening, and it's a lot of fun.

The next time we hear "The Company Way," it's as the instrumental underscoring at the opening of the mail room scene (Act I, Scene 4). After some dialogue, we hear the song for the first time in its full form. In the song, Twimble teaches Finch how to get ahead in a big company. Though Finch plays the good student, he already knows he will totally ignore Twimble's advice. The *real* way to get ahead is in Finch's little book. After Finch has successfully conned his way into an immediate promotion (after only two hours on the job), Frump is made the new head of the mail room and the entire company reprises "The Company Way," during which Loesser has some serious fun rhyming "Frump" with "*company.*" We hear the song again instrumentally as Finch gets Gatch transferred and himself promoted into Gatch's position. During the rooftop party for Ovington, the song returns again in a dance band arrangement. In Act II, as the executives file into the boardroom for the scene in which Finch will take his fatal misstep, we hear an organ playing a "Company Way" funeral march. Finally, as Finch takes the job of chairman of the board, the cast reprises "The Company Way" one more time. Though the song is originally Twimble's, *his* "way" is not the one that works. So Finch appropriates the song for himself and it becomes an ironic comment on Finch's "way" to the top. This final reprise also delivers the final joke—Bud Frump on the window washer's scaffolding, reading Finch's *How to Succeed* book. (Kinda leaves things open for a sequel, doesn't it?) Under the last notes of the finale, the orchestra quotes the "Company Way" vamp, and then the main motif from "How To."

The title song sets up the premise of the show, that Finch can learn everything he needs to know about succeeding in the business world from this little paperback. The song acts as a kind of summary of the events to come, including applying for the job, advancing from the mail room, and picking the right allies. The extended version of the song on the cast recording, part of which is not in the published score, even includes a reference to walking into a conference room with a brilliant idea. The melody of this song becomes a secondary motif for Finch's rise up the corporate ladder. It's used as a scene change as Finch sets up Gatch and gets him shipped off to Venezuela so he can steal his job. It's also quoted at the end of the first act finale, as Finch is finally promoted to vice president and gets his name on his office door and again at the end of the second act finale as Finch takes over as chairman of the board.

Character Through Song

"Happy to Keep His Dinner Warm" isn't used enough to be a motif for Rosemary, but it is reprised as Finch breaks his first date with Rosemary and again after Finch has promised that they will indeed get married. The lyric to this second reprise is another problematic moment for Rosemary. She sings of his "purpose in life and purity of soul." Surely she isn't blind and stupid enough to believe that. Is she being ironic? Is she laughing at the fact that she still loves him despite his relentless and less than ethical labors? Does she actually *admire* his determination and ambition? Reconciling her lyrics with her actions gets more difficult as the show progresses.

"Been a Long Day" is another interesting song. There are two instances of ostinato (long, repeated patterns) in the accompaniment—the first at the beginning, the other under the verses—that mirror the monotony and tedium of the workday. The lyric is funny and illuminating, but also very unusual. Finch, Rosemary, and Smitty are singing their internal thoughts, yet Smitty is a kind of narrator, knowing exactly what the other two are thinking.

"Rosemary" is one of the most fun numbers in the show, a love song so completely over the top it's both hilarious and thrilling. The number starts with a solo by Finch. When he gets to the line "what a crescendo," the orchestra (and the orchestra in his head, which he conducts) plays an excerpt from Grieg's piano concerto. It's a wonderful reference that perfectly conveys how melodramatic Finch is, hearing his feelings for Rosemary set to classical music. We, the audience, actually hear it, but he only hears it in his head. Rosemary enters and he tries to get her to hear the music in his head. She can't, until he proposes; then she hears it, only where he hears "Rosemary," she hears "J. Pierrepont." Loesser's greatest trick in this song is the way he plays with the second person pronoun. At first, Finch is singing, "There is wonderful music in the very sound of your name," referring of course to Rosemary's name. But after his promotion, the "you" becomes more general, now actually referring to anyone in his place, or more specifically, him. So in the second half of the song, when Finch tells the guy who'll paint his name on his door, "Boy, when you see it on your own door, there is wonderful music in the very sound of your name," he's referring to his own name. By this point, Frump has joined the action unseen by Finch and Rosemary, and he also joins the singing with a countermelody against the now strained love duet (actually, it's a triangle now—Rosemary in love with Finch, Finch in love with his name). The three characters end the act with a big musical finish, Rosemary's elation gone, Frump's resolve to defeat Finch renewed, and Finch more delighted with himself than ever. Under their last notes, the orchestra quotes "How To" as the curtain falls.

The love song in Act II belongs to Hedy and Biggley and, as might be expected, is not a traditional ballad. Biggley's overly dramatic lines leading up to the song are full of words of love for Hedy, but we know he's just blowing smoke. He'll say anything to keep her from leaving. His lines and the lyric he sings in the song are so devoid of real feeling that they're laughable (like everything else in the show). Biggley's only desire here is keep Hedy as a mistress. She is unhappy with her job and is threatening to leave town, so Biggley tells her what he thinks she wants to hear—that he loves her. What makes the song even funnier is that the lyric is peppered with money references—"gold," "treasure," "wealth." He's rich and he knows that's the only thing about him that keeps her there. When Hedy sings her own verse, using the same lyric, the money references jump out. Hedy is a gold digger, after all, just wanting to be taken care of by a rich old man. She is literally Biggley's "treasure" girl, as we'll see later in the act. Appropriately, the last word of the song is "gold."

Gotta Stop That Man

We first hear the "Gotta Stop That Man" vamp in Act I, when Frump gets the idea to set up Finch to be caught in Biggley's office with Hedy. An instrumental version with both the vamp and the melody opens the second act as the executives stand around whispering conspiratorially—about Finch, no doubt, and how to stop him before he gets them *all* transferred to Venezuela. By the time we hear the song with vocals, the vamp has already been established as the executives' revenge motif. After Finch's "I Believe in You," the executives end up singing counterpoint to Finch's electric shaver (how humiliating for them if they knew!). The two opposing camps come together and finish the song in gorgeous harmony.

Finch's "I Believe in You" is the proverbial icing on the cake. If we thought Finch was obnoxious up to this point, who would have expected he'd be singing a love song to *himself*? The genius of Loesser's twisted humor finds itself fully expressed as Finch looks into the mirror and begins singing to himself of trust, wisdom, and truth. There's not another moment like this in any other musical. His confidence and self-absorption are obscene. When he turns on his shaver and the members of the orchestra start playing kazoos, the moment gets even more hilarious. We know it's not the shaver we hear: it's kazoos, and the orchestra (and Loesser) knows we know. This is the moment when the outrageousness of the show reaches its pinnacle. It can't get more ridiculous than a group of men singing counterpoint to a Norelco triple-header. Later, as Finch prepares to be fired for the fiasco he's created, we get another shock as Rosemary sings a reprise of this song, only this time as a *real* love song (the movie version of the show destroys this by switching the order of the songs). With someone else complimenting him, it's actually touching. Once again, Loesser has caught us off guard. After two hours of each song's being more outrageous than the one before, he double fakes us by turning the most egocentric song yet into a genuinely sweet moment.

A Few Friendly Warnings

This is not an easy show to put together. I've seen productions that ran over three hours; no matter how charming Finch may be, no audience will sit still that long. I directed the show myself several years ago, and a few nights before we opened we were worried that we were running too long. We watched the show and couldn't find any scenes that were dragging and could find nothing we could cut. We eventually realized that it's just a really long show. But in order to keep your audience's attention, your Finch must be charming beyond words and a fearless actor. Finch is an outrageous character from the beginning of the show. The actor playing him can't be afraid to create an over-the-top performance (I usually have actors watch Jack Nicholson in *Batman*, Kevin Kline in *A Fish Called Wanda*, or Robert DeNiro in *New York, New York* to see what I mean by over-the-top). The rest of the cast must also be filled with first-rate comedians. This is not a normal musical. It's a farce and has to move like lightning. Not only do you want to keep the running time down, but you want the audience to be overwhelmed by Finch's rapid rise, leaving them literally breathless. If you find you have to cut for length, the "Yo-Ho-Ho" dance at the beginning of the treasure hunt show is the only truly expendable moment in the show and is often left out. As mentioned earlier, the recent Broadway revival cut "Cinderella Darling," probably to keep the overt sexism to a minimum. The other decision to be made is whether to set the action in the present or in 1961. Most directors set it in 1961, and some of the women's songs may work better that way, but the show can stand up to a contemporary interpretation.

Other Resources

The full piano score and vocal selections have both been published, although the script has not. There is a first-rate original cast recording as well as a revival cast recording. The movie soundtrack was released on LP. The movie is on video, but several songs were cut. Interestingly, though a scene from "Coffee Break" is on the videotape box and the song is on the movie soundtrack, it's not in the movie. The movie features Broadway cast members Robert Morse (Finch), Rudy Vallee (Biggley), Michelle Lee (Rosemary), Ruth Kobart (Miss Jones), and Sammy Smith (Twimble/Womper). Music Theatre International also offers a fascinating Study Guide on the show. Susan Loesser's book, *A Most Remarkable Fella*, is full of Frank Loesser's notes and letters and Susan's memories of her father's work on *How to Succeed*. Also of interest is "An Evening with Frank Loesser," a recording including early versions of "A Secretary Is Not a Toy" and other songs, sung and played by Frank Loesser, plus "Organization Man," a very early version of "The Company Way."

8 Into the Woods

Book by James Lapine
Music and Lyrics by Stephen Sondheim
Originally Directed on Broadway by James Lapine
Licensed by Music Theatre International

Into the Woods is one of Stephen Sondheim's big hits and is now a staple with community theatres, colleges and high schools, and other groups. The show is a "crossover" musical, combining the innocence of fairy tales, magic, and the mystery of the woods with the adult concepts of morality, sexuality, the consequences of actions, responsibility to the community, and the complexities of parent-child relationships. This is a different fairy tale world than we're used to, one in which wicked stepsisters aren't ugly and beautiful people can be bad, in which tough questions don't have easy answers. James Lapine's book and Sondheim's score provide a weird mix of escapism and hard-core reality, which manages to still succeed in creating a unified work. The show's book tells the convoluted plot, while Sondheim's score provides the themes and lessons.

Once Upon a Time

The show starts with the familiar phrase "Once upon a time," then hits the audience with a loud jarring chord and vamp, waking us up and telling us this is no ordinary children's story. *Into the Woods* is a fairy tale with a twist. During the first act the main characters all make wishes and all of them get their wish by the first act finale. Like *The Fantasticks*, the first act gives us a simple, traditional happily ever after, then the second act examines what happens *after* the happily ever after. Throughout history, literature has treated the woods as a dark place without society's rules where people find their true selves and learn important lessons before returning to the safety of the real world. This show acknowledges the fact that in the real world love is not ideal, princes are not perfect, choices are not easy, and every act has a repercussion. Human relations aren't simple. Even after these people get what they wished for, they want more. After the ball is over, Cinderella is bored. After Jack steals the gold from the giant, he goes back to steal more. After the Baker and his Wife get their child, they find they want a bigger house. After the Prince marries Cinderella, he still fools around with the Baker's Wife. When Cinderella confronts him, he tells her that he thought marrying her was all he ever wanted but instead he still wants more. He says, "I was raised to be charming, not sincere. And I didn't ask to be born a king. I'm not perfect." The condition of never being satisfied has serious ramifications in this very adult fairy tale world.

The plot is consciously chaotic. The Baker and his Wife, the only two characters not taken from traditional fairy tales, tie the other stories together but they also wreak havoc in these other stories. Connecting the stories gives each character's actions implications for everyone else. The Baker's Wife has an affair with Cinderella's Prince. Jack's theft from the giant brings danger to everyone in the woods. The added complications of these new combinations create new dramatic situations and tensions.

The music for the show is both very simple and very sophisticated. Sondheim has written short, jaunty melodies that sound very much like children's songs. Many of the songs in the first act are brief and self-contained, while the songs in Act II are longer and often interconnected. The lyrics have a great many rhymes and alliterations, which help make them sound even more like children's songs. For instance, in "On the Steps of the Palace" we hear:

> You'll just leave him a clue:
> For example, a shoe.
> And then see what he'll do.
> Now it's he and not you
> Who is stuck with a shoe
> In a stew,
> In the goo,
> And you've learned something, too,
> Something you never knew . . .

As well as:

> *'Cause you're still standing stuck*
> *In the stuff on the steps . . .*

Of course, because the lyrics are Sondheim's, there is important character and thematic development underneath the alliteration and multiple rhymes.

The End Justifies the Themes

The *Into the Woods* score uses music in various ways to unify the evening and to connect certain events and moments in the show dramatically. The most obvious unifying musical theme is the title song, "Into the Woods," which is used periodically throughout the show to support the concept of the quest or journey through the woods. The lyrics to this music change greatly as the mood of the show changes.

One musical idea used a great deal throughout the score is a "danger" leitmotif, often associated with the magic beans. It appears first in the accompaniment, as the Witch tells the Baker and his Wife how to reverse the curse on them, which connects to both where the beans came from and where they're going. We hear it next as five single notes played as the Baker counts out the five beans into Jack's hand, beans that already have caused much grief and will cause much more before the evening is over. Those five notes immediately become the basis for the accompaniment to the next song, "I Guess This Is Goodbye," as Jack says goodbye to the cow he's traded away for the beans. These notes become the melody of "Giants in the Sky," Jack's account of the danger and adventure up the beanstalk; "Stay With Me," the Witch's warning to Rapunzel of the dangers out in the world; and the Witch's "Lament," grieving over Rapunzel's death. It is also the melody of the wordless song Rapunzel sings from her tower, her song of longing for adventure in the real world—a world in which she will be killed. This melody that began with the beans also ties Rapunzel's imprisonment back to her father's stealing of the beans, which put Rapunzel where she is. This melody acts as a half-note accompaniment figure for "No One Is Alone" and is turned upside down for one of the song's key phrases, "People make mistakes."

Several other motifs and reprises also unify the score and create cohesion within this very complicated plot. The musical phrase accompanying the Prince's personality traits, "clever, well-mannered, considerate," shows up three times. The first instance occurs when the Baker's Wife asks Cinderella about the Prince. Strangely, though this section of "A Very Nice Prince" is on the original cast recording, it's not in the published score. The second occurrence is when the Prince describes himself to his brother. It occurs a third time in "It Takes Two," when the Baker's Wife describes the Baker. This last time is significant because the Baker's Wife uses the same music and some of the same words to describe both Cinderella's Prince and her husband, each of whom she sleeps with. Phrases from "Children Will Listen" appear earlier in the show in "Stay With Me" and the Witch's "Lament." Throughout the show, it is sung only by the Witch and only in reference to Rapunzel; but after Rapunzel's death, the Witch sings it for the first time to the Baker in reference to his child. There are also dissonant chords that accompany the Witch's comings and goings and those of the Mysterious Man. Indirectly, this foreshadows the fact that the Witch knows the Mysterious Man, who is in fact the Baker's father, who stole the beans from the Witch and set in motion most of the events that play out during the musical. Additionally, the Witch and the Mysterious Man are both parents who failed somehow in raising their children and lost them.

The Title Song

The opening sequence, which contains more than a dozen individual episodes all tied together musically, includes the title song, initially heard in bits and pieces. This sequence establishes not only the tone and style of the show, but also main characters, various story lines, and themes. The imagery of light and dark, used continually throughout the show, is established with the first occurrence of the title song. Red Ridinghood sings: "The way is clear, the light is good." In Act II, this line becomes "The way is dark, the light is dim," establishing the difference in mood between the two acts. With the line about her granny, "Never can tell what lies ahead. For all that I know, she's already dead," Sondheim has also set up the dark humor that will pervade the script and score and the fact that death will play a part in all the stories. The characters' moral ambiguity is established through the lines:

Into the woods,
To get my wish,
I don't care how . . .

The characters will lie, cheat, and steal to get what they want, and the apathy toward right and wrong that they display here will have great significance later.

The Woods Aren't Just Trees

Like Shakespeare and many other writers, Lapine and Sondheim use the woods as a place where the normal rules of civilization don't apply and where people learn important lessons about themselves and about life. The woods are a place of imagination where people find their true selves. The Baker's Wife sings to him in Act I, "You've changed. You're daring. You're different in the woods." Red Riding-hood's misadventure with the Wolf is a journey into the woods in miniature, going into "the dark" and later coming back into "the light" having learned a lesson. In the second act, Cinderella's Prince says to the Baker's Wife as he seduces her, "Right and wrong don't matter in the woods." The woods represent freedom from the constrictions of polite society but also the danger of the unknown in the world and in ourselves. The woods in this musical are just as dangerous, if not more so, than in Shakespeare's plays—here, people will die.

Jack sings a line in "Giants in the Sky" that aptly describes the experience of every character in the show: "And you're back again, only different than before." Each of the main characters has a song in which they describe the lesson they've learned in the woods. Each song has a similar accompaniment and each contains a variant of the line, "I [You] know things now." It's also interesting that all these songs except Red Ridinghood's are in the second person, a device that very effectively pulls the audience into the action and essentially makes *them* the focus of the songs.

Casting the same actor as the Narrator and the Mysterious Man (who is also the Baker's father) further supports the theme of learned lessons. As the Narrator, he knows everything but has come by that knowledge easily. He knows merely because he's the Narrator. As the Mysterious Man, he has learned his lessons the hard way, by losing his family through his own greed and misjudgment. As the Narrator, none of the characters want to listen to him. In fact, they willingly sacrifice him to the giant's wife in Act II. As the Mysterious Man, he can pass on his earned wisdom to his son, who is also learning the hard way, by losing his wife. When the Baker says to his infant child at the end, "Once upon a time, in a far off kingdom . . ." he is repeating exactly the lines that the Narrator—his father—said as the show opened (assuming the same actor plays both the Narrator and the Mysterious Man, as was done in the original production). The Baker has inherited the role of Narrator from his father. Sondheim further explored the passing on of stories from one generation to another in *Assassins*. Apparently in an early version of *Into the Woods*, it was revealed late in the show that the Narrator is actually the Baker's son, the baby the Baker holds at the end; he has heard the stories from his father and is passing them on. The line "Like father, like son" in the song "No More" means more than it appears to on first hearing. The difference between them, though, is that the Baker has learned that he can rebuild his life (to some extent) rather than run away from his pain like his father did.

Morals and Lessons

One of the major themes of the show is, as Red Ridinghood puts it, "Nice is different than good." People who are pleasant or polite on the surface are frequently immoral in their actions. The Witch is the most honest character in the show. She doesn't deceive anyone; she always lays her cards on the table. The Baker and his Wife lie and cheat in every case as they collect the items they need to reverse their curse. Jack steals from the giant. The Baker's Wife and Cinderella's Prince commit adultery. Cinderella wonders at great length about the insignificant rewards of being nice; no matter how nice she is, she is still treated poorly. In "Last Midnight," the Witch puts it most accurately:

> You're so nice.
> You're not good,
> You're not bad,
> You're just nice.

The show also examines the wishes that everyone makes at the beginning. Are these wishes really what these people want? Cinderella says, "What I want most of all is to know what I want." Is the realization of these wishes worth the price that must be paid? As the lyric to "Children Will Listen" says, "Wishes come true, not free." The Baker and his Wife get the child they wished for, but find that raising a child is not easy. The Witch gets the beauty she wanted, but loses her powers. Cinderella gets her Prince, but he cheats on her. Jack gets many treasures, but causes death and destruction. Everyone gets what he or she wished for, but it has thrown the woods into chaos. Everything bad that happens in the show is a direct result of an immoral act. The Baker can't have a child because his father stole the Witch's beans. Cinderella gets her Prince through deception and he turns out to be adulterous. The giant's wife comes down and kills for two reasons. First, the Baker cheats Jack by giving him only beans for his cow, and the beans grow into the beanstalk that provides the giant's wife the *means* to come down. Second, despite the giant's wife's hospitality, Jack steals from the giant and his wife and kills the giant, giving the giant's wife a *motive* for seeking revenge.

Everything boils down to a matter of responsibility. When the Baker becomes overwhelmed by the tragedy surrounding him, he wants to run away, leaving his child. Finally, all the characters learn that not only do they have the obvious responsibilities to family, they also have a responsibility to the community. No one is alone, as the song says. As they each committed their various wrongs, they had a responsibility to foresee the consequences they would force upon others. Regardless of whose fault it is, the giant's wife is a threat to them all. Only through cooperation can they survive. This concept of community responsibility is particularly applicable to issues in our contemporary world.

The Baker and His Wife

The story of the Baker and his Wife is the only one James Lapine created for *Into the Woods*. They are the audience's surrogates, representing middle-class working people. As with similar characters in many Sondheim shows, they are our way into the story. We can relate to their lives, desires, and values. Like the Balladeer in *Assassins*, Dot in *Sunday in the Park with George*, Robert in *Company*, they are our "viewers" through which we experience the story. Unlike similar characters in other Sondheim shows, the Baker and his Wife are not entirely honorable people. The Baker is weak. He is easily manipulated by his wife into lying and cheating, even though he complains about it afterward. His wife says, "Everyone tells tiny lies—what's important really, is the size" and "There are rights and wrongs and in-betweens," both very dangerous philosophies, so dangerous in this case that she will be killed in Act II. Analysts of the show have wondered if her death is meant as a punishment for her marital infidelity; but compared with her many other immoralities throughout the show, her one-time romp with the Prince seems almost insignificant. As in other fairy tales (and many horror stories), she dies because she is a bad person. Even after having sex with the Prince, which she knows was wrong, she wonders if there's a way to continue her infidelity without letting her husband know.

Once she's dead, the Baker is too weak to go on without her. Though they learn a lesson in Act I—that cooperation can be valuable—they don't learn the lesson that could save them. In Act II, in the song "No More," the Baker and his father sing about running away. The Baker's father left him and his mother when he was very young and the Baker has never forgiven him for it; yet, the Baker is contemplating doing the same thing to *his* child. He realizes that no matter where he goes there will always be questions to be answered and problems to be solved, that life is difficult. He realizes that he can't make the same mistake his father made. He has to make the difficult choice—to go back and deal with the situation he's been handed. He must raise his child, teach his child the lessons no one taught him. The last line of "No More" says a great deal in just two words. Despite the grief and pain the woods have given him, the Baker realizes there must be "no more" running away, "no more" selfishness and blame, "no more" destruction. Some battles must be fought.

Knowing a Lot

Like many of the other main characters, Red Ridinghood takes what is not rightfully hers; in the opening scene she steals numerous buns from the Baker and his Wife. Again, wanting outweighs right and wrong. Red Ridinghood grows up during her time in the woods and experiences a sexual awakening with the wolf she encounters. The original costume designed for the wolf on Broadway revealed a bare chest and stomach, tightly muscled, and included a large furry penis.

The wolf's song "Hello Little Girl" is bursting with sexual imagery—"flesh," "flowers," "exploring"—and she decides it might be okay to pick a flower. When she finally gets to her grandmother's house and finds the wolf, he literally takes her into his bed to eat her.

Her subsequent song, "I Know Things Now," is just as blatant: "He showed me things, many beautiful things"; "He made me feel excited, well excited and scared"; "But he drew me close and he swallowed me down"; and finally, "Even flowers have their dangers." Red Ridinghood is intelligent and learns her lesson quickly. She sings, "Though scary is exciting, nice is different than good." This is an important lesson for a young person to learn. Her song ends with a tremendously insightful line: "Isn't it nice to know a lot! And a little bit not." She has realized that *knowing* right from wrong means forevermore having to *choose* between right and wrong, an inevitable responsibility of growing up. She has also learned not to trust, to know when to protect herself; but the lesson is more severe in *Into the Woods* than it was when we read the story as children. For the rest of the musical, Red Ridinghood runs around wearing the wolf's pelt as a cape and brandishing a large hunting knife. Her reaction to the violence perpetrated against her is to become violent herself, very much like young people in our society today.

Different Than Before

Jack also has to grow up during his time in the woods. When we first meet him, he is having to let go of safety—his cow and best friend Milky White. His first adventure up the beanstalk, which he describes in the song "Giants in the Sky," is full of sexual imagery, like Red Ridinghood's sequence. He sings:

And she draws you close to her giant breast,
And you know things now that you never knew before . . .

(The original lyric about her "giant breast" was even more explicit.) Then her husband comes home and catches his wife and Jack. Before Jack escapes, he manages to steal some gold. He later decides it's not enough and goes back up to steal two more times. When the giant tries to follow him back down, Jack cuts down the beanstalk and the giant falls to his death. This episode is important is several ways. First, Jack is the one who is wrong. He is guilty of theft and murder.

When we read the story as children, we don't give Jack's slaying of the giant a second thought, but in the world of *Into the Woods* slaying is murder, no matter who is being killed. The giant isn't the monster here; Jack is. When the giant's wife comes down in Act II to seek revenge, it's a surprise to us (and the characters) that she's upset about her husband. It didn't even occur to us that the giant left behind a grieving widow. We don't think about it because they're giants and we've been conditioned to think giants are bad. Yet Jack has told us explicitly in his song that the giant's wife was very kind to him. Did Jack know the giant meant him harm or did he just assume that he was mean because he was a giant? Was that justification for stealing from him? Once again, a character's greed creates tragedy and will in time cause dire consequences to others.

The Choice May Have Been Mistaken

Cinderella embodies another of the major themes of the show—the burden of choice—that threads through every one of the main plots. The Baker allows his wife to choose for him. Jack makes choices about selling the cow, stealing from the giants, going back for more. Red Ridinghood chooses to go with the wolf. Making choices, making decisions is difficult and often frightening. Red Ridinghood finds that understanding right and wrong requires you to *choose* between right and wrong. Cinderella wants to leave the woods with its choices and decisions and return home "where there's nothing to choose, so there's nothing to lose." She hasn't yet learned what Dot learns in *Sunday in the Park with George* when she tells George, "The choice may have been mistaken; the choosing was not. You have to move on." Choices are a part of life, and avoiding them often can cause even more trouble than making a poor choice.

Cinderella's song "On the Steps of the Palace" finds her confronted with a big choice. Does she stay on the steps and let the Prince find her or does she go home and forget about him? As in other Sondheim shows, lyrics expressing deep sincere emotion contain less rhyme; lyrics of intellectual or critical analysis and comment contain lots of rhyme. Because the lyric to this song is analytical, it's full of rhymes and alliterations. The last stanza of the song contains nine "oo" rhymes in a row, indicating perhaps *too much* thought. Ultimately, her decision is not to decide. She will leave her shoe and take a passive role in the scenario, forcing the choice on the Prince. Cinderella is learning to flirt, to manipulate, and to be passive-aggressive, forcing others to make choices for her.

I Must Be on My Journey

In Act I, the action centers on several characters and their individual journeys or quests. Act II reveals the consequences of the actions these characters took in Act I in order to achieve their goals, and those consequences set in motion a collective journey that the characters must now take together—defeating the giant's wife. As "Your Fault" illustrates, everyone took some action in Act I that led to the situation in Act II, and only together can they make it through to the end. In "Last Midnight," the Witch points out that each of them must share in the blame and that trying to assign blame to one person is far less constructive than figuring out how to deal with the situation in which they now find themselves.

The woods are a place to learn, and as we move through Act II, we must learn the story's lesson along with the characters. Some critics of the show complain that it's too preachy, that a well-made musical or play doesn't tell the audience the point of the story, but instead allows them to discover it on their own. But *Into the Woods* is a fairy tale at its heart, and as such, must deliver a moral at the end. There are several lessons over the course of the evening: that there is no such thing as happily ever after; that every act has consequences for us and for the people around us; that there are no simple answers; and most important, that we never stop learning.

This last theme is the basis for the show. The journey through the woods is a metaphor for growing up, the kind of growing up we all do until the day we die. Going into the woods is something we must do over and over throughout our lives, just as the characters in the show make several journeys. As the finale says:

> *You think at last*
> *You're through, and then,*
> *Into the woods you go again*
> *To take another journey.*

The most important line of the song is "Everything you learn there will help when you return there." As in the musical, these growing experiences are cumulative. With each journey, you come equipped with all you learned the last time. It is also true that the first several times we go "into the woods," most of us take along a guide in the person of a parent or some other mentor. But "sometimes people leave you halfway through the wood"; at some point, we must begin taking the journey on our own.

Throughout the show, lessons are learned by the characters. Because there are so many stories, there are many lessons; but the overriding message is that there are no easy answers in James Lapine's woods (or in the real world). Things are not black and white. Red Ridinghood wonders about the morality of killing the giant's wife. She says, "But the giant's a person. Aren't we to show forgiveness?" How can her question be answered? In a standard fairy tale world, giants are bad and must be killed. In the real world—and *Into the Woods* is a frightening mix of both worlds—a person is a person, giant or not. Is it ever all right to kill? Red Ridinghood killed the wolf. The group killed the narrator by throwing him to the giant. The steward killed Jack's mother, and Jack wants to kill him in revenge. When is killing morally acceptable? It's a question the courts consider daily.

Children Will Listen

Lapine and Sondheim indirectly ask a very important question at the end of the show. What is it we teach our children? Do we teach them that it's all right for Jack to steal from the giant, that it's all right for Cinderella to be an imposter so that she can go to the festival, that the rampant killing is all right? Are we teaching them that immoral acts can be moral? When we tell children that people live happily ever after, are we imposing expectations on them they can never meet? Isn't this part of what has screwed up the characters who populate Sondheim's *Assassins*—the idea that if they can't find an ideal life, the American Dream, a happily ever after, that it must be *their* fault? Or is it better for children to learn the harsh realities of life only after they're older?

Sondheim warns us not only to be careful what we say to children, but also to be "careful the things you do; children will see . . . and learn." This applies to the drugs, violence, obscenity, and corruption that plague our cities. Can a parent smoking a cigarette effectively tell a child that drugs are wrong?

As the audience, we see that going "into the woods" is a metaphor for life, for every problem or difficult situation we encounter; and that people must go "into the woods" over and over throughout their lives. That's why it's the title of the show, why the title song weaves in and out of both acts, and why there are two acts with two separate journeys. No one makes only one trip into the woods. This show is a plea for us to examine our lives continually, our actions, our words, and our responsibility to our fellow human beings and to our planet. Nothing is as simple as it seems. Especially not a Sondheim musical.

Keep It Simple

Into the Woods is at its root a fairy tale. It's a show about imagination and internal journeys. The show can work well without elaborate sets. The stage can be decorated with big cardboard cartoon trees or even projections of trees. It can be very abstract with nothing at all that realistically represents trees. It can be done to look like the illustrations in a children's book. Because of the unreal nature of the story and the style of the script and score, you have tremendous freedom in the way you design the show. Likewise, the costumes can be as simple or elaborate as you want. In the original production, each story (the Baker and his Wife, Jack, Red Ridinghood, Cinderella) had its own style, each patterned after a different famous illustrator. You can do that or you can unify the costume design into one style. The simpler the physical design the less distracted the audience will be from following the psychological journeys each of the characters undertakes.

It's also helpful with this show to break the fourth wall. Bring the audience *into* these woods. Sondheim's lyrics do this quite effectively by setting all the "lesson" songs in the second person ("You know things now that you never knew before"). The audience is learning lessons along with the characters. Use the production design and the style of acting and staging to help them go on the journey with you. And keep the show moving like lightening. The energy level must be high, and you must be careful to retain the show's humor even in Act II; yet the characters can't become so broad that they're no longer believable. Even the more ridiculous moments, like Jack's love song to his cow or the Princes' competition to see who's suffering the most, should be treated with absolute sincerity. The Witch must be genuinely scary and must represent a genuine threat to the other characters. It's terribly important that we believe in these people and their dilemmas.

The issue of character motivation is important not only because it figures so prominently in the plot, but also because it will help ground the characters in this very unreal world and fantastic situations. The actors must always be asking themselves what their characters want and how far they are prepared to go (and how much they will lie) to get it. Why do they stay in the woods, despite all the dangers, both real and perceived? And why do they all go *back*? In some cases, the stakes are very high. With the Baker and his Wife, the completion of their task will mean they can have a child. In other cases, the characters are running away (like Cinderella) or are actually crazy (like Rapunzel). Each character grows and changes. Each one learns one or more lessons. How are they different at the end of the show—at the end of their internal journeys—from where they started?

Other Resources

It would probably be interesting to directors, actors, and designers to read the original Grimm fairy tales. In many cases, these stories are very different from the watered-down Disney versions we're all used to. The *Into the Woods* script, vocal selections, and full piano/vocal score have all been published (the song "Our Little World," added for the London production, is not in the published script and score but is available for rental on request). The Broadway production has been broadcast by PBS, and is now commercially available on videotape. Music Theatre International offers one of its invaluable Video Conversationpieces, an hour-long interview with James Lapine and Stephen Sondheim discussing the show and their intentions. Cast recordings are available of both the Broadway and London casts. MTI also has one of their Study Guides available for *Into the Woods*; designed to help teachers integrate the show's issues into their regular curriculum, it's also an excellent guide for the cast and production staff, with background on the show and its creators. Though extremely technical, Stephen Banfield's book *Sondheim's Broadway Musicals* offers some absorbing insights into the score (as well as other Sondheim scores). This isn't a book that should be approached without some music theory background, but it is an interesting read.

9 Jesus Christ Superstar

Music by Andrew Lloyd Webber
Lyrics by Tim Rice
Originally Directed on Broadway by Tom O'Horgan
Licensed by Music Theatre International

While it's true that the score of *Jesus Christ Superstar* is sometimes derivative—more so than most theatre scores—its greatest strength is that it's written in a musical language that we all know and recognize, tempered by infectious rock and roll harmonies and rhythms. Like most of Lloyd Webber's music, it's accessible and easy on the ear. *Superstar* was a hit as a record, first in America, then elsewhere. Mounted soon after the record's release, the misguided Broadway production was less successful, but *Superstar* fast became a worldwide phenomenon, largely because of its creators' fearless headlong plunge into a very controversial treatment of the last week in the life of Jesus Christ. It began a trend of musicals based on the Bible (*Godspell, Two by Two, Hard Job Being God,* among others), many of which were awful.

Today many people don't like Lloyd Webber's work, but the composer of *Superstar* is a different Lloyd Webber from the one who wrote *Phantom of the Opera*. When he began his career thirty years ago, he wrote in the rock and roll idiom, a musical language he knew and loved. No one can deny that he can still write a breathtaking melody, but his musical vocabulary is limited. Consequently, he excelled in the relatively simple repetitive language of rock and roll with *Superstar*, but when he tries today to write in a more classical, more sophisticated style, his limitations show through. What seems driving and primal in *Superstar* sounds merely repetitive in the classical European sound of *Phantom* or the pseudo-jazz style of *Sunset Boulevard*. His writing ability hasn't diminished, but when he changed styles our expectations changed as well, and he couldn't meet them. His critics believe that, unlike other theatre writers, Lloyd Webber has not grown as a composer over time. Luckily, we can still enjoy *Jesus Christ Superstar* and *Evita*, both set on the cynical, literate, and provocative lyrics of Tim Rice.

Rock of Stages

Rock and roll—*pure* rock and roll—doesn't usually make for very good theatre music. For most of this century, popular music and theatre music were the same. The musical theatre provided pop singers with hundreds of songs. But when rock took over the popular music scene, Broadway was slow to catch up. After the rock parody of *Bye Bye Birdie*, in 1960, and the first real rock musical, *Hair*, in 1968, Broadway composers tried to use rock and roll to give theatre attendance a boost. Unfortunately, in the early 1970s, the people who were listening to rock were not the people who were buying theatre tickets. A few shows succeeded with a mellower, hybrid "Broadway-rock" music (*Pippin*, *The Wiz*, and *Grease*, for example), but pure rock just didn't work on stage. More pop/rock musicals made it in the eighties, once rock and roll fans were old enough to be ticket buyers—*Dreamgirls*, *Little Shop of Horrors*, *Song and Dance*, *Evita*, *Cats*, *Starmites*, and others. Even today, the pop/rock musicals that succeed (*Les Misérables*, *Miss Saigon*, and *Blood Brothers*) employ a greatly altered kind of soft rock music.

The reason pure rock and pop music doesn't work in a stage show is largely due to its intrinsically repetitive nature. Rock music uses far fewer chords than classical or theatre music does; in extreme cases, an entire song can use only four chords (and many pop songs in the fifties did just that). The kind of musical development and invention necessary to hold an audience's attention over two hours is usually missing entirely. Likewise, rock lyrics are by their nature also highly repetitive. A typical pop song repeats its chorus many times, usually with the same lyric each time. Conversely, a theatre song has to convey a great deal of information about character, situation, subtext, foreshadowing, and plot elements. Because of its repetitiveness, a rock song just doesn't have the time and space to communicate that much information. Part of the appeal of rock and roll is its simplicity, our ability to sing along after hearing the first chorus; but theatre music that's too simplistic will put an audience to sleep.

Almost every musical or revue created around existing rock or pop songs has been a flop on stage—*Sgt. Pepper's Lonely Heart's Club Band*, *Leader of the Pack*, *The Night That Made America Famous*, *Beatlemania*, *Elvis: The Legend Lives*, *Rock and Roll: The First 5,000 Years*, and many others. In 1978, Stephen Schwartz enlisted a number of pop songwriters to write the score for a new musical called *Working*. They wrote pure pop and rock music, which was catchy and pleasant but conveyed very little information. Because *Working* had no plot, the show depended entirely on creating involving characterizations. With repetitive pop music and lyrics, that was never achieved, and the show left audiences cold, closing after only twenty-five performances.

The musicals of Rice and Webber also left some older listeners cold, but their scores were a hybrid of rock and theatre music. People who didn't grow up with rock still find Andrew Lloyd Webber's music too repetitive; but to younger ears—people who grew up in the sixties or later—the music of *Superstar* is in a familiar language, yet is still interesting enough to hold our attention. Adding immeasurably to the interest are Tim Rice's biting lyrics, written in the cynical, sarcastic tone of the post-Vietnam youth movement. Using contemporary slang and an often angry, decidedly smart-ass attitude, Rice also speaks our language. It is his irreverence that made *Superstar* an international hit and caused all the controversy.

What's the Buzz?

Jesus Christ Superstar set the world buzzing. When setting the story of Jesus' last seven days, lyricist Tim Rice approached the story as history instead of scripture and Jesus as philosopher and political leader instead of the son of God. Obviously, this approach was considered blasphemous by many people. Most of the show's critics believed that the story of Jesus should not be set to rock music, the music of rebellion. Of course, there are two problems with this position. First, merely because a music style is popular doesn't mean it can't treat serious subjects. Bach's music was popular in its time, yet no one today would complain that Bach's Passions are irreverent. The King James Bible seems old and formal, and therefore reverent, to us today, but when it was written its language was

contemporary. Unfortunately, many people today equate serious-
ness and import with antiquity. The second problem with the
stand against *Superstar* is that Jesus himself was a major rebel of
his time. He fought against the establishment, the high priests, and
the Pharisees. What better way to tell his story than with the contemporary sound of rebellion? Keeping all the stories of Jesus and
his views in antique forms takes the teeth out of his activism.
There's no reason why people should not celebrate their beliefs in
the language and music of their lives. Today, *Superstar* doesn't
seem so controversial because rock and roll is now the music of
adults and guitars are now allowed in mass. But imagine the up-
roar if the Catholic church began allowing rap music as part of the
liturgy.

The greatest objection of all was that the show did not include the
resurrection. Rice told an interviewer that he did not believe Jesus was
the son of God but, for him, that made the story all the more amazing.
Another bone of contention was the song "I Only Want to Say," which
Jesus sings in the Garden of Gethsemane. Though Jesus has some
doubt in the biblical version of the story, those doubts are articulated
so completely and so intensely in the song that to some they sounded
like more blasphemy. Also, Jesus refers to himself as a man, and the
hard-core critics maintained that he wasn't a "man"; he was the son of
God. This was obviously a matter of interpretation, but as overzealous
religious folks often do, they wanted to control not only what *they*
read and heard, but also what *everyone* read and heard—not unlike
the Religious Right in today's politics. They also found the relationship
between Jesus and Mary Magdalene very sexual. They were right. Her
physical attraction to Jesus is strongly implied. After all, she's a prostitute. Her attraction wasn't a bizarre detail dreamed up by Tim Rice; it
seems to make sense considering her vocation. For the first time she
finds someone who doesn't want her for sex and she falls in love with
Jesus' deep spirituality. Another complaint was the periodic humor in
the show, though it was minimal. The drunken apostles at the Last
Supper and King Herod's frighteningly wacky song and dance did not
amuse some people. Rice and Webber both felt the story of Christ, especially the crucifixion, had been too much romanticized into a beautiful, graceful event instead of the brutal, savage act it truly was. To
reopen our eyes to the horror of the story, they decided they needed to
shock the audience, and Herod's song was one of the biggest shocks
they delivered.

The Adaptation

Tim Rice has said in interviews that the story of *Jesus Christ Superstar* is fictional, a version of how it *might* have been. Because he treated the story as history, he took the facts he could establish and filled in the blanks himself. Several characters in the show are only sketchily drawn in the Bible stories—Mary Magdalene, Pilate, Caiaphas—but to bring them to life on stage (or on LP), Rice had to flesh them out, give them personalities, quirks, and motivation. The Bible is more event driven, where *Superstar* is character driven, focusing not on what happened but on why. As with most musicals or plays based on famous historical events (*Evita, 1776, Two by Two*), the audience already knows the basic plot, so more time can be spent on subtext, on what made these people act as they did. *Superstar* focuses on the doubt that all the characters experience—the apostles, Mary, the priests, Pilate, and especially Judas and Jesus—making these characters people we can relate to and understand. We are able to put ourselves in Jesus' place and understand his turmoil and terror. Because of the approach Rice took, it doesn't really matter in the context of the show whether or not Jesus was the son of God; he believed it, his followers accepted it, and that's all that matters. The issue of religion is all but absent from the show, a conscious choice on the part of its creators, and a contentious one.

Poor Old Judas

Originally, Rice and Webber had discussed writing a musical about Judas, in which Jesus was only a minor character. Though that's not what they ended up with, Judas remained a central character, at least as important and complex as Jesus. Judas is in an impossible situation; there is no easy way out. The dichotomy between Judas and Jesus is a fascinating one. Judas is practical, concerned with image, message, public opinion, and money. Jesus is concerned only with what's morally right. It's a tug-of-war between pragmatism, represented by Judas, and faith, represented by Jesus. Each of them is missing what the other has. Judas finds himself constantly frustrated and confused by Jesus' refusal to look at the practical side of their situation, as verbalized in "Heaven on Their Minds," "Superstar," and the fragment of "Superstar" at the end of the Last Supper. They fight because they both care passionately about the cause and about each other. Three main arguments break out between them: during "Strange Thing Mystifying" and "Everything's Alright" and at the Last Supper—the second two set to the same music. Judas acts as a kind of business agent and PR man, concerned about the political message they're sending out, the perceived inconsistencies in Jesus' teachings, and the money wasted on Mary's ointments and oils. He believes in Jesus' philosophy and in his ability to lead, but not in his methods and his choices.

Superstar

The lyric to the chorus of the title song originally just repeated "Jesus Christ" every time the melody repeated. But before recording it, Tim Rice wanted to give the lyric some variety. The word superstar was just beginning to be widely used, mostly to refer to rock stars. Rice changed the second repeat of the chorus to include the word "Superstar" because that's what Christ was, a superstar of his time, widely popular, complete with groupies. He was thronged when he went out in public, and like many rock stars today, he was considered dangerous and corruptive by the establishment. Jesus had a new message for the people, and they embraced it (for a while, at least). Despite his intentions to the contrary, he became a controversial political figure as well as a spiritual leader. The songs "Hosanna" and "Simon Zealotes" point out to Jesus the tens of thousands of followers who are hanging on his every word. Simon wants Jesus to use his power to bring about a rebellion against Rome, but Jesus doesn't want to be a political figure.

From the biblical perspective, an important question is ignored: why was he so "big," so successful, so influential? The Bible's answer is that he was the son of God. But from a purely historical, sociological angle, there's more to it. Like our country today, the people wanted a new message, a change, relief from the tyranny of Rome. Jesus came at the right time with the right message, just as the Religious Right did in the 1994 U. S. elections. Like Americans today, Jesus' followers wanted an alternative to the violence, corruption, and economic stranglehold against which they were straining. His message was one of peace, of morality and fairness. It's what the people wanted.

And Co-Starring . . .

Other central characters in the story are never fully drawn out in the Bible, so Rice had to characterize them more thoroughly in order for us to understand them and their relationship to Jesus and Judas. Though the Bible tells us that Mary Magdalene was a prostitute, how does that affect her actions, her personality, her motivation? Because secondary characters get very little "dialogue" in the Bible, those questions aren't really answered; but in *Superstar*, we see Mary as a complete, living person. She's a hooker, and the only way she knows how to relate to men is physically. She wants to comfort Jesus and help him relax; the only way she knows how to do that is by soothing him physically. She bathes him in ointments and oils, rubs his feet, massages his head and shoulders. She is a professional at relaxing men this way. But Jesus is different from the other men she's soothed. He treats her with respect, with genuine love. He appreciates her efforts. As she sings in "I Don't Know How to Love Him," this throws her completely. How does she respond to his treatment of her? Her first impulse is to return that affection physically, but she knows that's not appropriate. She doesn't know how to express love without physical forms of affection; she literally does not know how to love this man. Judas hates her because he sees her as a PR liability—Jesus preaches of morality, yet hangs out with a hooker. Judas also seems at times to be jealous. He is a man full of anger, anger that turns to jealousy of the one other person close to Jesus.

Pontius Pilate, the Roman governor, is a fascinating character, and is another person Rice and Webber discussed writing a musical about, again with Jesus as a minor character. Like Judas, Pilate finds himself in a no-win situation. The priests convict Jesus of blasphemy, but have no authority to put him to death as they would like, so they send Jesus to Pilate for execution. Pilate tries to pass the buck by sending Jesus to Herod. Since Jesus is a Jew, he falls under Herod's jurisdiction, but Herod sends him right back. Pilate doesn't really understand why Jesus is worth so much fuss, but the crowd has now turned on their leader and demands his crucifixion. Pilate even tries to convince the crowd that Jesus isn't worth their hatred. The song "Pilate's Dream" is one of the most disturbing pieces in the show and does a good job of painting Pilate as a politician trying desperately to avoid controversy and, more than anything, responsibility. He's not a bad person as much as gutless. In his dream he sees all that will happen and knows that despite his efforts to the contrary, he will end up being blamed for Jesus' death.

The Friendly Villagers

As in many musicals, the crowd is a character in and of itself. In most traditional musicals (*Brigadoon*, *The Music Man*, *Carousel*), the protagonist must either learn to assimilate himself into the crowd/townspeople or be removed from the community. In *Brigadoon*, Tommy assimilates. In *Carousel*, Billy can't, so he dies. In *Superstar*, Jesus can't assimilate, can't join the mainstream, so he must be removed—by crucifixion. But there's an extra element here; in *Superstar*, the crowd becomes one of the antagonists, actively demanding Jesus' death. The crowd starts off as followers of Jesus, a group whose loyalty the priests don't want to lose. The crowd gets in the middle of a tug-of-war between the priests and Jesus. They ask Jesus to heal them, to cure them, to feed them, and he complies in every case. Yet once the priests have condemned him as a blasphemer, the crowd turns on Jesus and demands that Pilate crucify him. As it still does today, public opinion swings quickly and unexpectedly from one extreme to the other. The loyalties of the masses change with the wind, and this phenomenon was just as dangerous and unpredictable then as it is now. The change in the crowd's position is seen through a series of songs: "Hosanna" and "Simon Zealotes" (all following him devoutly), "The Temple" (the moneylenders opposing him and the sick asking for healing), "The Arrest" (turning fickle, taunting him), "Pilate and Christ" (turning against him), and finally "Trial by Pilate" (demanding his death).

How to Succeed

Like Rice and Webber's later rock opera *Evita*, *Jesus Christ Superstar* follows two main themes. The first is success and the power that comes with it. As the show opens, Jesus has found great success in his ministry. He is reaching tens of thousands of people with his teachings and they are following him. Though his goal is not power, he finds himself becoming powerful enough to make the priests very nervous. The priests have great success and power as well. Their position in the church brings with it not only substantial wealth but also political power, which is now being threatened by Jesus. If people listen to his teachings, they will stop listening to the priests. Without followers, the church loses all its power—and money. As with any political struggle, including the current political landscape in America, there is a great battle fought for the hearts and minds of the masses. As the show opens, Jesus is winning, but before the show is over, fortunes are reversed and Jesus ultimately loses the battle. Herod and Pilate are also men of great power, and Pilate represents the inescapable responsibility that goes with power.

Kismet

The other main theme in the show is choice and the removal of choice by the forces of fate/God. Throughout the show, characters make choices that will greatly affect the outcome of events. Jesus chooses to keep Mary by his side despite her past, despite the fact that women are supposed to wear veils in public and are not to be spoken to, despite the bad image it may create. This is one of the things that drives a wedge between Jesus and Judas. Judas repeatedly chooses to ignore the mistakes he knows Jesus is making and to stay with Jesus anyway. Jesus' choices keep getting him deeper and deeper in trouble until finally, Judas betrays him to the priests. Here, fate plays a big part. Did Judas in fact have a choice or was he trapped into the events as they unfolded? If Judas had not betrayed Jesus, Jesus' role as martyr would've been subverted. Jesus knows from the beginning where everything will lead; he knows that Judas will betray him. These events are inevitable, so how much choice did Judas really have? In the Garden of Gethsemane, Jesus has serious doubts about what he's gotten into and considers whether or not he can choose to stop, to get out while he's still alive. He decides the choice is not his. After Jesus' arrest, Peter chooses self-preservation over loyalty as he denies Jesus; but again, Jesus knew this would happen, so did Peter really have a choice? Pilate tries to avoid making any choice at all regarding Jesus, but in the end the choice is forced on him by the priests, Herod, and the crowd. Everyone wants Jesus taken care of, yet no one wants to be the one who takes action.

Jesus Rocks

The music of *Superstar* is simple both harmonically and melodically. There is nothing too complicated, nothing that requires much of the listener. Lloyd Webber doesn't use reprises—repeated songs with the same or similar lyrics—except for a couple of fragments in Act II. Instead, he reuses music with entirely new lyrics, a device known as contrafactum. This works in much the same way as reprises, connecting characters or events by giving them the same music. He doesn't really develop musical themes or motifs, choosing instead to repeat them exactly or nearly so. Though it's not as sophisticated as other theatre scores, his use of contrafactum is interesting, and in most cases, dramatically motivated.

The first eight songs introduce eight melodies that will be used again and again throughout the score. The show starts with "Heaven on Their Minds," introducing Judas, his relationship with Jesus, his doubts about Jesus' approach, and even some information about Jesus' growing ministry. The song establishes Judas as the central character, an intelligent and perceptive man whose concerns are legitimate. The repeated ostinato vamp in the bass will later accompany the thirty-nine lashes and we will see that Judas was right all along about the dangers ahead. The next song, "What's the Buzz?" introduces the apostles and their collective character—curious, questioning, and basically ineffectual. Jesus sings for the first time here, treating the apostles more like dim-witted children than students of his teachings. The next song, "Strange Thing Mystifying," dramatizes Jesus and Judas' first confrontation in which Judas directly challenges Jesus' actions, specifically with regard to Mary Magdalene. In this song, he and Judas fight for the first of several times. Mary sings her first song, "Everything's Alright," defining her character, her relationship with Jesus, and her relationship with Judas. Jesus and Judas fight again.

The scene changes and we meet the bad guys, the priests, as they sing "This Jesus Must Die," establishing the central conflict of the show. The music to this song is the same music they will sing in almost every scene in which they appear. The crowd is introduced with "Hosanna," in which they show their blind enthusiasm for Jesus and his ministry; this is followed by "Simon Zealotes," in which Simon and the crowd offer Jesus their loyalty if he wants to seize political power as well. The song ends with Jesus singing "Poor

Jerusalem," realizing that his followers will never understand all they need to until he's dead.

Building on the Foundation

At this point, with all but one of the main characters and conflicts introduced, Lloyd Webber begins to reuse music, and the pace at which he does this increases as the show progresses. We finally meet Pilate as he sings "Pilate's Dream" to the tune of "Poor Jerusalem," and we see for the first time the inescapable grip of fate. Because we already know the story, we know that his dream will come true no matter how hard he tries to avoid it. The next scene, "The Temple," uses all new music, including a short fragment of "I Only Want to Say," which we'll hear in its full form later. It's interesting to note in this sequence that the music the moneylenders sing as they try to sell their wares is the same music the sick and crippled sing when they ask Jesus to heal them. Is Webber equating the two groups? Are the sick and crippled just as greedy and demanding as the moneylenders? Are they as upsetting to Jesus?

The next song is Mary's big number, "I Don't Know How to Love Him," in which her character's deepest conflict is expressed. As mentioned earlier, women were very much discriminated against in society, and Jesus' relationship with Mary went against all social conventions. Not only was she in love with him, but she had never been treated with any respect by a man. She didn't know how to deal with this. This is new music except for the fragment of "Everything's Alright" that opens the song. Judas' "Damned for All Time" is also new material, as Judas realizes the consequences of the actions he feels compelled to take. The priests convince him he's chosen the right path in "Blood Money," set to the same music as "This Jesus Must Die." The fact that the priests have only one piece of music demonstrates that they have only one thing on their minds—Jesus' annihilation. The drunken "Last Supper" is mostly new music—again portraying the apostles as relatively worthless, irresponsible men—but the scene also borrows musical fragments from other songs. Jesus and Judas argue again, to the same music they argued to in "Everything's Alright," even though the subject of their dispute has changed. The end of this argument uses a short fragment from "Superstar," Judas' posthumous song in Act II. Jesus then sings a short section, "Will no one stay awake with me?" that introduces a new melody that will be used again later as a betrayal motif. He goes out into the Garden of Gethsemane to sing "I Only Want to Say," his song of despair and doubt about the coming events. Though the song is mostly new music, a small fragment of the melody was used earlier in the temple scene. The song ends with one phrase of the betrayal motif, last set to "Will no one stay awake with me," this time as Jesus asks Judas why he has betrayed him. Jesus knows now that he can't count on anyone but himself; he is alone.

The Roman soldiers arrive to arrest him. As the drunken apostles wake, they sing "What's the Buzz?" The crowd that gathers uses the melody from the moneylenders in the temple as they taunt Jesus and demand he be taken to Caiaphas, who questions him and declares him guilty. The song ends with the crowd telling Caiaphas to take Jesus to Pilate for execution, singing the music from "Strange Thing Mystifying" in which Jesus accused the apostles of not caring if he lived or died. Apparently, he was right. Someone stops Peter on the street after the arrest and accuses him of being one of Jesus' apostles. Peter denies Jesus three times, as foretold. His melody is the main theme from "Strange Thing Mystifying," which originally accompanied Judas' criticism of Jesus' relationship with Mary, thereby connecting Peter with Judas, both of them now betrayers of Jesus. Mary points out that Peter did as Jesus said he would, singing to the betrayal motif from the Last Supper, underscoring Peter's betrayal.

The Beginning of the End

Jesus is taken to Pilate for a scene that employs three musical themes. The first is new, as Pilate expresses his disgust over Jesus. Then Pilate takes over Caiaphas' main theme from "Hosanna," followed by the crowd reusing their music from the same song, their sentiment the exact opposite of the first time they sang this melody; this time they want him dead. Pilate decides that because Jesus is a Jew, he's King Herod's headache, not his, and Jesus is led off.

The next song is new musical material, "King Herod's Song," Lloyd Webber's only obvious use of pastiche, a kind of raucous, blackly comic, music hall song and dance number. Though it's clear that Rice and Webber wanted to paint Herod as a grotesque man playing at being King, the use of such different music is a questionable choice. The song doesn't belong with the rest of the show, and certainly Herod isn't the only villain in the story. Why aren't the others portrayed with equally bizarre music? As unexpected as it is, introducing this kind of musical anomaly so far into the evening leaves the audience feeling disoriented and sometimes more hostile toward Rice and Webber than toward Herod. Merely using more rock sound in the instrumentation would have helped the number immeasurably, but as it stands, it just doesn't belong. In the 1994 recording *Jesus Christ Superstar—A Resurrection*, "King Herod's Song" is done as a fifties rock number in 6/8. Not only is it stronger dramatically, but it also fits better into the score. The next song, Peter and Mary's "Could We Start Again Please," was not on the original concept album, but was written for the Broadway production. The musical material is completely new. Peter and Mary express their desperation and confusion. They don't understand how things got so out of hand, and they don't understand why Jesus has taken things to such an extreme.

To the Bitter End

Judas commits suicide, angry at Jesus for using him for his martyrdom. All the music in this sequence is from earlier songs, musically looking back over the events that have led Judas to this point in his life. The music includes a fragment of "Damned for All Time," "This Jesus Must Die," an ironic and sad version of "I Don't Know How to Love Him," the vamp from "Heaven on Their Minds," and finally the choral tag from "Blood Money." Only this time the lyric "Good old Judas" becomes "Poor old Judas" and he hangs himself. Judas is dead and soon Jesus will be too. The "Trial Before Pilate" begins with the intro from "This Jesus Must Die," Pilate again appropriating the priests' music. New music accompanies Pilate's pleas with the crowd to forget about Jesus, but they want him crucified, and he gives in to them. The thirty-nine lashes are administered to the vamp from "Heaven on Their Minds," the song in which Judas predicted that Jesus' actions would lead to disaster. The vamp returns as Judas' prediction comes true. Pilate's music after the lashes is related to the melody of "Everything's Alright," but appropriately, it's now in minor, with the same rhythm and a somewhat similar melody line.

The next song finds Judas appearing to Jesus from beyond the grave to sing "Superstar," a fragment of which was quoted at the Last

Supper. This song sums up Judas' confusion throughout the show. He still can't understand Jesus' blind faith; he only understands reason and logic. As Judas said he would, Jesus has sabotaged himself. The battle between faith and reason has no easy resolution; both men's strategies lead to their deaths. The crucifixion is set to strange, atonal vocal clusters. The final moments of the show, "John Nineteen Forty-One," are underscored by the music from "I Only Want to Say"—Jesus has finally accepted his fate.

If You'd Come Today

Why produce *Jesus Christ Superstar* today? It's not controversial anymore. Using rock music to explore serious subjects is no longer novel. What does this counterculture rock musical have to do with our lives in the 1990s? Rice and Webber used the language they did to make the story live for us, to take Jesus and Judas out of the dusty language of the King James Bible and let us see them as real people with real triumphs and failures. Judas says to Jesus in the title song that if he had come today, to our modern society, he could've reached so many people through modern technology. It's an interesting moment conceptually because Judas has stepped out of the period; he's now speaking from the present. The word "today" in his lyric means the twentieth century, not 33 A.D. But had Jesus come today, what else would've happened?

How would today's world react to Jesus Christ? Would it be any different from how people reacted to him back in 33 A.D.? Some people would undoubtedly believe and follow him. Many would be skeptical, would refuse to accept him as Jesus Christ. The Church would surely denounce him; he would pose an enormous threat to their power, their control over their parishioners. What need would there be for a pope when the son of God is on earth? Today's religious and political leaders would probably react exactly as Caiaphas and his fellow priests did. Events in our contemporary world are *already* like events portrayed in *Jesus Christ Superstar*. Jesus was an activist, just like the activists in America today. Caiaphas claimed he was saving Israel by turning Jesus over to Pilate, just as today's Christian Coalition claims they are saving America by fighting gay rights, abortion, and the entertainment industry. Like Pat Robertson, Caiaphas is a savvy businessman, with an understanding of PR and marketing.

The show is called *Jesus Christ Superstar* for a reason. Jesus really was a superstar, enjoying a popularity equalled today only by rock and film stars. He was a celebrity of the highest order. Mary Magdalene's modern-day counterparts are obvious. The apostles are somewhat like contemporary fans of rock stars, New Age philosophers, self-help gurus. The moneylenders are like some businessmen today, looking for any way to make a buck. The lepers and sick are like our contemporary homeless people, living on the streets. The priests have obvious modern counterparts. The pharisees are like today's right-wing intellectuals, Rush Limbaugh, Pat Robertson, among others. The only element that is present today but missing in *Superstar* is the media. Today, Jesus would be a hotter story than even the various sensationalistic court cases being broadcast live on television. With so many clear parallels to our modern world, it's easy to see why many directors set the show in the present. Not only does it retain its power and its point, it helps make the story accessible to a contemporary audience.

Superstar's Difficulties

Superstar isn't produced as often as other classic musicals for a number of reasons. First, the show was recorded in the studio before it was staged, so it was originally written for the ears, not the eyes; and some of the score is very difficult to stage adequately. The piano/conductor score is very bare, and without musicians who can fill in what's missing, it's hard to make the score sound like the recording. Second, the show was originally done on Broadway as a spectacular, over-the-top, eye-popping extravaganza and everyone thinks that's the only way to do it. Every new touring company of *Superstar* is more high tech than the last, and Broadway's trend toward multimillion-dollar techno-musicals doesn't help. Directors forget that Rice and Webber didn't like the original Broadway production at all. It wasn't what they intended their show to be. Why must the crucifixion be a light show with fog pouring across the stage? This is a story with deep and profound human emotion, filled with passion, betrayal, death—*that's* the stuff of high drama. This is a story about people and faith, not theatrical wizardry. The audience should not be *impressed* by the crucifixion of Christ; they should be *upset* by it, *disturbed* by it. Some of the productions I've seen have made the gruesome practice of crucifixion into an exciting laser light show.

Any company that can find the singers can produce this show. Performers everywhere are dying to be in *Jesus Christ Superstar*, so the turnout at auditions should be huge, and even in the most conservative communities, the show should draw big audiences as well. The physical production can be as elaborate or as simple as you want, as long as you're true to the material. Remember that the score was a runaway best-seller before it was ever put on stage; sets and special effects are not what make people love *Superstar*. Approach it as you would any other serious musical or play. The first director hired to direct the show on Broadway, Frank Corsaro of the City Center Opera, saw the show as an intimate drama. After an auto accident, he had to be replaced by Tom O'Horgan, the man who had directed *Hair*. Lloyd Webber has said in interviews that he wonders what Corsaro's production would've been like and if he would've been happier with it. This is *theatre*, a medium of the imagination, and the greatest works of the theatre have always capitalized on that. Let the audience use their imagination. Ignore what has been done before with the show and approach it fresh. Focus on the characters and their inner struggles. Look at the material without preconceptions and make it your own.

Other Resources

Vocal selections from the show have been published, but the full score has not. The movie is available on videotape and is an interesting translation of this surreal material to the reality-based medium of film. Recordings are available of the original concept album—the definitive version—as well as the film soundtrack, a twentieth anniversary cast album, and a fascinating and wonderful new recording called *Jesus Christ Superstar—A Resurrection*. This last one features Amy Ray of the Indigo Girls as Jesus, along with other alternative rock artists. It's a different *Superstar*, but it's a great album. Depending on your concept for the show, it may or may not be worthwhile going back to the Bible (remember that Tim Rice said much of the story is his own creation). Either way, analytical works on Pilate and the other secondary characters might prove interesting. On the subject of Jesus as activist, the book *Jesus Acted Up* by Robert Goss, might be worth a look.

10 Man of La Mancha

Book by Dale Wasserman
Music by Mitch Leigh
Lyrics by Joe Darion
Originally Directed on Broadway by Albert Marre
Licensed by Tams-Witmark Music Library

No other musical—except perhaps Andrew Lloyd Webber's *Phantom of the Opera*—divides musical theatre enthusiasts so completely. *Man of La Mancha* is considered by many to be a masterful, deeply moving musical; to others, it's overly sentimental, obvious, cliché-ridden claptrap. It trades in unabashed optimism without apology. Perhaps this more than anything makes some people uncomfortable, since it's usually considered more "intelligent," more "sophisticated" to be cynical and jaded. This show sits at the far opposite end of the spectrum from shows like *Chicago* and *How to Succeed in Business Without Really Trying.* It's about the good in all people. Its language is that of pure, unconcealed human emotion, as extreme as Stephen Sondheim's *Passion*, which also made audiences uncomfortable. We're used to laughing at the sentimentality of musicals like *The Wizard of Oz* and *The Sound of Music.* In a sense, modern audiences are like Dr. Carasco in *Man of La Mancha*, afraid to expose their emotions for fear of being laughed at. Because "The Impossible Dream" (listed as "The Quest" in the show's program) was embraced by every two-bit crooner in the sixties and seventies, the song—and its lyric—have become a joke. As we must with shows like *Carousel* and *Show Boat*, we have to look at *Man of La Mancha* fresh, see the sophistication and truth in it, and give it another chance. There is much to admire and enjoy in this show if we only let ourselves.

Levels of Reality

In the novel *Don Quixote*, on which *Man of La Mancha* is loosely based, author Miguel de Cervantes plays with the form of the novel and with the nature of reality. He comments on literature *through* literature. He takes an elaborate potshot at chivalric romance novels, both directly and indirectly, through parody. Over the course of the novel, Don Quixote repeatedly comes across stories and storytellers. Each uses his own style of relating his tale, and with each, Cervantes comments further on the nature of narrative and on the relationship between writer and reader, performer and audience.

Señor Quijana is the man from La Mancha (a bare, monotonous plateau in central Spain), who collects chivalric romance novels, which he reads so obsessively that he goes mad and believes he is the knight Don Quixote. Quijana considers his novels reference works as well as entertainment. He uses them for the research that is part of his preparation to sally forth into the world. They are his only source of information on the life of knights, the life he is about to adopt for himself. To the soon-to-be knight errant of La Mancha, these books constitute his only reality. The world around him fades, and he molds what must remain so that it fits into his new reality. Cervantes has taken the convention of an author creating a reality in his book that the reader must accept and blown it up to fantastic proportions. Señor Quijana not only accepts the realities in his books, he believes them literally and adopts them as his own reality. His greatest problem is that those realities abide in the distant past. This reality he has adopted is at odds with the world around him.

After Cervantes had written the first volume of *Don Quixote*, another author wrote a sequel before Cervantes could. When Cervantes did publish his own second volume, he integrated the faked volume into his story. In Cervantes' second volume, Don Quixote is aware of the faked book and is incensed at the thought of a fictitious book being circulated about his squire and him. He is certain the "other" Don Quixote is an imposter and does not really exist. After all, he knows where *he* has been himself, what he's done, and who he is. Yet, the novel *Don Quixote* is already an account of a Don Quixote who did not exist and this nonexistent character is angry at the thought of another nonexistent Don Quixote. Cervantes' acknowledgment of the fake second volume within this work of fiction strengthens the book's reality for us. If Quixote interacts with the real world, it seems to us as if he really exists there.

In fact, *Don Quixote* the novel has a fictional author. According to the book, it was written by a Moorish enchanter named Cide Hamete Benengeli. So we have a real author (Cervantes) who's created a fictional author (Benengeli) to write about a fictional man (Quijana) who believes he's a real knight (Quixote), angry over a fictional imposter (another Quixote). It's a story within a story within a story. Don Quixote is both reader (of chivalric romances) and writer (a teller of stories of knights, chronicler of his own exploits, and alter ego of Cervantes); yet it is his voracious reading that has made him insane. How deep into these nested stories can we get before we forget where reality is?

In the case of *Man of La Mancha*, the three authors, Wasserman, Darion, and Leigh, have created a fictional character based on a real person (Cervantes), who plays a fictional man (Quijana) who thinks he's a real knight (Quixote); and additionally, the other fictional characters (the prisoners) play still other fictional characters in Cervantes' play (the Innkeeper, Aldonza, Dr. Carasco). Going one level deeper, Aldonza then takes on the new role of Lady Dulcinea when she finally sees the beauty in Quixote's view of the world.

The strange relationship between reality and unreality is what writing—and theatre—is all about. What is a novel (or a play or movie) but unreality commenting on reality, unreality acting on reality, unreality *posing* as reality. With the advent of "reality shows" on television, unreality and reality are often so alike that it's impossible to tell them apart. Of course, if we could easily tell them apart, the game would be over. Writers could no longer play with the two, juggling them back and forth, playing a mental shell game with the reader. The challenge is always the same: How extreme an unreality can a writer take and dress up as reality without the reader/audience knowing? Or, how close to reality can the writer shape that unreality, still keeping the two separate?

In a musical, the relationship is less that of writer versus reader and more actor versus audience. The actors in *Man of La Mancha* play the part of an audience for Cervantes' play and then that audience becomes actors by playing parts in his play. For added dramatic effect, the prisoners' personalities are like those of the characters they are given to portray. The Governor becomes the Innkeeper, the cynical Duke becomes Dr. Carasco, etc. So there are two audiences to be served—the prisoners who have put Cervantes "on trial" and us, the real audience in the theatre. Cervantes is trying to convince the prisoners of his story's value at the same time that the character he plays, Quixote, is trying to convince the characters *within* the play of the value of his view of the world and, it can be argued, at the same time that the director and actors of *Man of La Mancha* are trying to convince *their* audience of the value of the musical's story. The burden of suspension of disbelief falls on all these audiences. Cervantes must convince his audience that his tale is worth hearing, is worth caring about, and the actors in the musical must convince us of the same thing. Unfortunately, of Quixote's audience, only Sancho, and later Aldonza, believe in his story. With the addition of the "trial" aspect to Cervantes' play, he must please his audience in order to keep his possessions, just as a real actor must please an audience in order to keep his job. And though this isn't a formal trial (that awaits Cervantes when he is brought before the Inquisition), the idea of him being put on trial by his fellow prisoners is an interesting one. First, though they are prisoners, they have created their own system of trial and punishment within their prison. Second, a trial is basically a theatrical presentation after all, with a formal structure, specific parts to be played, and a formal set: the defendant's goal (or that of his attorney) is to convince the jury—his audience—that his story is worth believing and caring about. Cervantes telling a story as his defense isn't as unorthodox as it may seem.

Along with the various levels of reality at play in *Man of La Mancha*, there are also several kinds of truth. There is literal truth, the kind that Dr. Carasco and the muleteers see, the kind of truth based on observable, provable facts. But even in the world of fact, there is always room for interpretation. Any politician can attest that numbers, quotations, and other seemingly concrete facts can easily be twisted to support nearly any argument. *Man of La Mancha* has very little respect for facts. This musical instead centers on emotional truth, focusing on nobility, virtue, and integrity rather than identity, time, or place. The show also deals with universal truths, the things that are true for all people—the need for respect, compassion, and achievement. Just as the creators of the musical *Assassins* chose to emphasize psychological accuracy over historical accuracy, so does Don Quixote de La Mancha focus on universal truth over physical and temporal truth. It doesn't matter that knights no longer exist, that the dragon he attacks is really a windmill, that his lady Aldonza is actually a country whore. What matters is that he strives to make the world a better place; and we would be hard pressed to argue that his priorities are skewed.

The Spanish Inquisition—A Little Background

Man of La Mancha is set in a prison vault, a waiting room of sorts for those to be tried by the Inquisition. During the thirteenth century, opposition to the Roman Catholic church swept across Europe, and the church established a tribunal called the Inquisition to try people accused of heresy. The Inquisition judges, aided by local bishops and state authorities, would announce a thirty days' grace period for all heretics to come in and confess their crimes and be punished, after which the trials began. The names of witnesses were kept secret (not unlike the hearings of Senator Joseph McCarthy's House Un-American Activities Committee in 1950s America). Torture was often used to force confessions of guilt. At a grand ceremony, called an auto-da-fé (as immortalized in the satirical "What a Day for an Auto Da Fe" in the musical *Candide*), the names of the guilty were announced and punishments inflicted, ranging from fines and excommunication to imprisonment for life or burning at the stake—called "purification." Since canonical law forbade the clergy to participate in bloodshed, the more severe penalties were carried out by the state.

The Inquisition reached its height in Spain during the days of King Ferdinand and Queen Isabella. The crown exercised almost complete control over the Inquisition and carried it to outrageous extremes. The Inquisition was sometimes used as a cloak for political and private revenge, and the inquisitors were known for their fanatical zeal and great cruelties. It was a product of its time—the church and state were united closely and heresy was considered a crime against both, comparable only to high treason and anarchy. The Inquisition was created in 1478 and operated in southern Europe and in parts of Latin America. It continued in modified form in Spain until 1820. The Congregation of the Holy Office was established by Pope Paul III in 1542 to review the judgments of the Inquisition courts and to examine charges of heresy. It was supplanted during Vatican Council II (1962–1965) by the Congregation for the Doctrine of the Faith. Miguel de Cervantes, author of *Don Quixote*, was tried by the Inquisition in 1597 and excommunicated for "offenses against His Majesty's Most Catholic Church," barely escaping more severe punishment, which could've included being burned at the stake. He served several prison terms.

Knight of the Woeful Countenance

An actor portrays Miguel de Cervantes in *Man of La Mancha*, who in turn portrays Señor Quijana, who becomes Don Quixote de La Mancha. At the end of the show, the Governor says, "I think Don Quixote is brother to Don Miguel," in other words, all that is brave and good about the mad knight is also a part of Cervantes. When this story takes place (the late 1500s), there have been no knights in Spain for more than three hundred years, but this is entirely irrelevant to Quixote. What matters to him is what those knights stood for (at least as portrayed in his books). Most of the characters in the show think Quijana/Quixote is insane because he sees windmills as dragons, a kitchen wench as a high-born lady. He sees the world as he'd like it to be, as he thinks it *should* be, instead of as it is. Quixote says in the musical, "When life itself seems lunatic, who knows where madness lies?" Even more today than when the show opened in 1965, our real world *does* seem lunatic—urban gang violence, killer drugs, wars throughout the world. The only way to stay sane in our contemporary world is to see the world as it could be. Though *Man of La Mancha* is thirty years old and the novel is almost four hundred years old, the message is as timely today as ever.

One of the central questions of the play is whether it is crazy to see only the best in people and in the world. In Quixote's case, part of what people find insane about him is his utter selflessness, that everything he does is for others. It's not his optimism and his idealism that make people doubt his sanity; it's his extremism. Nothing in his life is done in moderation. As he sings in "The Quest," his goal is:

> *To dream the impossible dream,*
> *To fight the unbeatable foe,*
> . . . .
> *To right the unrightable wrong,*
> *To love, pure and chaste, from afar,*
> *To try when your arms are too weary,*
> . . . .
> *To fight for the right, without question or pause*

These are all noble aims, but ones that cannot be realized. Why should a person attempt something at which he can never succeed? Quixote (along with the musical's creators) believes that by setting your goals low, you won't achieve everything you're capable of, that the struggle is more important than the achievement. In the Padre's song, "To Each His Dulcinea," he suggests that perhaps people *need* a dream, that in fact, it is more healthy to have a dream to follow. Despite his "gentle insanity," Quixote has a genuinely good heart, which is why the Innkeeper is so nice to him, why he plays along with Quixote's belief that the inn is a castle, and why he agrees to knight him. Don Quixote's code of ethics is difficult, but he believes in the infinite goodness and purity of the human heart, and why shouldn't he? Though there are people like Dr. Carasco, the niece, and the housekeeper in the world, there are also people like Sancho and Aldonza, who, given the opportunity, can rise to the challenge Quixote puts forth.

The Duke asks Cervantes why poets are so fascinated with madmen. Cervantes answers that the two have much in common. The Duke replies, "You both turn your backs on life." Cervantes corrects him, "We both select from life what pleases us." This is an interesting exchange because it not only defends Quixote's mind-set, but it also defines quite clearly what it is that a storyteller does, an important theme in the show.

At the end of the show, Quixote is dead, but he lives on in those around him, those whom he has touched. He has transformed both Sancho and Aldonza, both of whom have become different people because of their association with the mad knight. Both of them have learned compassion, nobility, and integrity. In small ways, Quixote has changed the world. Similarly, if Cervantes is burned at the stake by the Inquisition, he will live on for the same reason. And though Cervantes is now dead, and even after the creators of this musical are dead they will all live on as people continue to perform and see *Man of La Mancha.*

The Skeptics

Though the Innkeeper thinks Quixote is insane, he sees no reason to change him. Most of the people who encounter Quixote know he's crazy, but figure he's harmless. But his insanity is a personal affront to the scientific logic of Dr. Carasco; he believes that Quixote must be forced to acknowledge his insanity. Carasco is the most narrow-minded of all the characters in the show. He believes that only his perception of the world can be accurate, that what is real is limited to that which can be proved. No other opinions or beliefs can be taken seriously. Though most intellectuals are not this extremely inflexible, Cervantes the poet uses an extreme view of this kind of man to offer a commentary on the struggle between science and art. Carasco also butts heads with the Padre. In this case, the friction is not between science and art, but between reason and faith. The Padre, as a man of God, must accept many things on faith, things that can never be proved. For him, it is easier to accept Don Quixote's world, one built on the unseen, on what is believed to be, one built entirely on faith in an ideal. Quixote says at one point, "Too much sanity may be madness." In other words, it's not wise to dismiss those things predicated on faith. Some things can't be proved, but that doesn't mean they're not real. In his own way, Dr. Carasco is as extreme in his view as Quixote, and that is why the show's climactic confrontation is saved for these two characters. It's interesting to note that Dr. Carasco/The Duke never sings (at least not alone). As the symbol of cold, hard reality, he does not participate in the very unnatural, very artificial act of singing in a musical.

When we meet Aldonza, she is a kitchen wench, a bitter and angry prostitute. By the end of the show, she sees what the world can be and she believes in it. We see this transformation when she volunteers to minister to the wounds of the muleteers after the attempted rape. But while ministering to them, they do finally rape her, and she learns the most important lesson—that it's not easy to aspire to such moral heights. At first, this makes her believe again that Quixote is merely insane. But after Quixote is defeated by the Knight of the Mirrors (Carasco) and taken home, Aldonza has time to think about what has happened and what Quixote believes in. When she comes to him on his deathbed, we realize that she has come to believe in his ideals. She has learned to have a dream.

Though he also thinks Quixote is nuts, the Padre is the one person who believes that perhaps he should be allowed to live in his dream. When Carasco promises a cure for Quixote's madness, the Padre says, "May it not be worse than the disease." He knows that taking a man's dream away from him can be devastating, or in this case, fatal. In our real world, the same is true of many people who retire from their jobs; without a goal to strive toward, without a purpose for being, they find nothing left in life. Similarly, when Quixote's quest, his "secret flame," is taken from him, he has no further reason to live. The death of his dream means the death of him. In "To Each His Dulcinea," the Padre sings, "And yet how lovely life would seem if every man could weave a dream to keep him from despair." The Padre knows Quixote is mad, but believes that madness to be in some way healthy. The Padre is the voice of the author(s), a position of moderation in the middle of the two extremes.

The Score

The critics all agreed that its score was what made *Man of La Mancha* a success. Most of the score is written in Spanish dance styles. For instance, Quixote's song "The Quest" (the show's biggest pop hit) is a bolero, an immediately recognizable style with a driving, persistent beat, embodying Quixote's determined quest. With a distinctly Latin quality and a subtle pop sound, the score not only adds an ethnic flavor to the show, but the driving rhythms also nicely offset the extreme sentimentality of the book. The music and lyrics are very intense, even unpleasant, as often as they are sweet and optimistic. The relatively small orchestra (sixteen players) includes two Spanish guitars, finger cymbals, castanets, and a tambourine, in addition to the more traditional brass and reeds. As with most musicals, the characters' emotions are most vividly represented in their songs; but in the case of Aldonza, her character is built almost *entirely* through her songs, including her birth and childhood (in "Aldonza"), her current vocation and life philosophy ("It's All the Same"), her confusion over Don Quixote ("What Does He Want of Me?"), and her eventual transformation and acceptance of Quixote (her reprises at the end). Two of her songs, "It's All the Same" and "Aldonza," share a similar rhythm, alternating between 6/8 and 3/4 meters. Interestingly, Quixote also shares this rhythm in his song about her, "Dulcinea." Giving these two characters similar music links them and shows that they are alike, and belong together. This rhythm is the same pattern Leonard Bernstein used in the song "America" in *West*

Side Story, another intentionally Latin-sounding piece. Aldonza's other song is in a highly irregular 7/8 meter, giving it a feeling of impatience, discomfort, uneasiness. Quixote's attentions have thrown her off balance, so she can't sing in a regular meter.

Like Aldonza's music, both of Sancho's songs share the same accompaniment rhythm. Appropriately, the instrumental music for "The Combat" and "The Abduction" both have constantly shifting meters to accompany the very explicit, violent staging. And in one of composer Mitch Leigh's most interesting moves, he takes the relatively innocuous "Little Bird" and turns it into the song the muleteers sing as they rape Aldonza later in the show. At the end, Aldonza uses songs from earlier in the show to jog Quixote's memory. She reprises "Dulcinea," the song that began her transformation, and "The Quest." He rises and with Sancho and Aldonza, begins to sing "I, Don Quixote," the song that began the whole adventure, but he collapses midsong and dies, a profoundly dramatic and unexpected twist. Back in the prison, as Cervantes climbs the stairs to the Inquisition, Aldonza and the other prisoners sing "The Quest" once again.

Only Flame and Air

The opening stage direction in the script describes the setting as, "A prison in the city of Seville and various places in the imagination of Miguel de Cervantes." Aside from the prison cell, the set cannot be realistic. Be careful too that the props and costumes for the story of Don Quixote (the play within the play) are not too realistic. They should look as if they've come out of Cervantes' theatrical trunk, saved from dozens of different plays. Part of the magic of the story is that things don't *have* to look realistic for Quixote to believe in them. His madness demands that the play be done with only the most minimal of physical trappings. It's also important that the cast be versatile enough to create two characters each, one in the prison and one in the story, and that these characters be similar, but separate.

Other Resources

The script and full score have both been published and are available. There is a movie version with Peter O'Toole and Sophia Loren, which is not quite as awful as many critics have written, but it's not great. If you've never seen the show, seeing the movie may turn you off completely. If you know and love the show, the movie is an adequate reminder of why the stage version works so well. Though the musical is not a faithful reproduction of the novel, reading the original *Don Quixote* will provide an excellent background in the themes, character motivation, and subtext that permeate the story.

𝟙𝟙𝟙 Merrily We Roll Along

Book by George Furth
Music and Lyrics by Stephen Sondheim
Based on the play by George Kaufman and Moss Hart
Originally Directed on Broadway in 1981 by Harold Prince
Revised 1994 version directed by Susan H. Schulman
Licensed by Music Theatre International

Merrily *We Roll Along* originally debuted in 1981, has been revised several times, and was revived in New York in 1994. The show traces the time period between 1957 and 1976, yet, it deals with some very nineties issues. One of the show's central themes is the loss of privacy in our lives; almost every scene in the show takes place in a public place, one scene even takes place on live national television. The more famous Frank becomes, the less privacy he enjoys. The disintegration of his marriage, his friendships, and his ideals plays out in front of the nation, making it that much more painful for him, and that much more relevant to our contemporary tabloid culture. But despite the cynical, headline-grabbing neurotics overflowing the TV talk shows and supermarket tabloids, this show reminds us that no one *starts* life that way. Something happens along the way that turns children into insecure, needy, manipulative adults. *Merrily We Roll Along* traces one path toward that unfortunate eventuality.

How Did It Get Here from There?

Though *Merrily We Roll Along* is widely regarded as a fascinating musical with a dynamite score, it was a tremendous failure when it first opened on Broadway. There were many reasons for its failure and they will be debated by musical theatre enthusiasts forever. So many mistakes were made and no one saw them until it was too late. The decision was made early on to populate the cast with young actors, many of whom were twenty years old or younger. Though they were full of energy and good intentions, most of them were just too inexperienced to pull off a major Broadway production; and audiences will more easily accept adults playing kids than kids playing adults. The set and costume designs were terribly inappropriate. The score was melodic and keenly sophisticated; unfortunately, it was lost in the disastrous physical production. The show closed after a long and frantic preview period and only sixteen official performances. The show was revised and revived at the La Jolla Playhouse in 1985, then again at the Arena Stage in Washington in 1990, and again in Leicester, England in 1992. Finally, in 1994, the "final revised version" was produced Off-Broadway to critical and popular acclaim.

One of the major problems the creators faced with the original 1981 version was that audiences didn't care about—didn't even *like*—Franklin Shepard. Because the story goes backward, we meet him for the first time as a real jerk, a bitter, commercialized, castrated artist. It wasn't until halfway through the second act, that Frank became likeable enough for the audience to get emotionally involved in his journey, but by this time, it was too late. One of the major changes throughout the several revisions is the softening of Frank's character. "That Frank" was written to replace "Rich and Happy," which demonstrated the duplicity of Frank's friends and Frank's descent into the pit of "selling out." Though it still paints an unflattering picture of Hollywood, it's a far less judgmental piece. We see that some of these people genuinely do like Frank because they think he's a nice guy.

Frank is also given the first appearance of "Growing Up," a song in which he gets to answer Charley's charges against him. Frank makes a legitimate argument that growing up must necessarily include giving up and/or adjusting dreams and he's right to an extent. What kind of world would it be if everyone was a ballerina, a fireman, a professional athlete, or a movie star? The dreams we set for ourselves in our youth aren't always mature, attainable goals. The rewrites make us realize that Charley's stand may be justifiable, but it's awfully extreme. The truth probably lies somewhere between Frank and Charley.

From Z to A

Merrily We Roll Along tells the story of Franklin Shepard, Charley Kringas, and Mary Flynn and the disintegration of their friendship and lives. Meeting and becoming fast friends in 1957, the three pursue their careers—Frank and Charley as musical theatre writers and partners, Mary as a novelist. What makes *Merrily* unique is that the story is told backward chronologically. The show begins in 1976, Frank and Charley no longer friends, and Mary a drunken movie critic. What is devastating for the audience is seeing these three people become more innocent and idealistic as the story moves back through time, until we arrive in 1957, our three heroes full of youthful hope and optimism. Though the last song, "Our Time," is inspiring and moving, it is terrible for the audience to know that those ideals will never be realized.

This backward structure also proves to be a director's worst nightmare. If the story were told from beginning to end, we would meet these sweet, idealistic kids and watch them lose their way; but we would care about them. As it is, we meet nasty, bitter people-users who think about nothing but money, power, and mourning the past. It's impossible for us to care about them until three-fourths of the way through the show when they become sweet kids. How do you keep the audience with you that long? Despite rewrites that have eased Frank's moral bankruptcy (including replacing "Rich and Happy" with "That Frank," and inserting Frank's new song, "Growing Up" in Act I), this remains *Merrily's* greatest challenge.

In each scene, we know what lies in the future, making the hopeful scenes later in the show that much more ironic. We see each misstep and we already know what the repercussions of each action will be. When Frank and Gussie meet, we already know she will ruin his marriage, marry him herself, and then divorce him. When Frank marries Beth because he thought she was pregnant, we know it won't last and that Frank will completely lose touch with his son. When Frank vows to change the world (and the musical theatre), we know that he'll sell out and abandon his ideals. When Frank promises Gussie that he and Charley will write her show without first consulting Charley, we know it's the beginning of a very dangerous trend (which we've already heard described in "Franklin Shepard, Inc."). By the time we get to the end of the show and "Our Time," we know they will never get to the future they envision.

In the first scene, during "That Frank," Frank introduces his girlfriend Meg to Mary:

FRANK: Mary is my deepest, closest friend in all the world. We go
      way back.
 MARY: But seldom forward.

Mary's right, of course. In a comically self-reflexive way, she's describing the unusual structure of the show, but there's a deeper meaning to her comment. Morally, ethically, emotionally, Frank becomes a confused, spoiled, frightened child as he grows older. He says in the final scene, ". . . we're going to be able to do anything. Anything we dream of"; but it's not true. So much will get in the way for both Frank and Mary. Charley is the only one who will hold onto his ideals. Though it isn't in the "final revised" script, Frank says on the 1994 cast recording, "Nothing's ever gonna be the way it was, ever again," and he has no idea how right he is. This musical is about the destruction of optimism and dreams, a theme that is subtly mirrored in the references to John F. Kennedy in "Bobby and Jackie and Jack." Now that Jackie Onassis has died, this song has an even more ironic feel to it.

Yesterday is Done

The show opens with the lyric, "Yesterday is done"; yet, the whole show is about going *back* to yesterday. These three words have tremendous import in the context of the show, so important that they return, though with very different meaning, in the lyric of the finale, "Our Time." What was once strong (friendship, ideals) is lost and can never be retrieved. What has happened can't be undone. The opening number repeats the phrase "Never look back" because the main characters can't look back without great regret. But as observers, the audience can and will look back in an effort to understand how these people got to the place where they find them as the show opens. The lyric traces the dissolution of the dreams. The first verse talks about "bursting with dreams." Then it tells us that "hopes go dry." It says you "bend your dreams." But, "merrily we roll along," moving too fast to see what's happening, too recklessly to see the dreams dissolving, blind to the compromises we make and the adjustments to our plans we allow the world to make for us. The title refers to the way so many of us breeze through life with no thought to what we do and what we lose. Even after we've lost what once made us happy, we go through the motions of happiness, still cruising through life, forgetting how happy we once were. This song comes back throughout the show in small fragments to remind us of the journey we're taking and the dangers that lie ahead. *Merrily We Roll Along* is a strange musical because, though it's about a very sad, disturbing aspect of the human condition, the end of the show is happy—only because the end is really the beginning.

In the song, "Like It Was," Mary makes a very interesting observation:

> *That's what everyone does:*
> *Blames the way it is*
> *On the way it was—*
> *On the way it never ever was.*

In other words, we find ourselves dissatisfied with our present situation because it doesn't measure up to our memory of the past. Mary suggests that we wouldn't be so unhappy with the present if it weren't for the fact that we can remember things being better "once upon a time." The danger in seeing life that way is that we don't often see the past with an objective eye. So we compare the present to our rose-colored memory of the past, a past that "never ever was." In *Merrily*, the audience has a chance to see the past the way it really was, warts and all.

That Frank

The show is about Franklin Shepard, a charming, talented composer who forgets the famous quote from *Hamlet*, "This above all, to thine own self be true." Every time he reaches a major juncture in his life, he either makes a corrupt choice or he allows someone else to make the choice for him (like Cinderella in Sondheim's *Into the Woods*). Despite his flaws though, he has an electric personality. Charley and Mary are both drawn to him; Mary soon falls in love with him (some would say that perhaps Charley does, too). Because Frank does not return Mary's romantic feelings, she turns to liquor. Frank wins Beth over easily. Gussie wants him later on. So many people are drawn to him ("That Frank"), both for his power and personality. The party go-ers sing, "He's the kind of a man that you can't resent."

Frank's "sidekick" Charley is the show's Donald O'Connor char-acter—the hero's best friend that we find in so many stage and movie musicals (*Brigadoon, Singin' in the Rain, Anchors Aweigh*, even Pickering in *My Fair Lady*). In many musicals, the hero has a best friend who never gets a girl of his own, who usually doesn't even no-tice the girls. He just faithfully sticks by his buddy, following his ro-mantic conquests. People joke that the Donald O'Connor characters were all gay and we just didn't know it. Here, Charley plays the same role. Of course, Charley has a wife, but his relationship with Frank—and its demise—seems to be so intense. It's not outrageous to think that perhaps both Charley and Mary are in love with Frank in some sense.

Frank doesn't only betray his friends; he betrays himself as well. He is a composer, and when he denies himself that by giving up his writing, he denies his very essence. In the rooftop scene at the end of the show, Frank says that if he didn't have music, he'd die. In the greenhouse scene with Gussie, he says his first love is music and his second love is music. Yet, by the time he's a big movie producer, he's stopped writing music. And despite what his sycophantic party guests say, it's obvious that Frank's movie is bad (it was more obvi-ous in the 1981 version—"When a movie's that bad, what on earth can anyone say?"). His rejection of his music is a symbol of all he has lost—not just the people he loves and his talent, but also the reason for what he does, the *soul* of his work. He becomes an imposter. His new friends aren't real friends. His new collaborators are not Charley. Charley knows that though Frank may be a good deal-maker, he's a better composer.

In the scene in Frank's new apartment in Act I, we see that, un-like the Frank in the original version, the new Frank knows that he's strayed from his dreams. After his friends leave, he sits at his piano and plays "Good Thing Going." As he plays the melody, he sings in counterpart:

Thanks, old friends . . .
Keep reminding me . . .
Frank's old friends
Always seem to come through . . .
Frank will too . . .

He appreciates their concern and knows that they only worry because they care about him. He believes, though, that growing up must involve letting go of childhood dreams. Frank sees the dreams of his youth as immature and unrealistic; he thinks adults should be "seeing things as they are" and "facing facts." To Frank, being an adult means knowing that life isn't as simple as it seems when we're young or as black and white as it seems to Charley. It's significant that the introduction to "Growing Up" is sung in counterpoint to "Good Thing Going," a song about a relationship (Frank and Charley's?) ending. But the fact remains that just because Frank *knows* that he's lost touch with his dreams doesn't mean he can reclaim them.

The musical and lyrical structure of this first appearance of "Growing Up" is fascinating. The musical use of "Good Thing Going" evokes Frank's partnership with Charley, and Frank's youthful dreams about writing musicals; "Good Thing Going" also stirs memories for Frank of his first success in the musical theatre, an art form which he has since abandoned. His singing of the "Growing Up" lyric evokes Gussie's influence on him (she first sings this song to him in the greenhouse). That "Growing Up" and "Good Thing Going" fit together so nicely demonstrates the differing influences on Frank that have come together to make him who he is. On top of all this, Sondheim also uses more road imagery ("Every road has a turning") to connect this introspective moment to the title song. There's even one line, "bending with the road," directly out of the opening number. Frank is choosing the road he will take, a road separate from Charley and Mary.

The truth is that Frank is no longer doing what he set out to do, what he does best. He says in the party scene, "If I could go back to the beginning . . . I'd give all this up." At this point, he finally knows what he's done, but it's too late to retrace his steps. Starting at the beginning of his career (and the end of the show), we see the germs of an ego out of control in the "Opening Doors" sequence. When he comes up with the idea to do their own revue, Mary suggests the title, "Frankly Frank." Why should it be named for him and not Charley and Mary? Both of them will be contributing to it as well. Later in the greenhouse with Gussie, the lure of writing a show for Broadway allows him to forget about the show he and Charley want to write in favor of the show Gussie wants them to write. It doesn't even occur to Frank to consult Charley on the decision. When Frank and Charley have their first Broadway success ("It's a Hit"), they sing, ". . . old friends don't need success to survive." They're right, of course; not only do they not *need* success to survive, success (or their handling of it) is what will destroy their relationship. Finally, when Frank and Charley go on the talk show, Frank's years of mistreating Charley explode in Charley's epiphanous "Franklin Shepard, Inc." Though it is true that Charley is somewhat at fault for losing control, it is Frank's behavior that precipitates it. Step by step, Frank leaves behind all that matters to him in his quest for the brass ring, and only when he has it does he realize it wasn't worth it.

There is an interesting question raised by the show: Is success a corrupting influence by its very nature or are these characters flawed, weak people? At times, the show seems to be telling us that success itself is a bad thing, but a closer look reveals that this is not really *Merrily's* message. Sondheim and Prince are too good for such a simple, clichéd statement. The critics who suggest the show is merely a tirade against success are missing an important detail: Charley realizes personal and artistic success without "selling out." Frank is the problem, not success.

There's No Business Like Show Business

Merrily provides a pointed commentary on show business and the people who populate it, as well as on Sondheim's career and critics. Charley is the only one of the three leads who ends up relatively happy, with artistic success and a stable, long-lasting marriage. Not coincidentally, he is the only one who has held onto his ideals. The show's creators clearly believed these two things were connected. More than any other artist in the musical theatre, Sondheim has stood firm in his desire to write interesting, challenging musical theatre no matter what the public or the critics may say. Though in many ways, Frank's early professional life mirrors Sondheim's, Charley's steadfastness is also Sondheim's.

In the "Opening Doors" scene, producer Joe Josephson complains that "There's not a tune you can hum," a not so veiled reference to criticisms of Sondheim's music. The humorous thing about Josephson's complaint is that it's set to the same tune as Frank's song, "Who Wants to Live in New York," the same melody Josephson says you can't hum, the same melody he will later love when it's set to the lyric, "Good Thing Going." Josephson compares Frank's music to Stravinsky's as an illustration of "unhummable" music; and lyricist Sondheim clearly intends the producer to look idiotic for disparaging the music of such an eminent composer. At the end of Josephson's scene, he leaves humming "Some Enchanted Evening"—presumably his idea of a melody that's easy to hum—but as he hums it, *he gets the melody wrong!*

Unable to find a producer, Frank, Charley, and Mary decide to produce their own topical revue, an arena in which many Broadway composers and lyricists got their first breaks. Sondheim himself didn't start this way (although he did write songs for one or two revues later), but many of the great theatre writers who came before him did, including Rodgers and Hart, Irving Berlin, Comden and Green and others. Josephson comes to see their revue and likes what he hears. But he doesn't want them to write the show *they* want to do; he wants them to write a show he already has planned with his wife in the lead. Again, this is vaguely reminiscent of Sondheim's career. He was offered two jobs as lyricist for other people's music (*West Side Story*, *Gypsy*) before he was able to write both words and music for a show. For *Gypsy*, it was because Ethel Merman, the star, didn't trust such an inexperienced composer. Gussie offers this opportunity to Frank and he agrees without asking Charley. If Gussie can get him to betray his best friend, can she also get him to betray his wife? Gussie represents temptation, glamour, the loss of artistic integrity and principle. She wants a show that's loud and funny, everything that Frank and Charley don't want to write. She needs a hit, and we see the gulf between her kind of theatre and Charley's. Frank has to choose between them because (according to *Merrily's* creators), he can't straddle them. Frank gets his first hit, but he's taken a really big bite out of the metaphoric apple.

Never Look Back...

The score to *Merrily We Roll Along* develops backward, just like the story. Reprises happen before full songs, melodies are quoted in bridges and accompaniments before we hear them as complete songs. Consequently, "Our Time," the last song in the score and the first song in the story, has to function as both opening number (plot-wise) and finale (effect-wise). The song "Old Friends" first shows up as a reprise and intro to "Like it Was." Later in the score, we hear the full song. A piece of "Our Time" first shows up in "That Frank" (and in "Rich and Happy" in the original version). This is an especially important instance of this device, because "Our Time" represents the ultimate in idealism, while "That Frank" represents the complete abandonment of those ideals. The fact that the two songs share material is particularly ironic. Gussie's song "The Blob" in Act II describes the phoniness of the people at the party. The music accompanying the guests' comments is used again later in the story (earlier in the show) in "That Frank" to remind us that these are the same people. The guests cling to Joe and Gussie while they're influential and later they cling to Frank when he becomes a movie producer. At the Act I party, Mary sees these people for who they really are, but Frank doesn't. In an earlier version of *Merrily*, Frank mentions at the Act I party that he's been asked to speak at his old high school, but hasn't decided if he'll do it. He says to someone at the party that he'll only do it if his life falls apart and he has no friends left by then—of course, because of the backward chronology, we've already seen him speak at the graduation, so we know that his life *will* fall apart and his friends will abandon him.

One of the accompaniment figures in "The Blob," which is later altered to become the verse melody in "Growing Up," is a slight variation on the accompaniment figure for "Franklin Shepard, Inc." This is a subtle but interesting way of telling us musically that Frank has actually become part of the Blob himself, with help and advice from Gussie ("Growing Up"). Charley will describe this transformation in "Franklin Shepard, Inc." Charley resents Frank's selling out not only because Frank has stopped writing, but also because Frank has dragged Charley into the world of the Blob as well ("And there I am in California, talking deals and turning pink . . ."). The Blob's accompaniment becomes Charley's accompaniment. The figure from "Franklin Shepard, Inc." shows up again underneath Frank and Charley's argument in "Old Friends." Sondheim has made it clear musically that the rancor Charley displays toward Frank on the television show is deeply rooted in the subject of their argument in "Old Friends"—Frank's having lost his way. The difference in the "Franklin Shepard, Inc." and "The Blob" accompaniment figures is that in "Franklin Shepard, Inc.," the figure is built on sixteenth notes that repeat their pattern every three notes; in "The Blob," the pattern is eighth notes that repeat their pattern every four notes. But the two intervals the figures are based on are the same. In fact, if you take out the first and fifth notes of the "Blob" figure, the two figures match exactly. Whether the audience actually registers this underlying musical connection consciously or subconsciously is certainly open for debate.

At Frank's first party in Act II, Gussie sings "Growing Up" to him, encouraging him to be patient, that his success will come soon enough. "Growing Up" shares a melody with "The Blob," presumably to link Gussie (and her advice) with the fake, ladder-climbing party guests. Her slant on growing up is to ignore your better judgment in favor of the "everyone does it" school of thought. After Frank has become a success and moves into a new apartment (in Act I) we hear the song again. Alone in his apartment, after a minor argument with Charley about his career choice, Frank sings "Growing Up," this time about learning that people change and that change isn't necessarily a bad thing, that dreams can be readjusted without being abandoned altogether. Gussie returns to tell Frank she's leaving Joe for him. Frank objects, but Gussie sings "Growing Up," now about the fact that no one can have everything they want. We all have to make tough choices, and have to accept the choices we've made. Frank can't have both Gussie and Beth. He has to choose.

One of the most interesting uses of the backward structure is Frank's melody that eventually becomes "Good Thing Going." In the original version of the show, we first heard the melody as "The Hills of Tomorrow," the song Frank wrote for his high school graduation. Because the original version began in the present and then told the story in flashback, this first appearance of Frank's melody was out of sequence. In the show's final version, "The Hills of Tomorrow" has been cut entirely, as has the high school graduation framing device. Working through Frank's career—and going backward through the show—we next hear the melody as a song Frank can't quite get right in "Opening Doors." As this song opens, Frank is at the piano toying with the melody, trying several variations. Later in the song, Charley finishes a lyric for the song and they audition it for producer Joe Josephson, its title now "Who Wants to Live in New York?" But Joe doesn't think it's hummable enough. As mentioned earlier, he proceeds to tell Frank and Charley why the song isn't commercial enough. Sondheim has set Joe's critique to the same melody, suggesting that the melody is more hummable than he thinks and that Joe doesn't really know what he's talking about. He complains, "There's not a tune you can hum"; yet, clearly there is. The next time we hear the melody is when it has become "Good Thing Going." (The final lyric of the song is a particularly apt description of Frank and Charley's relationship: "We had a good thing going . . . going . . . gone.") Frank and Charley play "Good Thing Going" at Joe and Gussie's party. Joe has decided he wants it in his new show, which Frank and Charley will write (presumably the new ballad accompaniment has made the melody more hummable . . .). In the newest version of the show, "Good Thing Going" appears once more, as we get a glimpse of Frank and Charley's first Broadway hit. As the second act of *Merrily* opens, Gussie is onstage singing a delightfully ridiculous, torchy intro that leads into a big, strutting arrangement of "Good Thing Going," for which the audience cheers enthusiastically. Frank has sold his melody—the symbol of his composing talent—to the highest bidder. He has cheapened it in exchange for commercial success on Broadway. Interestingly, though the music has become a cartoon of itself, the main lyric of the song remains unchanged—Charley has not sold out to the degree that Frank has. The last/first time we hear the melody is in Frank's apartment in Act I. Frank is sitting at the piano and starts playing the "Good Thing Going" vamp. He plays the melody as he sings in counterpoint to it the intro to "Growing Up."

As the "Good Thing Going" melody traces Frank's professional life, the song that follows Frank's emotional life is "Not a Day Goes By." Again, Sondheim uses the song throughout the show to achieve great ironic and emotional effect. The first time Frank sings it (the last time we hear it) is at his wedding to Beth at the night club. They sing the song together as their wedding vows. Significantly, Mary joins the duet from across the room, making it into a trio and a love triangle. She loves Frank desperately, and both women sing to him (Mary's singing is an internal monologue though, so Frank doesn't hear her). Already, his love life is precarious. Later, in front of the courthouse where Frank's divorce proceedings will take place, Beth sings the song to Frank again, but now the words take on an entirely new meaning. At the wedding, the lyric implied a deep and lasting love; at the courthouse, the song describes Beth's love for Frank, that won't go away no matter how painful it may be for her. Frank has destroyed his marriage, and with it, has made the words to his love song turn sad. In both cases, a child is part of the issue. At the wedding, Frank initially thought Beth was pregnant and that's why he agreed to marry her. At the courthouse, he doesn't want a divorce because he doesn't want to lose his son. In both instances, we can't be sure that his love for Beth is really his primary motivation.

Happily Ever After?

Toward the end of "Our Time" in the last scene, the young hopeful kids sing:

> *Years from now,*
> *We'll remember and we'll come back,*
> *Buy the rooftop and hang a plaque:*
> *"This is where we began*
> *Being what we can."*

Frank, Mary, and Charley all begin a life of following dreams, but only Charley will stay on that path. The last scene of *Merrily* takes place on the night that Sputnik flies over America, a symbol of the future, of unlimited possibility. "Our Time" is a beautiful and emotional tribute to the idealism of youth; but it is painful to watch because we know that this dream will not be realized for two of our three heroes. The last moment of the show finds the three friends joining hands in friendship. They are physically as well as emotionally linked; yet, we know they won't stay that way. The real ending of their story is the beginning of this musical, and it's not a happy one. Forearmed with that knowledge, this happy ending is very sad. Throughout the show, there are dozens of references to "time" in the songs and dialogue, and the lyric to "Our Time" brings the concept full circle. It is indeed their time we've been watching all night; we know that Frank and Mary will spend their time foolishly, while Charley will spend his wisely. The real world will take its toll on these three. What makes it even harder for us is the knowledge that we once felt as they did, and somewhere along the way, most of us lost our idealism, too. Finally, we identify with Frank; only we wish we didn't. Like many Sondheim musicals, the musical comedy happy ending is undercut by reality.

Keep It Simple

One of the mistakes made with the original Broadway production was the attempt to create a visual gimmick for it. The cast all wore sweatshirts proclaiming their characters' names or their relationships to each other. The set was big and abstract. My advice is to keep it small and to keep it real. Especially with a plot that moves backward and a story set in so many locations, help the audience to see where each scene takes place. You don't need elaborate sets, but you do need enough furniture to clearly define each setting, furniture that can be moved quickly so that scene changes don't take too long. Another mistake was casting the entire show with young people. In some cases that may be unavoidable, but when you can, use adults. It's easier for an audience to accept that a thirty-year-old is playing an eighteen-year-old than the other way around. The 1994 revival used older actors and the show worked much better. The brittle, world weary dialogue just doesn't sound real coming out of kids' mouths.

Avoid turning the songs into dance numbers or using cute staging gimmicks. Like most Sondheim shows, *Merrily We Roll Along* is about relationships and internal, personal journeys. The first choreographer of the original production was fired because he tried to make too many songs into dance numbers and it disrupted the impact of the scenes and songs. Don't let physical razzle dazzle distract the audience from the intricate lyrics—all of which provide lots of important information very quickly—or the substantial subtext. So much is going on in this show and the audience needs help to keep up. The transitions that track the years backward are possibly the most important lyrics in the show. If the audience doesn't understand that the show is going backward in time (and I've seen productions where they didn't), you've blown it. If you distract the audience visually or the actors don't enunciate lyrics clearly, the audience will get lost, and there's nothing more hostile than an audience who is lost. Despite your desire to have a happy ending, don't cheat the show out of its powerful and very real message: we all have dreams and we all mean to follow them, but most of us get lost on the way. Charley is evidence that it's not impossible to hold on to your ideals, but it's not easy. If you (or your audience) must have a happy ending, do another show.

Other Resources

The script to *Merrily We Roll Along* has not been published, but the original score and vocal selections have. The new script and the new score are available only through Music Theatre International. There are three original cast albums available. The original 1981 Broadway cast album is interesting, even though some of the music is not in the new version. The somewhat revised British version is interesting only to serious musical theatre buffs. The newest, 1994 revival cast album is the best recording of the score to date and the closest to the version available for performance. It will be interesting for the actors to hear the material on the 1981 recording that has since been cut, for some additional insight into the creators' intentions. It may also be interesting to read one or two of the books on Sondheim's career to see the parallels between Sondheim and Frank, and to read about his intentions for the show. The two best books are Joanne Gordon's *Art Isn't Easy* and Martin Gottfried's *Sondheim*.

12   Les Misérables

By Alain Boublil and Claude-Michel Schönberg
Music by Claude-Michel Schönberg
English Lyrics by Herbert Kretzmer
Original French Lyrics by Alain Boublil and Jean-Marc Natel
Originally Adapted and Directed in London by Trevor Nunn and
   John Caird
Licensed by Music Theatre International

In 1973, Alain Boublil was invited to the Broadway premiere of *Jesus Christ Superstar* and it changed his life. Already a big fan of musical theatre, here he saw a work that combined the conventions of grand opera, historical subject matter, and contemporary pop musical vocabulary. He decided instantly that he wanted to write in that form, and that same night realized the French Revolution would be a perfect subject. In collaboration with several friends (including Claude-Michel Schönberg), the pop opera *La Revolution Française* was written, recorded, became a best-selling album in France, and soon after was staged at the Palais des Sports for a full season's run.

Several years later, Boublil convinced Schönberg to make a pop opera of Victor Hugo's epic novel *Les Misérables*, which centered on the student insurrection of 1832, forty years after the French Revolution. In 1980, an album was recorded and sold 260,000 copies. That same year the show was staged at the Palais des Sports and played to more than 500,000 people. A friend brought the recording to Cameron Mackintosh, British producer of *Godspell, Cats, Little Shop of Horrors*, and other hugely successful musicals (including *Phantom of the Opera* a few years later). Mackintosh immediately decided to produce it, but it was restructured and further adapted as it was translated into English. Though French audiences knew the novel intimately, British and American audiences did not, so many scenes originally left out of the show were added, as well as a lengthy prologue. The show received generally scathing reviews in most of the London papers (British composer Andrew Lloyd Webber strongly disliked it), but within three days after opening, audiences had spread the word, ticket sales sky-rocketed, and it played to sold-out houses from then on.

An Epic Musical

Les Misérables is an epic theatre piece about history, faith, and humanity. It's a big show in its emotion and its sweep, but not a show that has to be physically big. Underneath the surface, woven through its various themes, the show is about perpetual motion—the inevitable flow of history, Jean Valjean's continual flight from the pursuit of Inspector Javert, Eponine's ever-growing love for Marius, and the quest for freedom. The show's motor, its pulse, can be summed up in one of the student revolutionaries' lines, "There's a river on the run, like the flowing of a tide. . . ." "One Day More," the show's Act I finale, illustrates this central metaphor. Every character in the show (including the chorus) is caught up in the sweep of events that leave love and life trampled in their wake. Yet through it all, they all maintain a faith in the future—"Tomorrow we'll discover what our Lord in Heaven has in store." Even the title of the song refers to the continuum of time, history, and fate. Like the show as a whole, this song displays the determination, hope, and faith of every character in the show.

Because of its epic scope, the lyrics in this show are unlike most musical theatre lyrics. They are bigger, more formal, more extreme, more tragic, more melodramatic. How many musicals could support the weight of a poetic lyric like

> *The very words that they had sung*
> *Became their last communion . . .*

Yet, it works here because the entire show is built on this bigger than life style. It is said that an audience will accept anything in a show as long as it's presented within the first ten minutes, and *Les Misérables* does just that, projecting its huge tragic language and subject matter from the first notes. Over the course of the show, we see great social injustice, a single mother reduced to prostitution, star-crossed lovers, war (on a small scale), the death of major characters, suicide, social reform, and marriage—all within the framework of a single musical. Boublil and Schonberg were told they were crazy for trying to bring such an epic novel to the stage, especially the musical stage; and they probably were, but they succeeded.

The Face of God

Director Trevor Nunn said that *Les Misérables* is a show about God. It is also a show about the nobility of the human spirit, faith, redemption, and other spiritual concepts. Religion and spirituality—as well as the distortion of it and the lack of it—informs most of the action of the show. Jean Valjean sings in Act II, "To love another person is to see the face of God." Valjean and Inspector Javert both believe fervently in God, but they believe in very different Gods. Javert believes in an angry, vengeful, Old Testament God, in the absolutes of right and wrong, good and evil. He believes that Valjean broke the law (which he did) and must be punished according to the law. In "Stars" he sings:

> And those who follow the path of the righteous
> Shall have their reward.
> And if they fall as Lucifer fell,
> The flame, the sword!

And later in the song:

> And so it has been,
> And so it is written on the doorway to Paradise,
> That those who falter and those who fall
> Must pay the price.

Though he is a man obsessed, he believes in the law, both man's and God's. How many people today—especially today, as everyone clamors for stricter punishment for criminals—would accept that some criminals shouldn't have to be punished according to the law? Today's audiences can look back now and say that the law of the time was too severe, but Javert has sworn to uphold the law and we can't condemn him for that. Yes, Valjean's family was poor and starving, but that isn't justification for breaking into someone else's home and stealing their food, and then later breaking parole. (Remember that Javert is pursuing Valjean not for the theft, but for breaking his parole.) Many people today believe that if our legal system was more like Javert's code of justice in its severity and consistency, crime might be reduced.

Javert is trapped by the strictness of his own beliefs, so that when Valjean turns those beliefs upside-down by releasing him in Act II, he has no alternative but to kill himself. He sings:

> And must I now begin to doubt,
> Who never doubted all these years?
> My heart is stone and still it trembles.
> The world I have known is lost in shadow.
> Is he from heaven or from hell?
> And does he know
> That granting me my life today
> This man has killed me even so.
>
> There is nowhere I can turn.
> There is no way to go on!

Javert's world, his convictions, and the rules by which he's lived his entire life are called into question, and because of the single-mindedness of his existence, he now has nothing left to live for. For the most part, Javert is portrayed as the villain of *Les Misérables*, but it's clearly not that simple. His sin lies in his extremism. He sees the world in black and white. He sees the divinity in the world and believes it is his duty to preserve it. In his song, "Stars," he sees the night sky as a symbol of the immutability of the universe. The stars represent God and the natural order of things, "filling the darkness with order and light." Valjean has violated Javert's view of what the world should be. There is no question that Valjean is guilty of the crime. In nineteenth-century Paris or in modern-day America, it is dangerous to apply the law only periodically. Like his descendant, Detective Gerard in *The Fugitive*, Javert doesn't care whether or not the law is fair; it's the law. Could he have tempered the law with mercy? Perhaps, but again, many people today would say we employ entirely too much mercy when dealing with crime; and after all, isn't that the job of a judge instead of a police officer?

In contrast to Javert, Jean Valjean believes in a benevolent, forgiving, New Testament God. He believes in redemption. When the bishop in the prologue not only lies to the police on his behalf, but also gives him the silver candlesticks, Valjean sees that he's being given a second chance, a chance to live life according to God's dictates ("My soul belongs to God, I know," he sings later). He has broken the law, has repented, and has been forgiven (by God, anyway). He aspires to goodness and he achieves it. The audience identifies with his desire to be a good man and lead a good life. He is the man we all wish we could be. He risks his life to find and protect Cosette. He actually offers up his own life to God in exchange for Marius, so that Marius and Cosette can be together. English lyricist Herbert Kretzmer sees "Bring Him Home" as Valjean's final transformation from selfishness to genuine altruism. The song is literally a prayer, and perhaps more than any other moment in the show, invokes the spirituality that lies beneath the entire musical. (When Colm Wilkinson, the original Valjean, first sang the song in rehearsal, a hush fell over the company. Trevor Nunn said, "See? I told you this show was all about God." And one of the company members said, "Yes, but you didn't tell us you'd engaged Him to sing it.")

Thénardier doesn't believe in God at all. He is completely amoral, living only by the rules of survival. He believes that it's every man for himself, and looking at his life it's no surprise that he feels that way. Again, it's hard to say he's a bad person; he lives outside the realm of right and wrong. Thénardier and *My Fair Lady*'s Alfred P. Dolittle are cut from the same cloth. In *My Fair Lady*, when Col. Pickering asks, "Have you no morals, man?" Dolittle replies, "No, I can't afford 'em, Governor." Audiences tend to impose their middle-class morality on Thénardier without a practical consideration of the difficulty of his day-to-day survival. He sums up his life in "Dog Eats Dog." When Thénardier sees the chaos, the injustice that runs rampant through the streets, he can come to only one conclusion:

> *And God in his heaven,*
> *He don't interfere,*
> *'Cos he's dead as the stiffs at my feet.*

If there was a God, Thénardier reasons, He would not allow a world as black and unforgiving as this one. The Thénardiers are even more despicable because they steal not only from the rich, but from the poor as well. It is truly a dog-eat-dog world.

So many morally ambiguous situations are scattered throughout the show—Fantine turning to prostitution in order to make enough money to support Cosette, the Thénardiers taking more of Fantine's money than they need to keep Cosette, the Thénardiers' looting of the dead bodies after the insurrection, even the insurrection itself. So many of these situations are neither right or wrong, and perhaps the message of Les Misérables is that people are basically good, that they do what they have to do to survive, that ultimately good always triumphs and we are judged not by each other, but by God.

Do You Hear the People Sing?

Some pop/rock operas, like Phantom of the Opera and Sunset Boulevard, use musical motifs at random. Melodies are repeated throughout the show, but not for any particular dramatic purpose. Other works, like Jesus Christ Superstar and Les Misérables, use musical motifs to connect characters, concepts, or dramatic situations, the way classical opera does. This use of motifs helps audiences recognize important dramatic and subtextual ideas, even if only on a subliminal level. In Les Misérables, there are two musical motifs that dramatize two of the show's primary concepts, moral dilemmas and loneliness.

The four-note accompaniment figure that opens Act I (after the Prologue, leading into "At the End of the Day") represents Jean Valjean and is used when he and other major characters grapple with difficult moral dilemmas. A slight variation of this figure appears underneath Valjean's first entrance in the factory scene ("Will someone tear these two apart..."), introducing him musically and connecting him to the textual theme of moral dilemmas. A minor version of this motif is heard later when Valjean stops Javert from arresting Fantine. Valjean is risking a great deal by talking to Javert, who might recognize him, but justice is more important to him than safety. It appears again as accompaniment to Valjean's greatest moral dilemma, "Who Am I?," in which he decides whether or not to reveal himself to Javert in order to save another man's life. In this case, the figure accompanies almost the entire song. The figure next appears when Marius first meets Cosette, foreshadowing the fact that this music will also underscore their farewell at the end of the act. In the "Rue Plumet" scene, Cosette sings her love motif as she thinks about

Marius. Valjean sings to her that he sees her loneliness, to the slightly altered melody of "On My Own" (which is used as a loneliness and separation motif), accompanied by his "moral dilemma" music underneath. He wants to protect her, but knows that he has to let her grow up at some point. Valjean's motif breaks out in full force as the accompaniment to "One Day More," in which all the major characters must make life-changing decisions. To reinforce the "moral dilemma" motif, the vocal melody from "Who Am I?" also reappears as the melody of "One Day More." In the second act, the decisions have all been made and Valjean is no longer the focus of the story; Cosette and Marius are. The only time the figure is used in the entire second act is when Valjean tells Marius the story of his life.

The loneliness motif is best remembered as the melody to "On My Own," but the song's accompaniment figure also appears elsewhere in the score. The accompaniment shows up for the first time in the instrumental tag at the end of Fantine's "I Dreamed a Dream," a song about losing the man she loved. This figure will come back in Act II in "On My Own," Eponine's song about never having the man she loves. The melody from "On My Own" first appears in Fantine's death scene, as she lies alone in bed, dreaming that Cosette is there with her. When the melody reappears as "On My Own," Eponine is alone on the street, dreaming that Marius is there with her. Though these two characters never interact directly, their music connects them, their loneliness, and their dreams.

There are a number of other musical motifs used to a lesser extent, which are effective in reinforcing dramatic concepts. For example, the show's Prologue acts almost as an overture, using several of the musical motifs we will hear later in the main body of the score. In this way, the Prologue not only introduces the plot, the character of Valjean, and the themes of God and destiny, but also some of the musical material as well.

Into the Words

In addition to the musical motifs, there are a great many textual themes woven throughout *Les Misérables*. As already discussed, God and religion figure prominently in every story line and most of the scenes, coupled with the concepts of fate and predestination ("Tomorrow we'll discover what our God in heaven has in store . . ."). Marius and Cosette sing, "I was born to be with you." Javert sings,

"And so it has been, and so it is written on the doorway to Paradise. . . ." It's interesting to note that Javert and Valjean share an important bit of music and lyric. At the end of the Prologue, Valjean sings the melody from "Javert's Suicide." In both songs, these men are questioning their view of God and the world, and both of them decide to end their lives, in Valjean's case by becoming someone else. Their lyrics are nearly identical:

VALJEAN	JAVERT
I am reaching but I fall	I am reaching but I fall
And the night is closing in,	And the stars are black and cold,
And I stare into the void	As I stare into the void
To the whirlpool of my sin.	Of a world that cannot hold.
I'll escape now from the world,	I'll escape now from that world,
From the world of Jean Valjean.	From the world of Jean Valjean.

Connecting them this closely through music and text is an interesting choice, especially since they both go through the show with a passionate devotion to God and to what they believe is right. However, the connection may be lost on an audience since the two occurrences of this music are so far apart.

The other major textual theme in the show is revolution and freedom. Jean Valjean's personal freedom is linked to the political and economic freedom the students are fighting for. We see that freedom is not gained or preserved easily. As the music indicates with the moral dilemma motif in "One Day More," the students' decision to fight is a difficult one. It will probably involve death for some of them, and they must each decide if their goal is worth such a price. This theme is also connected to the running themes of poverty and class inequality throughout the show. It is the poor, or *les misérables* (literally meaning the miserable or wretched ones), for whom the students are fighting, for whom they are trying to win a better life. Valjean, Fantine, and Javert all come from the ranks of "the miserable ones". Javert sings in Act I:

> *You know nothing of Javert.*
> *I was born inside a jail.*
> *I was born with scum like you.*
> *I am from the gutter, too.*

Javert rises to a higher social level by becoming a police officer. Valjean rises out of poverty by literally becoming someone else (as Eliza Dolittle does in *My Fair Lady*). But Fantine is hopelessly trapped there because she must support both Cosette and herself.

Why is *Les Misérables* embraced so fervently by audiences today? Most of the themes of the show are both timeless and universal. The concept of revolution is one that still today echoes around the globe. Americans will forever see themselves as the scrappy revolutionaries who fought for and won the world's first democracy. The poor people in nineteenth century France faced many of the same injustices and violations as the American colonists. Later in America's history, with the race riots in the mid-1960s, the riot at the Stonewall Inn in 1969, the riots over the Rodney King verdict, Americans have maintained their willingness to stand up for their rights through violent confrontation if necessary. In 1989, while *Les Miz* was playing around the world, Chinese students in Tiananmen Square staged an insurrection not unlike the one in the show and were similarly defeated. Throughout the world, there are "the miserable ones" like those in *Les Miz*, and as long as there are, there will also be revolutions and demonstrations. Audiences also find universality in the love story of Marius and Cosette, and in the unrequited love of Eponine, as well in the internal struggle of Jean Valjean to control the beast within him and live a good life. Victor Hugo populated his novel with universal archetypes, making his story one that will last indefinitely.

From Page to Stage

Les Misérables is a show about people and relationships, not about sets. Don't let the original two-ton, computer-driven set lead you to believe that this is a show that needs spectacle to work. Remember that even in the original production, the majority of the action takes place on an empty stage, or in scenes with one or two pieces of furniture. The revolve used in London and New York is a wonderful way to convey that sense of perpetual motion, of the chase, but you can do without it. Javert's leap from the bridge and the scenes in the sewers were achieved through ingenious lighting. The universality of the show will be communicated more easily if you *don't* clutter up your stage with sets and props. The costumes should be realistic and in correct period when possible, but even if you play fast and loose with period (the original designs for the "Lovely Ladies" costumes weren't strictly period), the clothes must look worn. It's all right to ask the audience to use their imagination, but don't pull their focus with bright, shiny costumes that contradict the mood of the show.

A decision must be made early on whether or not the actors should use accents. A case could be made that in a pop opera characters should be audibly as well as visibly distinct. In the London production, the Thénardiers had thick cockney accents that immediately branded them as lower class, distinguishing them from Valjean, Javert, and the students. But why should characters living in France have British accents instead of French accents? Realistically, why should they have any accent at all? People in nineteenth century France didn't speak with French accents; they spoke *in French*. A similar question could be asked about *Sweeney Todd*. Why did half the characters (in the original production) speak with British accents and the other half with American accents? In *Sweeney's* case, it helped characterize Mrs. Lovett. Perhaps it could work for the Thénardiers to have their cockney accents without giving the rest of the cast upper-class British accents. It's something to think about and maybe experiment with early on in rehearsals.

All technical considerations aside, your first priority must be to serve the show's score. *Les Miz's* greatest strength is the emotional power of its music. No matter what language the lyrics are in (they are now in many different languages), the same emotions are evoked—painful yearning in "On My Own," tremendous resolve and inevitability in "One Day More," and great optimism in "Do You Hear the People Sing?" Though people of the pre-rock generations may feel less of a connection to the music than those of us raised on rock and contemporary pop, the score still packs an undeniable punch. With or without giant sets and computer driven barricades, *Les Misérables* is a tremendously moving piece of theatre. You don't need Cameron Mackintosh to bankroll your production. You need only emotional truth, a sincere love for the material, and a cast that will dig down deep in their souls for the epic-sized passion of the piece.

Other Resources

There are several recordings of the score now available—the original French version, the original London cast, the Broadway cast, and the international cast (performers from various casts around the world). Only this last one contains all the music in the show. Vocal selections have been published, but not the full score. An interesting documentary called *Les Misérables: Stage by Stage* is available on video, including interviews with the creative team and footage of several different productions. Many musical theatre collectors also have on video a fascinating story on *Les Miz* done by the television show *20/20*. The tenth-anniversary concert performance of the entire score is also available on videotape. Music Theatre International has prepared a well-written Study Guide. Some people may want to read the original novel, but the musical is a very different kind of story with a very different tone, and the novel will offer only minimal insight into the stage piece. Edward Behr's *The Complete Book of Les Misérables* is a worthwhile book that follows the creation of the show from its inception, the mistakes made, and the creators' intent—it offers a number of very interesting insights into the show. It also includes the full libretto of the London production.

13 My Fair Lady

Book and Lyrics by Alan Jay Lerner
Music by Frederick Loewe
Based on the play Pygmalion (and its screenplay) by George
   Bernard Shaw
Originally Directed on Broadway by Moss Hart
Licensed by Tams-Witmark Music Library

Many people consider *My Fair Lady* one of the most perfect musicals ever written. It is thoroughly entertaining and at the same time a potent social commentary. Lerner and Loewe (and Shaw before them) explore and satirize the lines drawn between social classes. The idea that merely by learning to *sound* upper class Eliza Dolittle can *live* in the upper class—and the fact that Eliza actually has a lot more "class" than Higgins—says something about the standards upon which class distinctions are based. The show also explores the emotionally explosive relationship between teacher and student. In the Pygmalion myth, Pygmalion brings the statue of Galatea to life by loving her. In Shaw's *Pygmalion* and Lerner and Loewe's *My Fair Lady*, Higgins brings Eliza to life by *not* loving her. In other words, it is by ignoring Eliza that Higgins provokes the anger in her which pushes her to become an independent woman. It is this new, strong, self-reliant woman with whom Higgins finally falls in love. Though Shaw's play ended with a strongly nonromantic ending (Eliza leaves to marry Freddie), *My Fair Lady*'s ending is ambiguous, but indicates romance may be in the air.

One of the reasons the score is so masterful is that Higgins (and Eliza, to a lesser extent) sings words completely at odds with the truth, either trying to fool us or himself. Higgins tells Pickering he's "An Ordinary Man," yet, he's clearly not; he and Pickering sing "You Did It" when the credit really belongs to Eliza; Higgins sings "I've Grown Accustomed to Her Face," but we know it's not just her face he likes/loves. Similarly, Eliza sings about having Higgins killed in "Just You Wait"; yet, her vehemence betrays her interest in him. This device is relatively unusual in musicals and gives *My Fair Lady* tremendous emotional resonance and dramatic intensity.

Pygmalion seemed at first to be impossible to musicalize. Many people, including Rodgers and Hammerstein, turned down the chance to make it into a musical. Shaw's dialogue is packed with information, so a musical version had to incorporate the vast majority of Shaw's words. By the time Lerner and Loewe finally sat down to write it, many traditional rules of musical theatre were changing, making the play's problems easier to deal with. Before *My Fair Lady*, most musicals had to have a comic couple in a comic subplot, as well as a big chorus of townspeople opening and closing each act and showing up periodically throughout the show. By the 1950s, those conventions were slowly starting to change, and this opened up lots of possibilities for Lerner and Loewe to let the show's structure serve the story instead of merely serving convention.

An Ordinary Man

Henry Higgins has two passions: the English language and avoiding women at all costs. His primary personality trait is an absolute disregard for the rules of polite society and for the feelings of others. He sees the world only as it affects him. In some ways, he is like Eliza and her father in his straightforwardness, though his reasons for being so are different. Higgins doesn't lie to anyone because he doesn't give a damn what anyone thinks of him. He has no need to solicit other people's approval. Is there a contradiction in how easily it occurs to Higgins to perpetrate the dishonest act of passing Eliza off as an upper class lady? Perhaps it is easy to him precisely because he doesn't care about the people he proposes to deceive. He considers them all not worth his concern or his respect. The prospect of fooling them all and making them look like idiots has great appeal to him.

The only thing that Higgins cares about is speech and phonetics. It is important to note that his first song—the song that establishes his identity to the audience—is a song of anger and frustration over the way people pronounce words. Character must be driven by emotion, and Lerner and Loewe decided early on to base Higgins' songs primarily on these two emotions. Higgins' tunnel vision is comic to us, even as we recognize that he's right—most people don't care about the way they speak even though speech is the primary method of communication between them. It's also significant that his other two character songs involve the same emotions, but are about another topic—relations between men and women. Because Higgins spends 100 percent of his time studying speech, he has never taken the time to understand what we're all speaking *about*. He doesn't understand the dynamics between men and women because he's never considered it important enough to take time away from his phonetics studies. This will be his great character flaw, which will create a good deal of the dramatic tension in the story.

Higgins clearly did not have a normal childhood. Like other intellectual prodigies, he has focused so completely on his scholarly pursuits all his life that he never grew up. He knows that he can get his way by bullying those around him. It is ironic that Higgins' profession and great love is human language; yet, he cannot communicate. Unfortunately, he never changes. At the end of the show, there is the *possibility* that he has learned something, but we never really find out for sure. And even if he has come to a new understanding of Eliza, is that any guarantee that he will (or can) change his behavior?

Perhaps Higgins' most annoying trait is self-deception, as illustrated hilariously in "I'm an Ordinary Man." The song is constructed in two contrasting sections that repeat three times. In the first section of each pair, an easy going rhythm accompanies Higgins' claims that he's quiet, easily contented, humble, that he never raises his voice. The second section of each pair explodes into a driving, pounding rhythm as Higgins bellows about the way a woman would turn his quiet world upside down. What the audience can see that Higgins cannot, is that his unilateral prejudice against women is irrational, ignorant, and mean-spirited. He is, in fact, not easygoing or quiet; he is a loud, screaming brat. After this has all been established in this masterful character song, Higgins' bewilderment throughout the play whenever anyone criticizes him is even funnier to us. We know that he really doesn't know what a jerk he is.

Higgins as Brat

Henry Higgins has the emotional level of a child. He's never grown up. He pouts, he throws temper tantrums, he listens to no one but himself, and he can never understand when someone tells him he's done something wrong. He sees the world only as it affects him. Even at the emotional climax of the show, "I've Grown Accustomed to Her Face," he still cannot consider how he's hurt Eliza or why she's left him. He can think only about how lonely he'll be without her and how much he'd like to see her hurt and humiliated. We're supposed to feel sorry for him here, and though we shouldn't (after all, he brought it all on himself), we do because he is a funny, familiar, and very human character.

It's important to focus on why everyone in the show so strongly dislikes being around him even though the audience likes him. Mrs. Pierce clearly disapproves of most of what he says and does. Mrs. Higgins doesn't want him to meet any of her friends. He's rude, self-centered, and thoughtless. Those traits can often be ignored or at least understood in children, but not in adults. But only the rudeness is spelled out in the dialogue. The other traits are implied in his reactions and others' reactions to him. Peter O'Toole still ranks as my favorite Henry Higgins, in a production of *Pygmalion* shown on Showtime in the early 1980s. He acted literally like a child throughout the play, sticking his lower lip out when he pouted, slouching when he sat, sometimes even throwing his leg over the arm of a chair, getting too close to people when he talked to them, and getting a tremendous thrill out of showing Pickering his "toys" (his recording cylinder, etc.). His relationship to Pickering was that of a playmate, and Eliza was his new pet. Despite his very extreme performance, his Higgins was the most likeable I've seen, precisely because he was a child. He wasn't mean and never had the slightest idea when he had hurt or offended someone. He was all innocence and naïveté, and thereby escaped blame. All this is evidenced by one of Higgins' most telling line:

PICKERING: Does it occur to you, Higgins, that this girl has some feelings?
HIGGINS: Oh, no, I don't think so.

Higgins is not being mean or insulting. It honestly hasn't occurred to him that Eliza has feelings, and even someone bringing it to his attention doesn't help. He simply doesn't think about other people. The key to creating a Higgins that is realistic, funny, yet still sympathetic is to look at the show from his point of view. He doesn't know when he's being rude, when he's hurting someone's feelings, or when he's being selfish. He is a genuine innocent, and this makes it easier to forgive (and laugh at) his behavior.

The Act II song "Without You" is an important moment for both Higgins and Eliza. When the song was initially put into the show, Rex Harrison refused to stand on stage and let Eliza blow up at him. He threatened to simply leave the stage while Julie Andrews sang the song. Finally Lerner and Loewe realized what the scene lacked. Lerner wrote a new section in which Higgins interrupts Eliza at the song's climax with the line, "I did it! I did it! I said I'd make a woman and indeed I did!" Eliza's explosive anger at him proves to Higgins that she has become an independent, thinking woman. Harrison finally agreed to stay while Andrews sang.

A Good Girl

From the moment we meet Eliza, we like her. She's strong, self-sufficient, and a comically manipulative passive-agressive. Notice the way she consciously makes a scene at the beginning when she thinks Higgins is trying to arrest her. She makes sure she inovlves everyone in the crowd, hoping to embarrass and bully Higgins into leaving her alone. She screams, protests, begs those around her to save her. What she doesn't count on is the fact that it won't help her to leverage "public opinion" against Higgins. He cares even less than she does about what other people think.

Shaw's play *Pygmalion*, on which *My Fair Lady* is based, is primarily a social commentary/satire about the artificial barriers between social classes. In fact, Shaw wrote repeatedly that *Pygmalion* was not a love story and that Eliza goes on after the play is over to marry Freddie. But the musical version is the story of the bizarre relationship that develops between Higgins and Eliza. The musical is at its most basic level the story of two adults who don't act like adults. One grows up, the other doesn't (or barely begins to in the last moments of the show).

Eliza Dolittle has been on her own since she was a child. In many ways, she also probably never got to have a real childhood. Yet, she's learned (like Higgins) that she can manipulate people through temper tantrums. Any time Higgins is doing anything she doesn't like, she screams or cries. But she learns from Col. Pickering that there are better—and easier—ways to get by in life. Because he treats her like an adult and like a lady, she wants to be those things. At the beginning of the show, we laugh at Eliza, objectifying her just as Higgins does. But soon we see her strength and her tremendous desire to escape the squalor of her life and realize that this woman of character and intelligence has been condemned to the life of a flower girl. Finally she becomes a person to us, one worthy of respect and of a happy ending. Her first song, "Wouldn't It Be Loverly" describes what she wants most—a better life, including the basic creature comforts she lacks. Most of her subsequent songs are based on two emotions, hurt and fury, based on perceived obstacles to getting the better life she wants. The one exception to this is "I Could Have Danced All Night," in which Eliza's emotion is unbridled joy. She's happy because she's in love with Higgins, but she doesn't know it yet. Her outburst is primarily about her linguistic triumph on the surface, though we know there's much more bubbling underneath. Yet, Lerner has inserted one line at the song's climax that hints at Eliza's real joy. She sings, "I only know when he began to dance with me, I could've danced, danced, danced all night!" It was not her success in saying her vowels correctly, but instead the sharing of that success with Higgins that has excited her.

Eliza is honest, a trait she has learned from her father. Though Alfred Dolittle is lazy and a drunk, he is absolutely honest. The people in Eliza's social class have no use for false modesty; there is no ego or pride to cause people to lie. It is an interesting irony that Eliza is far more honest and straightforward than the people she wants to be like, yet her desire for a better life is strong enough to convince her to be an imposter. Higgins' goal of passing her off as a duchess at the embassy ball is a huge deception and Eliza agrees to it—against her nature—in order to receive lessons from Higgins. Not only does Higgins make her into a lady, but he also makes her into a phony in the process, a biting commentary by Shaw on the British class structure.

The Undeserving Poor

Alfred P. Dolittle, Eliza's father, is the exact opposite of Higgins. He knows exactly how far outside society's rules he lives. But he is sympathetic because he's really thought about his philosophy of life and has made an informed, conscious decision not to live by society's dictates. When challenged he can quite eloquently explain his philosophy. He is a member of the "undeserving poor," does not work, and does not look for work; and as he says, he intends "to go right on being undeserving." Dolittle's deliberate rejection of polite society appeals greatly to Higgins, so Higgins happily gives him the money he asks for. Unfortunately, Higgins then sends Dolittle's name to the American millionaire—again without any regard for the consequence of his action—and indirectly destroys Dolittle's idyllic world by making him into the millionaire's heir and—subsequently—a rich man.

Dolittle's music is all written in the style of British music hall songs for two reasons. First, Dolittle is a member of the working class (despite the fact that he doesn't actually work himself) and the British music hall was an entertainment for the masses. This is the kind of music Dolittle would be familiar with and it nicely represents his nature—loud, brash, predictable, comic, lots of fun, and not at all subtle. Second, Stanley Holloway, the original Alfred P. Dolittle, was himself a veteran of the music halls, so he was right at home with these kinds of songs.

A Non-Standard Musical

When Lerner and Loewe first began discussing musicalizing George Bernard Shaw's play *Pygmalion*, they quickly discovered that this was a play that did not want to be a musical. First, it was a very talky play with only three locations, two of them drawing rooms. Lerner and Loewe faced many tough questions: Who would the ensemble be (every musical had to have a chorus at that point); How could they "open up" the play and use more locations; and How would they wrestle a love story out of the play? Lerner asked "How does one write a non-love song?" Of course he found the answer with "I'm an Ordinary Man," "Just You Wait," "A Hymn to Him," and "Without You." Each of the two main characters gets two songs to rail on the other. Only two songs in the score approach being real love songs. The first, "On the Street Where You Live," is sung by the purposely shallow Freddie and was described by lyricist Alan Jay Lerner as "the flagrantly romantic lyric that kept edging on the absurd." Lerner wrote Freddie's lyrics as if he were a teenager, because

Freddie is still an adolescent emotionally (of course, that still puts him ahead of Higgins). The other almost-love song was "I've Grown Accustomed to Her Face," which never really says outright that Higgins cares for Eliza, though it is implied in his rage over her betrayal. Lerner realized that Higgins' lyrics had to be written in a rhythm that exactly imitated normal speech. This helped smooth the transition from dialogue to song, while it also made it much easier for Rex Harrison, a non-singing actor, to learn—and effectively act—his songs.

Two Worlds

Their are two worlds in *My Fair Lady*, illustrated as vividly in the music and lyrics as in the dialogue. The upper-class society is characterized by very controlled, operetta-style music, relying more heavily on the strings and woodwinds. Rhythms are generally more regular, yet the structure of these songs is often intricate and sophisticated. The lower-class society is characterized by songs in the style of the British music halls, using brass more than strings, louder, less controlled, with simpler chords, less counterpoint, and a more simplistic structure.

To portray the conflicts in both Higgins and Eliza, they are each given a song that is schizophrenic in its musical style. Lerner and Loewe did a masterful job of translating Higgins' annoying character traits into wonderful music and lyrics. Higgins' personal anthem, "I'm an Ordinary Man" has a comically split personality just like Higgins, charming and quiet one moment, then explosive, arrogant, and abusive the next. Of course, Higgins sees no contradiction in the lyrics or music. Eliza's angry "Without You" also operates in two distinct styles, illustrating the fact that Eliza is now caught between the two worlds. Though the song is predominantly in a graceful, classical style, the music and lyric move completely into the music hall style for the line "If they can live without you, Ducky, so can I," then goes right back to the more restrained style.

Higgins' second tirade against the female gender, "A Hymn for Him," is written as a 6/8 march—music that is manly, reminiscent of soldiers, man-to-man camaraderie, a society without women. Remember, too, that he is singing it to Col. Pickering, a retired military man. Though Higgins would probably never survive in the army, he believes he is that kind of man.

It's significant that Higgins hears the music of spoken language; he lives submerged in the world of language and phonetics. He talks about the rhythm and musicality of Dolittle's speech pattern. In his impassioned speech to Eliza immediately before "The Rain in Spain," he speaks of the "extraordinary, imaginative, and musical mixtures of sound." It's amusing that Higgins finds music in spoken word since Rex Harrison (and most actors since him) *talked* most of his songs in the show. The most surprising thing is that talking the songs works so well. It more closely connects the spoken dialogue with the sung lyrics; and it makes the sometimes awkward switch from speaking to singing far less jolting. As with Lerner and Loewe's *Camelot* (in which Richard Burton talked most of King Arthur's songs), Alan Jay Lerner's lyrics are so expertly written that they sound good either spoken or sung. Try talking the lyrics to other show tunes sometime and see how rare it is that lyrics work when they are spoken.

Eliza in Conflict

In Act II, after Eliza has exploded at Higgins for ignoring her after the embassy ball, Lerner and Loewe have written a sequence of reprises for her and one new song that beautifully characterize her despair. The sequence begins with a reprise of "Just You Wait," allowing her to vent her anger again at Higgins' heartless treatment of her. This segues directly into the next scene, out on the street in front of the house. Freddie is singing "On the Street Where You Live" again. Eliza enters and though Freddie is delighted to see her, she shows him nothing but contempt. Freddie is as worthless to her as Higgins. Freddie's love is merely infatuation, and though Higgins' feelings go deeper, his fear of those feelings makes him ignore her completely. Despite her disdain for Freddie, she still looks to him for assurance that she's not "a heartless guttersnipe." Even this late in the game, Eliza still relies on others for her feelings of self-worth. Freddie launches into another ridiculous declaration of his love, which Eliza interrupts mid-sentence (but notice that Lerner still makes the rhyme work through the interruption). She begins the one new song in the sequence, "Show Me," in which she tells Freddie to stop *telling* her how much he loves her and to demonstrate his love instead. At the song's end, she hits him with her suitcase and leaves. The music continues into a scene change to the flower market Eliza has left behind. Four men are singing "Wouldn't It Be Loverly," the same four who sang it with her in Act I. She goes to them, but they don't recognize her anymore; she's not the same woman who left the market not that long ago. There is a brief conversation as the music continues underneath. The men leave her alone in the market and she sings the end of the song, standing alone in the home she can never return to. This sequence of songs is important in that it shows us the primary conflict of the show. In the Pygmalion myth, the story is about making the statue into a woman. In *My Fair Lady*, the story is about what happens to the woman after she comes to life. Eliza can't stay with Higgins, she can't go with Freddie, and she can't go back home. Early in the first act, Mrs. Pearce had asked Higgins, "What is to become of her when you've finished your teaching?" This is the problem that must be resolved before the play is done.

Higgins' Transformation

The final sequence cleverly and artfully ties the score together, gives us the most penetrating look at Higgins yet, and provides an emotional and musical climax like few others. After Eliza tells Higgins she's not coming back, Higgins leaves his mother's house in anger. In his mind, he has given Eliza everything and has asked nothing in return. Of course, the one thing he hasn't given her is respect, which is what she most deserves and needs. As the scene changes to the street, the music explodes in anger with a chromatic line building to a musical quotation of the angry "But let a woman in your life . . ." sections of "I'm an Ordinary Man." The song initially characterized him for us in Act I, but only from Higgins' point of view. Now in Act II, the music is used again, but this time we see inside him, deeper perhaps than he can even see himself. But there's something wrong. In the first measure of the quotation, the music drops a beat, throwing the whole phrase off balance, just as Higgins has been thrown off balance by Eliza's anger toward him.

The music stops and Higgins says "Damn! Damn! Damn! I've grown accustomed to her face," and we hear new music, the melody for the last song. It is the most lush, rich music we've heard yet and is the most genuinely heartfelt love song in the show. But Higgins' feelings for Eliza make him even angrier and he vows that she'll regret her decision. The music changes to a new driving melody that is a close variant of the melody to "Just You Wait," Eliza's Act I song of revenge. Now the music accompanies Higgins' revenge, to see Eliza (if only in his imagination) reduced to rags and heartbreak. The first verse of this section is in major, but as the fantasy gets more grim the second verse is in minor. Higgins ends the verse with the lines:

Poor Eliza!
How simply frightful!
How humiliating!
How delightful!

She has hurt him and now he wants to see her hurt. The farther he takes his fantasy, the darker it gets and the more he enjoys it. He imagines her coming to him for help and him turning her away. The music changes again, this time to the music of the slower sections of "I'm an Ordinary Man." Higgins insists that he's "a most forgiving man," but as the music returns to the angry melody, he repeats that he will never take her back. We know this is not the truth; that in fact, he has fallen in love with her. Why else would his reaction be so strong?

The music returns to the main melody of "I've Grown Accustomed to Her Face." This establishes that the root of all his anger, his hurt, and his revenge fantasy is his very deep love for her. Though he insists his feelings for her are merely those of a pleasant habit, we know they run much deeper. Higgins has finally let a woman in his life, and appropriately, the melody of "I've Grown Accustomed to Her Face" is a barely altered melodic variant of the melody to the words, "But let a woman in your life . . ." in "I'm an Ordinary Man." The difference is that it's beautiful passionate music here, instead of the angry battering ram of its earlier incarnation. The scene changes to the interior of Higgins' house as the music continues. Higgins goes to his recording machine and turns on the recording he made of Eliza the day she first came to him. Underneath, the orchestra segues into a reprise of "I Could Have Danced All Night," though it has been altered. It's quiet and peaceful now, not giddy and passionate like the first time we heard it. Eliza has grown up since then, and her signature song has changed with her. Higgins sits down to listen to the cylinder, and behind him, unseen, Eliza enters the room and goes to the machine. She listens for a moment, then turns it off and says the line herself. Higgins perks up but does not turn to her. He slumps down into his chair and says, "Eliza, where the devil are my slippers," and the orchestra swells in a big finish based on the melody of "I Could Have Danced All Night." This is Eliza's music, not Higgins', and it shows us that she has come back on her terms, not his. They obviously love each other, but their relationship will no longer be dictated by Higgins.

Happily Ever After... or Not?

Because both actors and audiences want Higgins and Eliza to end up together, George Bernard Shaw wrote an afterword to his play that declared emphatically that they never marry. In fact, he says, Eliza marries Freddie Eynsford-Hill. Shaw wrote an elaborate summary of Eliza and Freddie's married life. The play, unlike the musical, ends with Eliza leaving Mrs. Higgins' house as Higgins laughs.

Shaw allowed a happy ending to be used in the film version of *Pygmalion*, in which Higgins and Eliza clearly will live "happily ever after." When asked why he allowed a happy ending, he replied, "I did not. I cannot conceive a less happy ending to this story . . . than a love affair between the middle-aged, middle class professor, a confirmed old bachelor with a mother fixation, and a flower girl of eighteen." So much for happily ever after. . . .

In *My Fair Lady*, the ending is ambiguous. After Higgins and Eliza's fight, and after we find that Higgins does indeed have feelings for her, Eliza returns to him in the last moment of the show. When she returns, Higgins acknowledges her but doesn't welcome her back or apologize. The stage direction in the script after Higgins' last line says "There are tears in Eliza's eyes. She understands."

But what does she understand? Different productions of the show interpret this last scene differently. In some, it is clear that they will now confess their feelings to each other. In some, we know that they will learn to deal with each other, but no romantic relationship is possible between them. In one production I saw recently, Eliza picks up the slippers and pretends to throw them at him (as she did in Act II, scene 1); he ducks, then realizes she's just kidding. This showed us that not only will they learn to get along, but that they're now able to look on their past conflict with a sense of humor. Which ending is best? That's your choice. But beware of making it a happy ending merely because you like happy endings. Discuss it with the actors playing Higgins and Eliza. Decide which interpretation makes the most sense for the characters as they are playing them. Shaw may be right, that a romance between Higgins and Eliza could be the greatest tragedy of all.

Other Resources

Try finding a videotape of Showtime's production of *Pygmalion*. It's a very different, but extremely intelligent and insightful study of Henry Higgins. There are also film versions of both *Pygmalion* and *My Fair Lady*, but be careful not to let the actor playing Higgins copy Rex Harrison's performance without the understanding behind the performance. The Broadway cast recording, the movie soundtrack, vocal selections, and the full piano/vocal score are all available. Also available is a volume of the scripts for both *Pygmalion* and *My Fair Lady*, with interesting commentary on the two works published by Signet Classics. Alan Jay Lerner's book *The Street Where I Live* is a riveting and very funny book about all of Lerner and Loewe's musicals and provides some wonderful background on the creation of *My Fair Lady*.

14! Pippin

Book by Roger Hirson (and Bob Fosse, according to many sources)
Music and Lyrics by Stephen Schwartz
Originally Directed and Choreographed on Broadway by Bob Fosse
Produced on Broadway by Stuart Ostrow
Licensed by Music Theatre International

Pippin is a largely underappreciated musical with a great deal more substance to it than many people realize. Because it rejects a Happily-Ever-After in favor of a real world ending of compromise and doubt, and because it is happening in real time and on a stage, it may also be one of the most realistic musicals ever produced (Fosse also toyed with realism in a musical with the film version of Cabaret). Though it is set in Charlemagne's France, it is about the here and now. Sprinkled with anachronisms in the costumes and dialogue, it makes no pretense at actually being a period piece, despite its characters' names. It is about America as much as The Music Man or Oklahoma! The show deals with the coming of age, the rites of passage, the lack of role models and guidelines for the young adults of today's society, and the hopelessness that has become more and more prevalent among young people. Because of its 1970s pop style score and a somewhat emasculated licensed version, which is very different from the original Broadway production, the show has a reputation for being merely cute and harmlessly naughty; but if done the way director Bob Fosse envisioned it, the show is surreal and disturbing. Even people who've done the show often don't realize the depth of meaning and subtext in Pippin.

When Leading Player says to the audience during the final sequence, "Why we're right inside your heads," the implication can only be that the Players are all in Pippin's imagination (and/or our collective imagination). If you read the script carefully, it's hard to imagine that this interpretation was not intentional. So much of the show's surrealistic moments make more sense if the whole thing is happening in Pippin's head. Of course if we accept that premise, then Pippin is making himself fail at everything and convincing himself to commit suicide by self-immolation. Many of Fosse's friends say Fosse himself had considered suicide on several occasions. Like Pippin, the audience gets caught up in the literal images onstage and forgets the metaphorical and symbolic significance of the characters and events in the show.

The show may actually have even more resonance today than it did when it ran on Broadway in the 1970s. As we approach the end of the twentieth century in America, the teens and young adults of our culture find themselves without a road map, without any discernible guidelines for growing up and making their way in the world. The American Dream doesn't exist today in the same way it did in the earlier days of this century, yet young people are still sold on the Puritan work ethic that promises rewards for those who work hard. Graduating from college, hip deep in student loans, many people reaching adulthood now are finding it impossible to achieve what their parents did; so they "drop out" of society and stop trying. They work at McDonald's and stay up late watching television sitcoms from their childhood on Nick at Nite. The media have dubbed them "Generation X."

Pippin is a young man just out of college with plenty of energy but no idea where to direct it. He wants complete fulfillment, the too-hyped "American Dream," and has been told that he can have it all if he just works hard enough. When Pippin is confronted with the mundane realities of life and finds that he can't have his ideal life, he is angry and bitter. His contemplation of suicide is tremendously potent to contemporary audiences as the murder and suicide rate among teens and young adults soars. Our increasingly secular society has lost touch with the myths and lessons that guided earlier generations and that still guide people in other cultures. Pippin is lost. All he needs is a guide to point him in the right direction, but how will Pippin know when the right guide has come along?

The Birth of Pippin

After *Godspell* had opened, its composer Stephen Schwartz returned to looking for a producer for a show he had written called *Pippin*,

Pippin. Stuart Ostrow agreed to produce it, but wanted a new script. By the time the new book was written by Roger Hirson, now called *The Adventures of Pippin*, an entirely new score had to be written as well. The show now told the story of a young man named Pippin going on a quest for fulfillment and self-awareness, and the traveling troupe of Commedia dell'Arte players who play out his life for him, so that he can experiment in relative safety.

To direct the show, Ostrow hired the respected director/choreographer Bob Fosse. But Fosse didn't like the show. It was cute and very sentimental, and Fosse had developed a reputation for dark, often disturbing musical theatre. He wanted to make *Pippin* more into his kind of show. He created the character of Leading Player, a narrator and Best Buddy, who accompanies Pippin on his quest and who also controls the events as they are played out. In Fosse's version, Leading Player and his troupe want Pippin to do their Grand Finale—setting himself on fire—and they make sure that Pippin fails at everything he tries, so that the finale will be his only remaining option. The show became dark and cynical.

Originally opening with the troupe of players arriving in a field with their wagon of props, Fosse's opening set them on the stage the audience was watching—complete realism. The original happy ending became a compromise instead of a victory. Instead of finding true happiness, Pippin finds he must settle for less than he really wants. Fosse turned the love song "With You" into an orgy. He remade the entire show as a parade of frightening, disturbing incidents in which Pippin finds less and less satisfaction. Historians and people involved with the show say Fosse greatly rewrote Hirson's script, but he asked for no official credit. Hirson strongly denies that Fosse wrote any part of the show.

Intrigue, Plots to Bring Disaster

Neither Stephen Schwartz, Roger Hirson, nor John Rubenstein who played Pippin, liked the rewrites or the style of the show as it was finally set. But it opened in October of 1972 and was generally regarded as something genuinely innovative and exciting. The reviews were positive, admitting that though the score was mediocre, Fosse's unusual conception and direction had made the show into an incredible piece of theatre. *Pippin* won five Tony awards that year, including Best Director and Best Choreographer for Fosse and Best

Actor in a Musical for Ben Vereen. Neither the show's script nor its score won Tonys. After the Broadway run, Schwartz had much of Fosse's material taken back out of the script and his and Hirson's work restored. It is this tamer, watered-down version that is now available for amateur productions. Though the 1981 videotaped production of the show that was released commercially does include many of Fosse's rewrites, remember that you can't change the licensed version without permission.

If you follow Fosse's darker vision of *Pippin*, the show must be unsettling, decadent, outrageous. For community or school groups, directors may be hesitant to stage a genuinely perverse orgy or to allow the actress playing Fastrada to be too sexually explicit in her incestuous relationship with her son Lewis. But there are ways to communicate the extreme and frightening nature of Pippin's adventures without offending your audience. For instance, in the orgy, the performers don't have to be half-naked. You can dress them all as common sexual fantasy figures, a cop, a construction worker, a Catholic school girl, a hooker, a dominatrix, or a sailor. Instead of Fastrada actually kissing or rubbing up against Lewis, their dialogue can be merely infused with sexual undercurrents. It's important for Pippin to be unnerved, even repulsed, by much of what he experiences, but you can let the audience's imagination fill in some of the gory details without compromising the intent of the material.

Breaking the Rules

Fosse dealt with the score he considered weak and often treacly by creating a show that ridiculed itself. Fosse had a kind of self-loathing for his kind of razzle dazzle show business, and like *Chicago* several year later, *Pippin* became a show that made fun of its own artifice. In Fosse's version, we're not supposed to hear "Corner of the Sky" as Stephen Schwartz' song for the Broadway musical *Pippin*; we're supposed to hear it as a ridiculous statement by an immature young man in the troupe's musical, *Pippin, His Life and Times*. In that context Fosse could actually let characters make fun of the songs. Before the overly sentimental "Love Song," Fosse added a speech that ends by telling us that Pippin and Catherine are "struck" by a love song, showing again Fosse's distaste for traditional happily-ever-after musicals (of course, this line was removed from the licensed version).

Thus, Fosse dulled the clichés of "Love Song" by letting us laugh at it and, therefore, at Pippin, too.

Because of this self-awareness, we become a part of the event, a part of the action, more so than with any other musical. Not only do characters interact with us throughout the show, but we also become a reason for Pippin to kill himself in the finale, as Leading Player tells him he's going to disappoint the audience if he doesn't set himself on fire. We witness Leading Player losing control of the show, so that the show both admits its artifice and pretends to reality simultaneously. Catherine rebels by taking control of her scene and singing a song that Leading Player doesn't know she's going to sing (the song is traditionally not listed in the program for this reason). Then Pippin rebels by refusing to do the finale. Finally, Leading Player loses all composure and has a temper tantrum, signalling a total loss of control. Leading Player then involves us again by inviting one of us to take Pippin's place. We become the show's only hope of going on as planned. Our decision affects how the show will end (although what would happen if one of us volunteered?).

Leading Player is doing something you usually only see in straight plays by writers like Edward Albee or Eugene O'Neill. Leading Player lies, not just to Pippin, but to us as well. We can't trust him as we would a normal narrator, and unlike a normal narrator he manipulates events for his own purposes.

Some Days He'd Scowl and Curse

One of the problems with having movie or video versions of shows available is that people tend to imitate performances without understanding why choices were made in the first place. The role of Pippin demands reexamination, bearing in mind the framing device already discussed. If this is all in his mind, he's not a very stable guy and has very little self-knowledge. He must be intelligent or he wouldn't be asking these existential questions to begin with, but he's also demanding, childish, selfish, moody, and most significantly, suicidal. Many people in the audience will ask why they should feel sorry for him; he's a rich, educated, white male. What's he got to complain about? It's an important question to consider.

Pippin is also very passive. Throughout most of the show, things happen *to* him rather than because of active decisions on his part.

This is part of what makes the show so interesting. Instead of watching the standard happy, sincere lovers, we're watching someone who has all our faults and more, someone who is profoundly real and *ordinary*. We see ourselves in Pippin, and though we don't pity him—after all, he brings everything on himself—we do identify with him. We see in him our own desire to find perfection in our lives.

Pippin is in many ways the generic adolescent. He wants complete fulfillment and he wants it now. He thinks no one else is at all like him and no one can understand him. He tells Catherine she couldn't possibly understand what's wrong with him.

It's important not to sugar coat the characterization of Pippin. Make him too good-natured, too innocent, too wronged, and you lose the impact of his journey. He is a child when the show opens and he is an adult—or at least on his way to adulthood—when the show ends. Don't romanticize his childishness or you'll lose the value of what he's learned (or is about to learn). Don't be afraid to let Pippin be a selfish jerk sometimes. He is, because he's real; and what's more important, so are we all from time to time.

Why, We're Right Inside Your Heads

At the end of the show, after Pippin has refused to do the Grand Finale, Leading Player turns to the audience for a volunteer to do the finale in Pippin's place. He knows that there are people in the audience who feel like Pippin, like they deserve better than they've gotten from life. He tells us that if any of us wants to do the finale, that the Players will be waiting for us, that in fact they are inside our heads. We can only assume from this last statement that the Players are all in Pippin's head, too. If we accept this premise, so many of the characters and events in the show make more sense.

Pippin's family is made up entirely of stereotypes. Pippin's father Charles is the ultimate authority figure—the emperor of the Holy Roman Empire—whom Pippin describes as the most powerful man in the world in Scene 2. Charles is the father figure to whom Pippin can never measure up. By having Charlemagne for his father, Pippin has guaranteed that he can never be as smart, as powerful, or as successful as his father. Fastrada is a typically evil stepmother who loves her own son (Lewis) more than her stepson. Lewis is the half-brother who is obviously (from Pippin's perspective) not half the man Pippin is, yet has a much easier life. Fastrada and Lewis represent a frightening and too explicit sexuality, something else of which Pippin is clearly afraid As players in the troupe, Pippin's entire family is part of the plot to sabotage his quest and to encourage him to kill himself. Why has he created such a monstrous family in this hallucination of his? Perhaps it's a way for him to not accept blame for his failures. Perhaps they are obstacles he believes he *could* overcome if only he were truly extraordinary.

Lewis is Pippin's opposite. He is animal, physical; while Pippin is cerebral, spiritual. Yet, Pippin envies Lewis' prowess in battle, his strength, his confidence. Lewis is the kind of man Pippin thinks Charles wants him to be—brave, proud, never questioning. The part of Lewis is often played as a homosexual because of one line in the second scene. Pippin tells Lewis he's shocked he's interested in women. However, Pippin isn't shocked that Lewis is interested in women instead of men; he's shocked Lewis is interested in women *instead of war and killing*. If Lewis were gay, it would undermine the impact of the incestuous relationship clearly indicated between Fastrada and Lewis. It would also subvert Lewis' position as the masculine soldier Pippin aspires to be, yet never will be.

Because everyone is in Pippin's imagination, you can play fast and loose with period. In the original Broadway production, costume designer Patricia Zipprodt intentionally dressed Charles in period garb and Fastrada in a modern cocktail dress. Some productions go even further, putting Lewis in the military uniform of yet another time period. As Zipprodt tells the story, Bob Fosse's directive to her was to do something magical, anachronistic, something like Jesus Christ in tennis shorts. Along with the costumes, props and set pieces can also be from various time periods. Charles can carry golf clubs or a newspaper (like *Le Monde*, since they're French). Fastrada can have a martini. Essentially, anything goes.

Pippin chooses for his only confidante the Leading Player, who betrays him at every turn. In several recent productions, Leading Player has been cast as a woman to add a sexual element to Pippin's seduction. This casting of a woman in the position of authority also gives the show a much more contemporary feel. Leading Player is the person Pippin should trust least, yet is the one he trusts most until he meets Catherine. But Pippin is afraid to trust Catherine because everyone else has betrayed him. He must learn to have faith in her as he learns to have faith in himself.

The Players

False appearances and artificiality play a big part in *Pippin*. Pippin's whole life is just a play, populated by stage sets, props, and actors. Nothing is real. He is surrounded by a family who isn't really his family; they're just portraying his family. Fastrada is never what she seems to be. She pretends to love Charles, yet helps Pippin plan his assassination, and she continually calls herself an ordinary housewife and mother, which she clearly is not. In the production I directed for New Line Theatre, we cast the same actor as both Charles and his mother Berthe to remind the audience that these people are only actors and not Pippin's real family.

But nobody pretends more than Pippin himself. He pretends to be a soldier, yet with Vietnam still fresh in the original Broadway audiences' minds, Pippin finds he has neither the stomach or enthusiasm for it. The show's antiwar statements are particularly disturbing considering the time frame, most notably in "Glory" and its softshoe dance break through a battlefield of dismembered limbs—as with most of Fosse's work, it's both funny and macabre. Pippin pretends to be a politician yet has absolutely no understanding of being a leader. Despite Charles' attempt to teach Pippin a last lesson in being king before Pippin kills him, Pippin still believes being king will be easy. Yet, when he has to make life and death decisions, when the full responsibility of leading an empire bears down upon him, he crumbles under the weight. He wants the power and privilege, but not the accountability.

Pippin's biggest masquerade is as a monk in the chapel at Arles. Pippin enters dressed in monk's robes in order to get close enough to Charles to kill him. Compounding the charade is the fact that it isn't really Charles—it's a player playing Charles. Charles pretends not to know it's Pippin, although he must know. Why else would he offer Pippin this last lesson in being king? Pippin's monk disguise also reverses the roles of father and son. Charles calls Pippin "Father" as he would a monk or priest and Pippin calls Charles "my son." The icing on the cake is that Charles' death isn't even real— Pippin later asks for his dagger back and Charles stands up and gives it back to him. The entire scene is filled with deception, contradiction, and falsehood except for the truth that Charles tries to pass on to Pippin in his monologue about the price that must be paid for order. Like all leaders, Charles knows there are always sacrifices necessary to achieve progress, but Pippin doesn't understand that. His inability to see both sides of issues will bring about his failure as king.

Think About the Sun

There are several important images running through *Pippin*, the most noteworthy of which are the metaphorical references to the sun (and "son"). As the first-born son of Charlemagne, Pippin is connected repeatedly to sunrise, while Charles is sunset. The use of sunrise and sunset is symbolic of beginning and ending, life and death, an image used in many cultures throughout history, and this image ties the whole show together. If everything goes as Leading Players plans, *Pippin* the musical will encompass Pippin's entire life, from his birth to his death in a fiery suicide in the finale.

At first, the sun references are made by other players, but later Pippin begins associating himself with the sun as well. Perhaps the connection comes from Pippin's desire in his first song to find his "Corner of the Sky." Leading Player knows from the first moment of the show that Pippin is primed to be led into the flame of the Grand Finale. He knows that Pippin is considering suicide and needs little help to take the final step. The first reference to the sun comes in Pippin and Charles' first conversation. Charles tells him that though sunrise and sunset are similar, they are not identical. Of course, what he means is that Pippin (sunrise) is like Charles (sunset) in many ways, but would be a very different kind of king, as we'll see in Scene 5.

Fastrada continues the sun metaphor with her song, "Spread a Little Sunshine." She sings in one verse about lighting a fire, presumably with an eye toward the impending finale. She reinforces the sun metaphor and even gives us a hint of the nature of the finale by connecting sunshine and lighting a fire with fulfillment.

Charles' comment about sunrise and sunset in Scene 2 apparently makes quite an impact on Pippin. When Pippin comes disguised as a monk to kill Charles in his chapel at Arles, Pippin says he sees in Charles' eyes a sunset. This is a symbol both of Charles and the old regime. Pippin stabs Charles and becomes the new king. Pippin sees his ascendancy to the throne as a new beginning—a sunrise—as he sings "Morning Glow." Charles, as sunset, is at the end of his reign. Pippin's discontent is also seen as the phantoms that will fade away in the light of the sun; but he thinks that sun is his reign as king. He will find later that it's really his suicide. Charles' death has spawned the birth of a new world under Pippin's reign, and has simultaneously presaged Pippin's own death. Not surprisingly, like everything else Pippin tries, he's a dismal failure at being king too, because he has such a superficial view of what it means to be a leader.

In Scene 7, Catherine makes a surprisingly prescient comment about Pippin in her song, "I Guess I'll Miss the Man." She sings that though some men can outshine the sun, Pippin is not one of them, despite what Leading Player will later suggest. Catherine, the only one in the show who genuinely understands Pippin, knows that he's *not* supposed to do the finale. She knows that he's not extraordinary and, therefore, not a proper candidate for the finale. As the rest of the troupe tells Pippin he can be as brilliant as the sun itself, only Catherine knows that it's not true.

Meanwhile, the company is preparing Pippin to do the Grand Finale. The sun and sunrise now also represent death and suicide. But by refusing to do the finale, he finally realizes that he is in fact *not* the sun, not extraordinary. For the first time, Pippin is actually taking action, making a decision. After feeling suicidal and out of control, Pippin has finally regained some control over his life.

God

Like *Les Misérables*, *Fiddler on the Roof*, *Sweeney Todd*, and other musicals, *Pippin* has the themes of God and religion running through it. As Emperor of the Holy Roman Empire, Charles is of necessity a religious man (though only to a degree). Pippin tells Charles early in the show that he thinks Charles in the most powerful man in the world, even more so than the Pope. Charles humbly agrees. In the same scene, Charles tells Pippin that he and the Pope have dedicated themselves to bringing Christianity to the world, even if that entails killing anyone who doesn't believe. Charles may believe in religion, but the basic tenets of Christianity have apparently escaped him.

Before the battle with the Visigoths, Charles asks Pippin and Lewis to pray for victory with him. As kings (and presidents) have done throughout history, Charles believes that God will help them in their killing, raping, and pillaging. But as a university student,

Pippin has learned to question everything, and it occurs to him that the opposing king must also be praying, also believing that God is on *his* side. Like the young adults of today's world, Pippin won't blindly accept everything he's told. He's more educated than his father, but with that education comes a built-in skepticism. Pippin asks Charles if the other king is also praying for God's favor in the upcoming battle. Charles says with a bit of admiration that in fact the Visigoth king is a real pro at praying for victory. Pippin's confidence is shaken. If God isn't on their side, will they be killed? He realizes that surely God isn't on the side of *both* kings, in fact maybe God isn't on *either* side. But they win the battle anyway and in their victory song ("Glory"), they make references to a number of religious images. Charles is seen as a minor deity himself, throwing wide the gates of heaven for his people. After the battle, Pippin has a discussion with a decapitated head about the hereafter. Pippin asks if the head will go to heaven and the head says that his king has promised him he will, though that is small consolation. Pippin begins to think dying for your king may not be all it's cracked up to be, heaven or not.

Later, in the chapel scene, Pippin comes disguised as a monk to kill his father as he prays. As many authors have throughout the ages, the creators of *Pippin* found the mystery and secretiveness of the church a perfect place for a murder. Charles' belief that God is on his side is certainly called into question if his son can stab him to death while he prays. Then again, perhaps we're to believe that Charles might have been spared if he prayed more than once a year. Maybe God and religion aren't being called into question here as much as man's faith and dedication to God. Pippin has seen that which side wins in a battle probably isn't connected to praying (since both sides pray), and that maybe violence shouldn't be perpetrated in God's name, as Charles has done for so long. Yet, the only way for Pippin to stop Charles from killing is to kill him—another moral gray area. Pippin kills Charles, believing that he can start a new era of peace, but it's not that simple; peace doesn't begin with an act of violence.

Pippin's faith in religion is shaken. He realizes during "On the Right Track" that the church is not serving the people, but is instead stuffing its own pockets. When Theo's duck dies later in the show, Pippin tries prayer as a last resort ("Prayer for a Duck"), but his failure only reinforces his observation earlier that events don't change merely because you ask God. The Visigoth king prayed but was defeated; Pippin and Theo pray, but the duck dies.

All these experiences form the basis of his conviction at the end of the show that the angels of the morning are *not* in fact calling him to dance, that death—his or anyone else's—is no solution. He begins to see that religion and God are not necessarily connected, that what other people tell him about his life and destiny may not be as true as what he knows himself. Of course, if we accept that the show is happening entirely in Pippin's mind, then what others tell him is actually coming from his own mind. Like his other dilemmas, this too is an internal conflict between what he has been taught (organized religion) and what he has learned from experience (a spirituality independent of man-made institutions).

The Trouble with Catherine

The "Hearth" sequence, in which Pippin becomes involved with Catherine, is unlike the rest of the show and consequently, it is also problematic. It can easily be long and boring, and one remedy many directors have found is to eliminate Theo, Catherine's son (again, you have to have permission from the licensing agent to do that).

There are several things that don't seem to make sense about Catherine. She's the only character who narrates her own segment. Is this a clue that she's going to rebel against Leading Player or is it just a poorly written sequence? Catherine is a player just like everyone else in Pippin's "life"—she isn't really a widow any more than Fastrada is really Pippin's stepmother. Why, at the end, does Catherine end up on Pippin's side?

We can assume that, like all the other players, Catherine starts out the show working toward Pippin's failure. At some point though, she begins to have genuine feelings for him, and decides she won't work against him anymore. This interpretation makes sense if you leave in the interruptions by Leading Player that have been cut from the licensed version of the show. Catherine asks Pippin very sweetly if he will stay with her to run her very large estate. Suddenly, Leading Player appears out of the shadows (or from out in the house) and reminds her that the line is to be read naggingly; they even argue briefly. Later, Catherine accidentally says a line incorrectly, and again

Leading Player appears and corrects her. And—here's the significant part—Leading Player warns her that she'd better stick to the script from now on. He senses her reluctance to follow the plot as it's laid out, and he's not happy about it.

After Pippin has left Catherine, the lights begin to go out on the scene but Catherine asks for the lights to be held for a moment and sings "I Guess I'll Miss the Man." In the Broadway production and in most other productions, this song is not listed in the program because Catherine is not supposed to be singing it. Leading Player doesn't know she is going to sing it. It's not in Leading Player's script. In the New Line Theatre production, Leading Player and a few of the other Players began to come out on stage during the song to see what was going on. When Catherine finishes, she suddenly sees Leading Player is standing right next to her, glaring. Catherine quickly leaves the stage.

Her actions show us that Catherine is straying from the plot and Leading Player worries that Catherine may be a threat to his control. It's a perfect set-up for Catherine's unexpected appearance during the final sequence, which makes Leading Player terribly angry. Catherine's appearance here needs to be set up earlier in order for it to make any sense. Her decision to stand by Pippin is a tremendous defiance of Leading Player, and the audience needs to be prepared for this turn of events. We need to see her growing fondness for Pippin over the course of several scenes and her reluctance to see him kill himself.

The Grand Finale

The end of the show is genuinely bizarre and unlike the ending of any other musical. It is important to remember throughout *Pippin* that each event, each episode not only must be disturbing to Pippin, but also to the audience. They have to feel the disgust and dismay Pippin feels. If the battlefield is not disturbing, if Fastrada and Lewis aren't intolerable, if the orgy isn't frightening, if Catherine's estate isn't claustrophobic, the audience won't accept that Pippin has come to the extreme position of considering suicide.

Once he has failed to find fulfillment in anything he's tried, Leading Player leads Pippin gently toward the Grand Finale. When Pippin finds out the finale involves setting himself on fire, he resists.

To convince him, the company sings the "Finale" and Pippin slowly gets sucked into their enthusiasm. When the players launch into a majestic four-part quotation of "Corner of the Sky," we think Pippin may actually get into the fire. But suddenly he realizes the magnitude and finality of what he's considering and he stops.

This sequence involves many subtextual implications. First of all, if this is all happening in Pippin's imagination, then he is actually trying to convince *himself* to commit this fiery suicide. The finale is symbolic of Pippin's interior struggle over whether or not to kill himself. It seems logical to assume from Leading Player's rage and surprise over Pippin's reticence that the players have done the show many times before (earlier, Catherine says in the original version that "they" don't usually touch her hand, indicating that other men have done this show in Pippin's place), but no one has ever refused to do the finale until now. If that's true, then they have never needed to sing this song before—it is, in fact, being made up on the spot. The song's structure is consistent with this interpretation—Leading Player sings the verse first alone, then Fastrada joins, then the rest of the company joins (it's helpful to keep this is mind while choreographing the finale). Fosse told the original cast that the Players wanted Pippin to kill himself in order to achieve a kind of group orgasm, a final realization of their desires. In the original production, the Players all started masturbating themselves as they convinced Pippin to get in the fire box, rubbing themselves, sucking their fingers, literally miming masturbation in some cases. Like the bulk of the show, sex was a barely concealed subtext to everything that happened.

But Pippin decides he doesn't want to set himself on fire. This is a great breakthrough for him, and once Catherine has joined him on stage, it appears that his decision is final. Leading Player still tries to bully and shame him into the fire. The entire company turns on him, calling him a coward and a compromiser. This is the moment toward which the whole show has been building, the true test of Pippin's resolve. He makes the bravest choice yet—he chooses to ignore the peer pressure, the allure of fame and admiration, the abuse of Leading Player, and the players' ridicule of Catherine. He accepts that he is not extraordinary, and in that moment, he finally becomes an adult. He leaves the childish fantasy and dreams behind and faces the real world for the first time, a life with Catherine that is not part of the play. By admitting that he is ordinary and by facing up to the realities of his life, he is finally truly courageous. He is, perhaps for the first time in his life, genuinely extraordinary. His ordeal throughout the show has been his rite of passage.

How Do You Feel?

The last line of the show has been a cause for debate since the show opened in 1972. After the Players all leave, Catherine asks Pippin how he feels. Pippin's original reply was "Trapped . . . but happy." According to most sources, Bob Fosse thought the "but happy" was a cop out. After all, Pippin can't yet be sure his decision was the right one. He hopes that it will be, but surely he hasn't gone from having no idea what he wants to knowing exactly what he wants in only a few minutes. Pippin has made a choice, but he is still scared. He knows that he has given up some of his ideals and must accept compromises for the first time.

Fosse cut the "but happy." Neither composer Stephen Schwartz nor John Rubenstein, who played Pippin, was happy about the change. They both already felt like Fosse was making the show too cynical. But Fosse was the director and was also very intimidating, so the line was changed. After the show's Broadway run, Schwartz had the two words put back in the last line. So the standard licensed version contains the original line. Because the word "happy" carries extra baggage in the world of musical comedy in which so many shows must end happily ever after, it is dangerous to use that word carelessly. So the debate rages on. Is Pippin really happy? Can you feel trapped and happy at the same time? Can he acquire that much wisdom and self-knowledge that quickly? It's a decision you have to make.

Other Resources

Vocal selections for *Pippin* are available, but the script and full score are available only by renting them from the licensing agent for performances. The original Broadway cast recording is available on the Motown label, but with several of the shorter songs missing ("Welcome Home," "There He Was," "Prayer for a Duck"). A videotape is also available, but it's important to note that the video is not the original production. It's a production done in 1981 in Ontario,

Canada, directed by Kathryn Doby, a dancer from the original Broadway cast, with several other members of the original cast. People who saw the Broadway production say there are some significant differences, including some added bits of schtick, and that the video version seems to lose sight of many of the show's important themes and subtext in favor of glitz and laughs. Martin Gottfried's book *All His Jazz: The Life and Death of Bob Fosse* and Kevin Royd Grubb's *Razzle Dazzle* are both extremely interesting books looking at Bob Fosse's work from very different angles and both worth reading.

15   Sweeney Todd

Book by Hugh Wheeler
Music and Lyrics by Stephen Sondheim
Originally Directed on Broadway by Hal Prince
Licensed by Music Theatre International

Sweeney Todd is one of only two musicals that Stephen Sondheim has initiated himself (the other was *Passion*). He has said that he intended it to be a small chamber musical with few sets. But Hal Prince went in another direction with it on Broadway—big and epic. The set of the Los Angeles production, which is preserved on videotape, is only slightly less cavernous. Though it does work, Sondheim meant the show to be done small, and that may be the way it is the most effective, the most chilling, the most personal. At the end of the show, the cast points to the audience and accuses them of being like Sweeney and Mrs. Lovett, just as easily motivated by revenge and greed. This is not a show intended to leave an audience happy and safe in the knowledge that good always triumphs over evil. *Sweeney Todd* is meant to disturb. It is both social commentary and horror story, a musical *Twilight Zone* set in nineteenth century England. Like a good horror movie, there is a great deal of underscoring and foreshadowing; the music in this show is almost continuous and filled with leitmotifs that identify important concepts and plot elements. The show even opens with pipe organ music, reminding us of films like *The Phantom of the Opera* and other horror classics.

Attend the Tale . . .

Storytelling is one of *Sweeney Todd*'s primary themes. The opening number, "The Ballad of Sweeney Todd," establishes both mood and presentation style for the evening. It is formal, gothic, ominous. By the time the song reaches its first chorus we hear the first quotation of the *dies irae*, a traditional melody from the Mass for the Dead. *Dies irae* is Latin for "day of wrath" or "judgment day." What could be more appropriate for a story about a madman who takes it upon himself to dish out justice as he sees fit? Sweeney isn't just a murderer; he's a self-appointed judge and executioner, doling out his wrath and judgment with the blade of his razor. At the climax of the song, the chorus repeats Sweeney's name over and over, an incantation that conjures the demon barber himself, rising up from his grave to address the audience directly. At the same time, the audience is reminded, as they will be throughout the evening, that this is a story, that it's not real. When Sweeney rises from the grave, he speaks of himself in the third person; this is not the real Sweeney, only an actor.

Storytelling continues to dominate the structure of the show, but also the action. In the first scene, Sweeney tells Anthony the story of what Judge Turpin did to him. He sings "There Was a Barber and His Wife," but the story ends halfway through because Sweeney doesn't yet know the ending. In fact, the story of the Barber and his Wife won't be finished until the action of the musical is played out completely. When Sweeney returns to Mrs. Lovett's meat pie shop, he pretends not to know her and gets her to tell him the same story, hoping she'll know more than he does. She tells him the story to the same music, but with significant differences. The story of Sweeney's arrest becomes like Rashomon— Sweeney and Mrs. Lovett see events from two entirely different viewpoints. Where Sweeney began with how beautiful the wife was, Mrs. Lovett tells how beautiful the barber was. What Sweeney saw as Lucy's virtue, Mrs. Lovett sees as fatal naïveté. In the basic facts, the two stories are the same—though Mrs. Lovett has more information—but their interpretations are totally different. It's here for the first time that we see how different Sweeney and Mrs. Lovett are, a fact that will prove very important later on. Other instances of storytelling in the show include Toby's accounts of satisfied customers, Pirelli's stories of popes and kings, and the Beadle's ballads at the harmonium.

The German director Bertolt Brecht was famous for developing what is sometimes called the "Alienation Effect," a highly formalized, presentational style of theatre in which the audience is supposed to understand the play intellectually instead of becoming emotionally involved. Though Sondheim has frequently said quite strongly that he does not think his shows are Brechtian, many of them do follow Brecht's precepts. In the case of *Sweeney Todd*, the repeated return to the narrative "Ballad of Sweeney Todd" continually reminds the audience that they are watching a play, that the action is not real. The actors address the audience directly and the chorus comments on the action. Sweeney even threatens the audience directly during "Epiphany." They refer to Sweeney as if he were real ("He wouldn't want us to give it away."), yet they make no pretense that *this* is the real Sweeney. It is this theatrical, presentational format that would seem to suggest a minimalist production. Realistic sets could not be in synch with this style of storytelling. The material consciously breaches the line between fiction and reality and the physical production should follow suit.

To Seek Revenge May Lead to Hell

Sweeney Todd has its roots in melodrama, a form in which emotions are bigger than life, and motivations are clear and uncomplicated. The text of the show explores a number of themes. At its core are the themes of revenge, obsession, and justice. Sweeney has created an "illegal" justice of his own, which contrasts starkly with the "legal" though immoral justice of Judge Turpin. Though he says he tempers his justice with mercy, we see the Judge condemn a boy to hang. Conversely, Sweeney pretends no mercy, knowing the gravity of the death sentence he has pronounced against the Judge. After years of rotting away in prison on a false charge and returning home to find his wife dead (he thinks) and his daughter the ward of his persecutor, we understand Sweeney's taste for revenge. It is only when his revenge is thwarted that it turns to obsession, so much so that eventually his love of Lucy and Johanna is replaced by an even greater love of revenge.

The other theme at the core of this story is greed and covetousness. Mrs. Lovett's first words in the show are "A customer!" Her primary goal at all times is to make money; it is all she thinks about. Through her first song, "The Worst Pies in London," we learn almost everything we need to know about her greed. After seeing Sweeney again, she decides she also wants him. Through the rest of the show, those two goals alone will drive her every action. The Judge is guilty of tremendous greed as well. He wants Lucy, so he sends her husband to prison and rapes her. He wants Johanna, so he legally adopts her and then plans to marry her. Both Pirelli and the Beadle are motivated by greed as well; in the Beadle's case, he wants both money and power.

Once the story is underway, another theme develops—madness. We see two sides to Sweeney. His good side is represented by his love of his family and his friendship and gratitude to Anthony. His bad side comes through in his willingness to kill at random when his revenge isn't fully realized. As the story moves forward, we see Sweeney's madness progress. In the opening "Ballad," the lyric tells us that "Sweeney heard music that nobody heard"; in other words, he's crazy. Later the song says, "Like a perfect machine 'e planned," suggesting that rational thought is gone and that he acts without thought, without mercy, without conscience. We can assume his madness began while he was incarcerated. When Mrs. Lovett tells him what happened to Lucy after he left, he suddenly screams out, "Would no one have mercy on her?" Everything he loved has been taken from him. He has nothing left, and his mind takes its first visible step into insanity. He gives his razors human characteristics. He sees them as his friends, imbuing them with patience, luck, and other human traits. He holds his razor and declares, "At last, my arm is complete again." He is no longer completely human. He is now part machine, a commentary on the dehumanization of the industrial revolution. Then, when Sweeney loses his chance to kill the Judge, his mind snaps and he goes over the edge into madness. Not only does he lose his opportunity to kill Judge Turpin, but he knows that he will never again see his daughter, his only remaining family member. He explodes in a musical mental breakdown, "Epiphany." It is at this point that his love for Lucy and Johanna is transformed into a love for revenge. His morality has been destroyed. Only killing matters to him now. The transformation is complete with "A Little Priest," in which he finds humor in the grisly random murders he plans to commit. The fact that he will now kill indiscriminately is funny to him. His obsession has destroyed what little good was left in him, and he will realize this only at the end of the show when he finds out he's killed Lucy.

Madness is also represented in the tragic figure of the Beggar Woman. She switches back and forth from begging for money to offering sex. One second, she's a pathetic, broken down woman in rags, the next a pushy whore spouting vulgar comments. Like Sweeney—like the show itself—there are two very distinct personalities to the Beggar Woman. In Act II, Sondheim returns to one of the themes of *Anyone Can Whistle*, that only the insane can really see clearly. The Beggar Woman is the one character who seems to know that there is evil at work. She tries to warn everyone, but she is ignored because she's crazy. Johanna, daughter to Sweeney and the Beggar Woman, has obviously inherited her parents' proclivity to mental instability as evidenced in the song "Kiss Me." She decides to kill herself, then changes her mind. She hears noises. She sings, "I think I heard a click. It was the gate. It's the gate. We don't have a gate." The difference, of course, is that Johanna's mental state is played for laughs.

The last presentation of madness is in the last moments of the show, when Toby finds Sweeney surrounded by dead bodies, including that of Mrs. Lovett, who Toby had vowed to protect. The awful knowledge of what has happened—indeed, what has *been* happening—is more than Toby's mind can handle. His mind takes the only possible recourse; it shuts down. He begins chanting a children's rhyme, absently turning the handle of the meat grinder. He knows that he has been a part of this atrocity; he has cooperated by selling the meat pies filled with human remains. He knows he can't separate himself from the crime that has been committed, so he cranks the meat grinder, physically connecting himself to Mrs. Lovett and Sweeney's horrible crimes.

Another theme throughout the show is that knowledge is dangerous, often fatal. Mrs. Lovett and Judge Turpin are the ones with the most knowledge. They both know where Johanna is, that Lucy lives, and they are both killed. Mrs. Lovett also knows that Sweeney is really Benjamin Barker, and the Judge finds out just before he's killed. Pirelli also knows Sweeney's real identity and is killed because of that knowledge. After Sweeney finds out the Beggar Woman's real identity, he is killed. When Toby finds out what's been going on, he goes mad. In contrast, Anthony and Johanna are essentially idiots; they know nothing and they survive.

One-Track Minds

Sweeney Todd is melodrama, and as in a well-constructed farce, each character in the musical has clearly defined wants: Todd wants revenge, Mrs. Lovett wants money and sex, Anthony and Johanna want each other, and the Judge wants Johanna. Sweeney's motivation is spelled out beautifully in the music. His desire for revenge is driven by the loss of his family at the hands of Judge Turpin, so his love of Lucy and Johanna are often linked in the music with Sweeney's obsession for revenge. "Epiphany" is the show's obligatory moment, the moment toward which everything that comes before builds and from which everything after follows. It is the moment at which Sweeney makes a choice that will lead inexorably to a tragic end. The "obsession" motif, which appears in the accompaniment of Sweeney's "There Was a Barber and His Wife" and in "Wait," shows up again here, tying the loss of his Lucy to his desire to kill. Likewise, the two sides of his personality are portrayed in the music, which switches back and forth from the plaintive grief over Lucy to violent rage. Like the Beggar Woman's music, it has two sides, a very literal description of his mental state. Also, the music that accompanies the lyrics about Lucy and Johanna, Sweeney's "loss" motif, is the same music that accompanies the Beggar Woman's "Alms, Alms" lyric. Not only are Sweeney and the Beggar Woman/Lucy connected by the schizoid nature of their music, but they also share this musical motif. When Sweeney sings in "Epiphany" about Lucy, he's actually using her music. He says she "lies in ashes" and he's right, though not in the way he thinks. Lucy, as the Beggar Woman, sleeps in the streets and alleys, among the ash cans. She literally "lies in ashes" every night. Sweeney doesn't know how accurate he is.

As mentioned earlier, Mrs. Lovett has one motivation—greed—aimed at two targets, both money and Sweeney himself. Her plot to use Sweeney's victims as meat pie filler will get her both things she wants, a partnership with Sweeney and a boost for her business. She complains of how disgusting it is that Mrs. Mooney puts cats in her pies, yet she also inadvertently tells us that she's considered doing the same. The only reason she hasn't is that she can't catch any cats. Despite what she says, any moral objections can be put aside easily in the name of money. In fact, later on when she finds out Sweeney has killed Pirelli, she's outraged only until she finds out Pirelli was threatening Todd with extortion. Once she discovers it was a matter of money, she finds the murder perfectly justified.

Sweeney's primary motivation is a moral one (though his methods are decidedly immoral), while Mrs. Lovett's motivation is purely materialistic and selfish. She is his comic counterpart. Neither of them have misgivings about what they're doing, but for different reasons. His morals have been destroyed along with his life, his family, and his sanity, by the Judge. Mrs. Lovett is a member of the poor working class, living by her wits. Like *My Fair Lady's* Alfred P. Dolittle and *Les Misérables'* Monsieur Thénardier, Nellie Lovett can't afford morals. Mrs. Lovett's meat pie scam provides a perverse social justice for Sweeney and a booming business for her. As they sing at the end of Act I, "those above," the customers upstairs in the barber shop "will serve those down below," the customers downstairs in the pie shop.

Anthony's only motivation is to marry Johanna. His near-obsessive love (what is it about this girl that inspires such obsession?) is introduced in his song, "Johanna." Despite the fact that Anthony and Johanna are portrayed as fools throughout most of the show, it's important that their love is real. So Sondheim has written a big, sweeping, romantic love song for Anthony to sing to/about Johanna. It returns several times, during "Kiss Me," also in counterpoint to Sweeney's own "Johanna" in Act II, and again at the end of the show after Sweeney has recognized Lucy and killed Mrs. Lovett. When Toby comes down to Sweeney we hear the "Johanna" melody in the accompaniment, perhaps reminding us that Sweeney's love for Johanna became twisted; only Anthony's love remained pure. Sweeney's heart is black with hatred and so he cannot survive. Of the central characters, only the young lovers will live.

Of course, both Sweeney and Judge Turpin also want Johanna, so they are each given their own distinct "Johanna" motifs. The Judge's was cut from the original production, but is still included on the Broadway cast recording and in an appendix in the published score. As already mentioned, Anthony's and Sweeney's "Johanna" motifs appear in counterpoint early in Act II, but only Anthony's version makes it to the end of the show.

"He Wouldn't Want Us to Give It Away . . ."

A great lover of games, puzzles, and mysteries, Sondheim has sprinkled clues throughout the show, giving the careful listener hints about what's to come. He uses a number of musical fragments throughout the show as leitmotifs—musical motifs that identify a person or object. The Beggar Woman has two distinct motifs, the "loss" motif and the "madness" motif (my labels), both of which tell us about her personality and give us important clues when used elsewhere to show us that the Beggar Woman and Sweeney's long lost Lucy are really the same person. The "loss" motif accompanies the Beggar Woman's pleas for "Alms, alms, for a pitiful woman . . . ." This music is also sung by Sweeney late in Act I in his "Epiphany," accompanying the line "And my Lucy lies in ashes." The lyric about Lucy set to the Beggar Woman's music tells us that they are connected.

The "madness" motif that immediately follows the other motif in the Beggar Woman's first appearance, accompanying her sexually explicit offers (" 'Ow would you like a little muff, dear, a little jig, jig"), is the same music as the minuet accompanying Lucy's rape by Judge Turpin in the Act I flashback. The music tells us not only that this is the same woman, but also that the moment in which she lost her mind (the rape) has stayed with her, haunting her all these years. The moment of her attack has become a permanent part of her personality—a dark, sexual side—displayed here both verbally and musically. This motif also underscores Anthony's conversation with the Beggar Woman outside Johanna's window. He asks her who Johanna is, and following the "madness" motif, the underscoring changes to a strange, dissonant, waltz version of "Green Finch and Linnet Bird," implying a connection between the Beggar Woman and Johanna. But having spoken of Judge Turpin, the Beggar Woman is reminded of her rape and becomes the whore again, propositioning Anthony yet again. The "madness" motif also begins the organ prelude at the beginning of the show, alerting us right away that this music is important and will figure prominently in the show. The use of both of these motifs together illustrates the Beggar Woman's "wandering wits" and split personality, again an important clue that she is two people—a beggar and Lucy. She even sings to Sweeney, "Don't I know you, mister?" And after she leaves in the first scene, Sweeney says, "I feel the chill of ghostly shadows everywhere"—he feels the ghost of Lucy in the Beggar Woman. Sondheim gives us every opportunity to recognize this vital piece of information, yet we are still surprised at the end when Sweeney kills the Beggar Woman and only afterward recognizes her as his Lucy.

Mrs. Lovett is also provided with several bits of foreshadowing. Within moments of her first entrance, she tells Sweeney she thought he was a ghost (perhaps because she recognizes him) not unlike Sweeney's reference to ghosts after seeing the Beggar Woman/Lucy. When she mentions the high price of meat in "The Worst Pies in London," Sondheim is setting us up for one of the central premises of the show and will come back to this reference—using almost exactly the same words—in the introduction to "A Little Priest." The fact that she would use cat meat in her pies if she could only catch them partially prepares us for the fact that she won't mind using human meat later.

Mrs. Lovett's attraction to Sweeney is also no secret, beginning with her alteration of Sweeney's lyric to "There Was a Barber and His Wife," which she changes to ". . . and *he* was beautiful." It's also reasonable to assume that her line "Ooh, Mister Todd, you're warm in my hand," in the song "My Friends" may well be a sexual comment. Later in the show, she will make no secret of her sexual attraction to him, including the phrase "rumpled bedding" and other less overt references in "By the Sea."

Tying the Score

Like most of Sondheim's scores, *Sweeney Todd* makes use of numerous musical motifs to provide unity to a very busy, complicated story. But the *Sweeney* score is also unlike Sondheim's other scores in a number of ways. Several of the characters in the show speak in their own unique musical languages. Pirelli sings entirely in mock Italian opera style to characterize his fake Italian ethnicity. Mrs. Lovett generally sings in a raucous, British musical hall style, particularly in "A Little Priest" and "By the Sea," the songs that illustrate her two primary motivations—money and sex. Anthony and Johanna sing in a big, overblown, operatic style when they sing about their love. Notice how unlike the rest of the score "Green Finch and Linnet Bird" is in both its vocabulary and its music; it's almost a classical art song. Yet, in its yearning for happiness and freedom, its emotional content is like some of Sweeney's songs. Notice also the long, high notes and simple accompaniment in Anthony's "Johanna," again not like most of the rest of the score.

This score also uses more underscoring than most Sondheim shows. Like a movie score, the *Sweeney* orchestra provides atmosphere (the church bells, Johanna's birds, etc.), tension, surprise, even clues to the mystery, often without vocals. Though *Sweeney* is not an opera, the music only occasionally stops; the underscoring is nearly continuous. And when it does stop, it's to make a dramatic moment (like Sweeney's death) stand out from the rest of the show. Unlike much musical theatre underscoring, this music is thematically connected to the events happening on stage. It's not just an instrumental reprise of the last song or the song coming up.

Not surprisingly, Sondheim actually includes a lot of stage action in the actual music. In "The Worst Pies in London," Mrs. Lovett's pounding of the dough, swatting of flies, plucking, flicking, and smacking are all rhythmically incorporated into the music and the lyric, providing even more comedy in the number. Similarly, Sweeney's shaving of Judge Turpin is an inseparable part of "Pretty Women." Without the onstage action, it would be an entirely different song. "The Contest" is a song entirely *about* the action onstage, as are the Beadle's "Parlor Songs." "God That's Good" at the beginning of Act II also interweaves several different pieces of stage action into a visually exciting number that would not work (and would be virtually unnecessary) without the physical action.

Of the many musical motifs used in *Sweeney Todd*, one of the most interesting is the *dies irae*. As mentioned earlier, this chant melody from the Mass for the Dead has been used for centuries in music about death and dying. Because death is at the center of the story of *Sweeney Todd*, the use of the *dies irae* is particularly interesting. It first appears in "The Ballad of Sweeney Todd" as the melody to the chorus ("Swing your razor wide, Sweeney . . ."). It's also found throughout the show—inverted—as the accompaniment to "The Ballad of Sweeney Todd," sometimes with the melody from Anthony's "Johanna" added in counterpoint (as in "There Was a Barber and His Wife"). The "Ballad" accompaniment, slightly altered, also becomes the melody to "My Friends." These uses of the *dies irae* connect the opening number describing Sweeney with both his song about *why* he will kill ("Barber and His Wife") and his song about how he will kill ("My Friends"), lending great unity to the score as a whole and to the character of Sweeney.

The "Ballad" is a strange piece musically. It follows almost no "normal" rules of harmony. In many spots, the song has no traditional chordal harmony at all. It sounds very modal, like a folk song, which adds to the period feel and the storytelling style of its lyric. Whereas the majority of western melodies end on the first degree of the scale, this melody ends on the second degree, an unsettling ending, but also the same note the accompaniment figure is based on. Like some of the music in *A Little Night Music*, this song is harmonically stagnant much of the time, not changing harmonies for long stretches at a time, parallelling Todd's single-minded pursuit of the Judge and the fact that society's injustices never change. The highly repetitive nature of the accompaniment figure, or "ostinato," not only creates a profound unity, but also holds our attention as we wait for the music to change, to resolve itself.

Bookends

The opening and closing sections of *Sweeney Todd* are almost mirror images of each other. The show opens with "The Ballad of Sweeney Todd," and we then meet Anthony and Sweeney in an extended musical scene. It's interesting to note that when Anthony sings about London, the word "London" falls on major harmonies, but when Sweeney sings about it, the same word is accompanied in minor—two very different views of the same city. Sweeney's "Barber and His Wife" is first heard here, though it doesn't really end; it just stops midstory, midmelody, because the story isn't over yet. The "Ballad" accompaniment is used here again, which also sets up the melody of "My Friends" that will be in the next scene. Sweeney's dissonant "obsession" motif is heard just before the end of "Barber and His Wife" and again at the very end of the scene, setting us up for all that lies ahead.

The next scene introduces Mrs. Lovett and centers on "Poor Thing," the story of Lucy. As part of the "Poor Thing" sequence, her rendition of "Barber and His Wife" echoes Sweeney's version in the preceding scene, connecting them both in the past and the present, but it also shows their differences. The creepy ostinato accompaniment from Todd's version is missing when Mrs. Lovett sings it; to her, it's just a story, without the emotional baggage that Todd carries. The scene ends with "My Friends," (using the inverted *dies irae* for the melody) as Sweeney formulates his plans and reunites with his razors.

The final scene reverses the opening sequence. "Pretty Women," the song that was interrupted in Act I, is finally finished—and so is the Judge. The final sequence is set in motion. After the murder, Sweeney sings "My Friends," again investing the razors with human qualities, but this time putting them to rest now that their work is done. Mrs. Lovett returns to "Poor Thing" as she tries to justify not telling Sweeney the whole story of Lucy. After killing Mrs. Lovett, Sweeney is finally reunited with Lucy—though only in death—and he sings "Barber and His Wife," finally knowing the end of the story. Toby enters and kills Todd, and finally he and Lucy are together. The show ends with "The Ballad of Sweeney Todd," creating perfect symmetry and closing the show's framing device.

There are other songs used in both acts. Toby's selling song in Act I, "Pirelli's Miracle Elixir," becomes "Mrs. Lovett's Meat Pies" in Act II, underlining the similarly false claims of greatness for the two products. In Act I, Toby is hawking fake hair tonic, in Act II, meat pies made of human flesh. Neither product is actually what he claims and the over-abundance of rhyme proves it. Sondheim has pointed out that his use of rhyme is usually associated with the character's intelligence and presence of mind; the more intelligent and lucid they are, the more rhyme they use. In *A Little Night Music*, for instance, Frederick, a lawyer, rhymes more than any other character; in "Getting Married Today" from *Company*, Amy is so flustered that she rhymes almost not at all. There are sections in Sweeney's "Epiphany" (and some other moments in the show) without any rhyme. Yet, Toby's selling songs contain *too much* rhyme, connoting not just presence of mind, but premeditation, calculation. In other words, Toby—or more likely, his employer, who probably writes his sales pitch—is a con man.

In both acts, "A Little Priest" accompanies Todd's decision to take action by taking lives. In Act I he decides, at Mrs. Lovett's urging, to take the lives of random strangers. In Act II, he decides to take Mrs. Lovett's life in revenge for her deception. Anthony's "Johanna" is used in both acts for Johanna's incarceration and Anthony's promise to rescue her. In Act I, she's locked up in Judge Turpin's house. In Act II, she's locked up in Fogg's Asylum.

Sweeneys, Sweeneys, Everywhere ...

Sweeney Todd has several things to say about human nature and about society. The most obvious statement the authors are making is that we all have the capacity for revenge that Sweeney has. In the last song, the chorus sings to us, "Perhaps today you gave a nod to Sweeney Todd," and later in the same song:

Sweeney waits in the parlor hall,
Sweeney leans on the office wall.
No one can help,
Nothing can hide you.
Isn't that Sweeney there beside you?

They point to people throughout the theatre, shouting, "There! There!" Toward the end of the song they sing, "To seek revenge may lead to hell. But everyone does it. . . . ." To some extent they are saying we all live in the past, we all make mistakes we regret, and we all have revenge in our hearts at one time or another. Perhaps we don't go to the extremes that Sweeney does; but then again, how often are we put in the very extreme circumstances into which Sweeney has been thrust? Like Sondheim's later show *Assassins*, *Sweeney Todd* also makes the case that society is to blame for the unfair class structure, exploitation of the lower classes, the abuse of power, and a corrupt government and justice system. We do nothing about these social ills, so we are just as guilty. Like *Assassins*, the black humor in *Sweeney Todd* allows us to distance ourselves from the horror of what's happening, but it also makes us realize how easily we can trivialize murder and brutality. Is "A Little Priest" all that different from Oliver Stone's film *Natural Born Killers* or Quentin Tarantino's *Pulp Fiction*? As a society, we have grown numb to death; we see it so much on the news, in television shows, in the movies, that it hardly phases us anymore. Through wars, urban riots, and "ethnic cleansing," killing has become an impersonal act. And perhaps that's one of Sondheim's points—the fact that Sweeney and Mrs. Lovett can joke about the brutal murders they will commit is an indictment of our culture. But remember that they're not the only ones laughing; so are we.

Mrs. Lovett is, after all, the ultimate capitalist, literally feeding off her fellow human beings. Business by its nature is about money and often lacks morality and humanity, and this is personified in Nellie Lovett. She is not immoral; she is amoral. She cares about nothing other than surviving; and of course, this is the only way she *will* survive. Money can make us do horrible things, the show seems to be saying, and a quick look through *USA Today* or *The Wall Street Journal* will bear witness to that.

So society is to blame not only for Sweeney's situation, but also for the monster he becomes. We have made him a murderer by refusing to fix what's wrong with our society, by allowing the corruption and abuse of power to continue, in fact, by rewarding corruption and abuse with money and fame. The story goes that while working on the show, people asked Hal Prince what was made in the factory that dominated the Broadway stage set and Prince would reply, "They make Sweeney Todds." So many of the incidents and themes in the show are a growing part of our contemporary world. The show is set in the nineteenth century, but it's very much about our world today, the lower classes striking back at the upper classes, the homeless woman begging on the streets, a justice system that too often protects the criminals at the expense of the victims. Sweeney believes in "a dark and a vengeful God," not unlike religious conservatives who believe that God has sent AIDS down to earth as punishment. Though it is unusual for a musical (though not for a Sondheim musical), *Sweeney Todd* looks into the darkest corners of the human existence, a darkness that exists in any time period. It is a show about what happens when people are pushed too far. In this age of armed youth gangs, mad dictators in the middle east, and economic and social unrest throughout the world, that is a theme worth exploring.

Other Resources

The script and score to *Sweeney Todd* have both been published (though the score is expensive because of its size), and the original cast album is available on tape and CD. There is a videotape commercially available of the Los Angeles production with Angela Lansbury (of the original Broadway cast) and George Hearn, Len Cariou's replacement on Broadway. The differences in Cariou's performance on the CD and Hearn's on video are fascinating to observe. Cariou's Sweeney is more inwardly tormented, his madness boiling just beneath the surface, while Hearn's is more external, more melodramatic from the beginning. Which road you take is up to you and will define to some extent the overall style of your production.

Though the L.A. production is smaller than the Broadway version, it's a pretty good record of Hal Prince's direction. MTI's Study Guide, designed to help teachers integrate the show's issues into their regular curriculum, is an excellent guide for the cast and production staff as well, with background on the show and its creators.

Also available are earlier versions of the Sweeney Todd story, including Christopher Bond's version (on which the musical is based) and the (possibly) original version by George Dibdin Pitt, called *A String of Pearls*. A look at how Bond, and Hugh Wheeler and Sondheim transformed the story is fascinating and will give you additional insights into the beauty of the Sondheim/Wheeler version. As mentioned earlier, Stephen Banfield's book *Sondheim's Broadway Musicals* offers some valuable insights into Sondheim's scores—and traces the dozens of musical motifs throughout *Sweeney Todd*—but it isn't a book that should be approached without some music theory background.

16 West Side Story

Book by Arthur Laurents
Music by Leonard Bernstein
Lyrics by Stephen Sondheim (and Leonard Bernstein, uncredited)
Originally Directed and Choreographed on Broadway by
*   Jerome Robbins*
Licensed by Music Theatre International

West *Side Story* is the American musical theatre's only great tragedy, a story in which a happy ending is not possible, a musical about hatred and prejudice, a musical that says that love cannot triumph over all. It is also a perfect blend of the many disciplines that make musical theatre. More than in most musicals, the book, music, lyrics, and staging come together as a perfectly unified whole, speaking with one voice.

Musical theatre is by its nature a collaborative art form, but rarely do the many parts make such a consistently crafted statement. Driven by the vision of Jerome Robbins, the greatest talents on Broadway created a musical that is specific yet universal, as current as today's headlines yet also timeless. As long as there are differences between groups of people, as long as there are haves and have-nots, there will be resentment and hatred; as hard as it may be to accept, *West Side Story* will always be timely. It was written in 1957, yet it describes most metropolitan cities today just as accurately as it did then. It is a musical whose final curtain brings not hope for tomorrow but inconsolable grief over today; what little hope the final moments may imply, we know that hatred does not die. In a country where hate crimes multiply exponentially each year and gang warfare has turned our streets into war zones, *West Side Story* is heartbreaking and also somehow cathartic.

West Side Story was a big shock to the Broadway audiences of

1957, with its intricately integrated dance, dissonant, driving, jazz-inspired score, its gritty, frightening sets, its assault on the well-protected sensibilities of theatregoers. It was not a big hit. Lyricist Stephen Sondheim wasn't even mentioned in the *New York Times'* generally positive review, though Brooks Atkinson did see the innovation and brilliance of the show. On the other hand, the *Herald Tribune* said the show was "almost never emotionally affecting." The critics mostly applauded the show, though audiences favored the concurrently running *The Music Man*, which swept the Tony awards that year. *West Side Story* went on tour and then returned to Broadway again in 1960. It wasn't until the release of the 1961 film version that it finally captured the hearts of the public. Subsequent New York revivals in 1964, 1965, and 1980 fared better with audiences, who were now presumably better equipped to deal with its unconventionality.

Happily Never After

There had been serious musicals before—*Show Boat, Carousel, South Pacific*, and others—but none with the in-your-face anguish of *West Side Story*. Here was a musical with the unheard of message that love not only *will not* triumph over all, but *cannot*. This was a show with more violence and death than any other musical before or since. The Act I curtain fell on two dead bodies, both of them leading characters. The audience went out into the lobby for intermission knowing that there could not be a happy ending.

In addition to this, *West Side Story* used dance to a degree never before attempted in the musical theatre. Though George Balanchine and Agnes DeMille had succeeded in integrating dance into musicals, even advancing the plot with it, Jerome Robbins took their tradition to new extremes. There were twelve major dance sequences in the show, providing most of the exposition—Tony and Maria's meeting, the deaths of Riff and Bernardo, Anita's foiled attempt to deliver the message to Tony, and other important moments. The show had one of the shortest books ever written for a musical, leaving much of the plot and characterization to the songs and dance. Dance had become an element every bit as important as the book, music, and lyrics. But this was not an act of egotism on the part of director/choreographer Robbins; the material demanded it. The characters were inarticulate kids. They could not express their love, their anger, or their fears through words, but all that and more could be expressed through dance. Dance, however, was not the only element that gave *West Side Story* its unique look. The singers never broke the fourth wall; songs were not sung to the audience as they were in most musicals. It was closer to reality—painfully so—than other shows, yet also more stylized, more theatrical with sets flying in and out, an invented slang, choreographed knife fights, and several extended musical scenes.

Endless Night

Unlike most musicals of the time, *West Side Story* pulled no punches. This was a musical about death as much as love. In addition to the staged deaths, references to death are scattered throughout the script and score. These kids think about death all the time. For them, it is an inseparable part of life. Tony and Riff's pledge to be friends forever invokes images of birth and death—"womb to tomb" and "sperm to worm." Tony and Maria sing of endless night, but though they mean endless moonlight and romance, they get a very different kind of endless night—death. In the "Jet Song," Riff promises that the gang members will be Jets until they die. When Doc is told he doesn't "dig it," he responds that what he will dig is their early graves, and he's more right than the kids want to admit. Before "Cool," Riff tells the Jets that if they let the Sharks know how much they bother them, they're dead. In the lyric to "Cool," Riff talks about living it up and dying in bed. Schrank tells the gangs he hopes they kill each other, so he won't have to deal with them anymore. In "One Hand, One Heart," Tony and Maria sing that only death will part them, and later, that even death won't. Maria and Anita discuss death and killing explicitly in "A Boy Like That." Anita even lies about Maria's death to the Jets in Act II, causing Tony to actively seek out his own death.

West Side Story vs. *Romeo and Juliet*

West Side Story has been compared to *Romeo and Juliet* since opening night, for obvious reasons. Almost always, people begin with the "obvious" statement that the poetry of the musical can never outshine the poetry of the Bard; but perhaps that assumption is a hasty one. Though Shakespeare's words are magnificent, there is a strong case to be made that the addition of music and dance adds a new dimension that words alone—even Shakespeare's—cannot achieve. The music of *West Side Story* heightens emotion, adds subtext, and adds irony. The music of the song "Cool" is anything but calm; the wacky music and lyrics of "Gee Officer Krupke" ironically oppose the serious subject of the song. Leonard Bernstein's music creates dramatic connections through the use of motifs, adding to the dramatic impact and to the audience's understanding. The music that underscores Tony and Maria's meeting at the dance is so dramatically different from the rest of the music in the scene, immediately showing us that they are different, that they belong in another world, that their love does not, maybe cannot, exist in the real world. Without any words, Bernstein has dramatized love at first sight more effectively, more powerfully than mere words could.

Arthur Laurents adds to the tragedy by making the man Tony kills Maria's brother instead of her cousin, as in *Romeo and Juliet*. Maria is forced to accept that the man she loves killed her brother, who was in many ways like a father to her. Laurents also fixed some problems in Shakespeare's version. First, there's a *reason* the two "families" are fighting. In *Romeo and Juliet*, it's just an old feud. There is no explanation why they're feuding or what started it. In *West Side Story*, the feud is over turf, prejudice, and other social problems. The working class Americans resent the immigrants even though they are immigrants themselves. The Jets' fathers tell them the Puerto Ricans are the reason their economic situation is so bad. The Sharks have been brought to America without their consent, by parents hoping to find a better life, yet all they find is hatred and violence. None of these kids had any choice about being where they are. Can we wonder why they're angry?

Also, sleeping potion doesn't figure into the plot anywhere in *West Side Story*. Maybe audiences in Shakespeare's time would accept sleeping potions, but they won't today. Also, the failure of Maria's message to reach Tony is not merely due to coincidence, as in *Romeo and Juliet*; it's due to prejudice. The Jets don't trust Anita merely because she's Puerto Rican. Everything in *West Side Story* happens as a result of racial prejudice. The interception of the message is society's fault, as are the deaths of Riff, Bernardo, and Tony. *Romeo and Juliet* is not true tragedy because the main characters have no tragic flaws; they make no tragic mistakes. The unhappy ending is due to chance. Unlike its Elizabethan predecessor, *West Side Story* is a social document as much as a love story. In *Romeo and Juliet*, the background of the feuding that begins everything is unknown and apparently unimportant; in *West Side Story* it is clearly articulated and is the catalyst for every single event in the story. Doc says to the Jets, "You make this world lousy." Action replies, "That's the way we found it, Doc." Though the ending of the show is profoundly unhappy, there is still the tiniest hope of resolution as the two gangs come together to carry Tony's body out. Just maybe things have finally gotten bad enough that the kids might change.

From a dramatic standpoint, the biggest improvement Laurents made is in the character of Maria. It is significant that she lives at the end. This one detail makes *West Side Story* so much more tragic than *Romeo and Juliet*. Unlike Juliet, Maria must go on without Tony. Traditionally, the central character in a play or story learns something by the final curtain, but neither Romeo nor Juliet learns anything— they are the same at their deaths as they are at the beginning. In contrast, Maria does learn something. She says to the two gangs as she brandishes Chino's gun, "We all killed him . . . I can kill now because I hate now." She has lost her innocence. She has seen the real world for what it is—ugly, violent, dangerous, and ultimately uncaring. She knows now that love cannot triumph over all. As an audience, we grieve not only for the loss of her beloved, but also for the loss of her idealism. She is no longer a child.

Timeless

Why is *West Side Story* timeless? Why does it stand up today as well as it did in 1957? There are several reasons. Laurents' invented slang keeps the dialogue from becoming dated; it has no period. It's both mythical and real at the same time. It's also important to remember that the central story is as old as storytelling. The story of star-crossed lovers goes back long before Shakespeare's time; his version was not the first, and *West Side Story* has not been the last. *West Side Story* is as relevant now as ever, maybe more so today. America today is besieged by violence on the streets, gang war, murder, bigotry and prejudice. White supremacists, the Ku Klux Klan, neo-Nazis, and other groups are as zealous as ever, as well as groups all over the world advocating race purification. The issue of race, of prejudice against immigrants, may never go away.

It is unfortunate that the social problems of 1957 are even more prevalent today, yet our only hope of erasing them is to understand them. Why do gangs exist? Why do they have turf? The Jets and the Sharks feel helpless, impotent. They feel they have no control over their lives, destined to live the same horrible lives their parents do. They want to feel power, to feel they have control over their surroundings. Without money or connections, their only tool to gain that power is violence. Just as countries fight over land, so do gangs. More than anything, this is why Tony and Maria need each other—to escape this existence (as illustrated in the dream ballet, "Somewhere"). That's why "Somewhere" is an important musical motif running throughout the show. It represents the hope that there is some place in the world where the violence is not necessary.

In all fairness, we have to put ourselves in Bernardo and Anita's place. Would we feel any differently if we were them? They are outsiders, they were taken from their homeland and deposited in a place where they are surrounded by hate and the constant threat of violence, even death. Is there a foreseeable end to this awful situation? No. Throughout the history of the world, there has always been the battle between the haves and the have-nots; ironically, in this case, both sides are have-nots. That's precisely why both groups feel the need to look down on the others, why they hate and resent them.

Music and Lyrics

The music and lyrics shoulder the lion's share of the characterization in the show. Sondheim's lyrics accomplish this by using a simple vocabulary and by almost cursing in "The Jet Song" and "Gee Officer Krupke." Bernstein's music is heavily jazz inspired and, here and there, borderline rock. Again, this is a language familiar to us, unlike the Elizabethan English of *Romeo and Juliet*. Bernstein uses lots of minor chords, and the lowered third and seventh scale degrees, a device common to jazz and blues. In some cases, he uses both major and minor sounds at the same time, making chords with both the natural third degree and the flatted third in the same chord. In "Something's Coming" he uses the lowered seventh frequently, and even ends the song on this pitch, never resolving the melody, letting it just hang out there, waiting like the song's lyric. Unfortunately, in the movie, they wrote a final phrase onto the song, resolving the melody, and ruining the effect.

Bernstein also uses "hemiola"—he sets a melody in duple time against an accompaniment in triple time, or he sets 3 against 4, etc. The Prologue contains many instances of a duple meter over a triple meter. The "Jet Song" sets a melody in 3/4 time over an accompaniment in 6/8. "Something's Coming" does the exact opposite setting a 6/8 melody against a 3/4 accompaniment. "America" alternates every other measure between 6/8 and 3/4. All this gives the score a sense of restlessness, of unease, the feeling that something isn't right.

Bernstein also based the entire score, particularly the romance, on the tritone. A tritone is the musical interval of a raised fourth—from C to F#, for example. Historically, it's been used to characterize danger or evil. In the Middle Ages, the tritone was called *Diabolus in musica*, or "the devil in music," and its use in composition was strictly forbidden. It is the most dissonant interval in Western music and Bernstein uses it in *West Side Story* to great advantage. The very first vocal phrase in "Something's Coming" starts with a descending tritone; this same phrase opens the "Dance at the Gym" music. If you drop the first note down an octave, it becomes the first phrase of the main melody of "Maria." Therefore, this one phrase accompanies Tony's hopes of falling in love, the meeting of those expectations at the dance, and their full realization in his new love. Almost every song in the score contains the tritone at some point (the beginning of "Cool," for example), but none as prominently as the songs that chart Tony and Maria's love.

Instead of an overture, *West Side Story* begins with a choreographed Prologue in which the tensions between the Jets and the Sharks over the course of many months are dramatized in music and dance. Just as the dance in the Prologue illustrates the violence and hatred between the two gangs that will fuel everything in the show, the music similarly sets up the rest of the score. The very first chords set up the simultaneous use of the natural third and flat third, the sounds of major and minor together. These chords will be significant throughout the score. The Prologue also sets up the extensive use of the flat seventh and other dissonant jazz sounds, preparing the audience for the rest of the score. Within the first seventeen measures, the Prologue has quoted part of the melody from the "Jet Song," establishing this as an important musical motif. Midway through the Prologue, it jumps from the key of C to the key of F#—a tritone.

Something's Coming

The first song, the "Jet Song," is important in several ways. Although the two gangs have been introduced to us in the Prologue, this song tells us why belonging to the gang is important to these kids. It also sets up what separates the Jets from Tony. Tony is no longer an active part of the gang. He has grown out of the need for the gang, past the mentality that needs to find a group to belong to in order to have an identity and that needs to hate those that don't belong to that group. Conversely, the lyric of the song says that once you're a Jet, you're a Jet forever; and as far as the Sharks are concerned, Tony is a Jet whether or not he's an active member of the gang. He's still one of "them." The song begins with the Prologue accompaniment, reminding us of the violence and fierce hatred between the gangs. The vocal melody repeats phrases we've heard in the Prologue. In many ways, this song says verbally things that the Prologue hinted at choreographically, that the gang represents security (physical and emotional), power, and territory. The song's bridge, about going to the dance, also introduces a melody that we'll hear later at the dance (this section of the song is not on the cast recording or in the movie, but it is in the published score).

During the previous scene, we learned about Tony, a close friend of Riff's who co-founded the Jets but is no longer active. Now we meet him. He has outgrown Riff and the Jets to an extent. He's more concerned with making a life. It's important that this is established because it allows for Tony, the only one of the Jets who can get past his prejudice, to fall in love with a Puerto Rican. As mentioned before, Tony's song begins with a musical phrase that is almost exactly the same as the main melody of "Maria," approached from above here and from below later. The lyric is strangely like the title song from Sondheim's later musical *Company*. Here, Tony mentions both the phone ringing and door being knocked on; Robert uses the same two images in the song, "Company." Any good dramatic piece sets up expectations; here, it couldn't be any clearer. Tony's expecting something wonderful to happen to him, and the music that expresses that expectation is going to stay with him throughout the show.

Twitchin' at the Dance

At the dance at the gym, the music begins with the opening melody of "Something's Coming." This is where Tony will find what he's looking for. The music in this scene is chromatic, dissonant, jazzy, driving, loud, articulating the anger, restlessness, and raw sexuality of these teenagers. The opening bars of the scene begin in plain octaves, but add dissonance and chromaticism with each successive bar of music until it's nearly deafening. There is also rock and roll here. The bass line in the Blues section is a standard blues/rock bass. One of the early segments in the Blues is even marked "Rocky" in the score. Within this piece is the accompaniment figure from the Prologue and the "Jet Song," indicating perhaps that there may be conflict here tonight. This dance is very American in its jazzy blues/rock flavor, but the Mambo is unmistakably Latin. Yet even in the Mambo, there are quotations of the "Maria" melody, as well as some alterations of this motif, in the trumpets and later in the lower brass. Up until this point, the orchestration of the music at the dance has been heavy on brass and percussion, giving the music a slight rock and roll feel as well. Once Tony and Maria see each other, that changes.

The Cha-Cha, which underscores Tony and Maria seeing each other and falling in love, is orchestrated mainly with the woodwinds and strings. It is a very different sound because Tony and Maria's love exists on a different plane; it can't exist in the worlds of the Jets and Sharks. Its music must be different. The melody of the Cha-Cha is a variation on the melody of "Maria." Tony has only just seen her and already her name sings to him. It is this music that he hears forever more when he thinks of her, that he hears in the next scene as he roams the streets thinking of her. But their music cannot exist independently of the real world, and the music of the earlier Promenade begins to encroach on their love motif. As they kiss, Bernardo steps in between the lovers and separates them. Riff joins them and the real world has taken over. The music gets louder and louder until, like the Promenade, it is interrupted by a whistle—the sound of authority (Schrank and Krupke), of unreasonable repression, of the uncaring adult world. The music returns to the intense jazz of earlier, but this time with the orchestration from the love motif, a mix of the real world and the ideal world of romance.

The music of their meeting stays in Tony's ears after he leaves the dance. He begins the next song, "Maria," with an introduction of repeated notes, almost chantlike in its solemnity. Soon it explodes into the main melody, which we've heard in several forms since the beginning of the show. His expectations have been realized. His song of love for Maria has a strongly Latin beat, of course. His love is so consuming, so overwhelming, that halfway through the song he can't stay with the music anymore, and he spins off into a high, free musical line as the accompaniment takes over the melody for him. Finally, he returns to earth (and the melody line) and finishes the song. In the last phrase of the song, he alters the "Maria" motif, so that instead of going up at the end, it now comes down, finally feeling resolved now that they can be together. The last sound we hear is the orchestra quoting the "Somewhere" motif, the music that will represent their dream of a life together and their inability to ever find that dream.

The music having continued without interruption through the dance at the gym and "Maria," it now continues this extended musical sequence, moving directly into the Balcony Scene. As Tony and Maria meet and talk, the underscoring repeats the intro and main melody of "Maria"; her love is still singing in his head. They begin to sing new music, to a breathless accompaniment, with a lyric invoking a number of heavenly images—suns, moons, stars, space. This segues into "Tonight," an important song that will be used again later. The Balcony scene goes through two unusual key changes that are worth noting. In each case Bernstein uses the raised fourth degree of the scale—the tritone—to move into the new key. At the end of the scene, as they sing the last verse, the orchestra sneaks in a quotation of the melody to "Somewhere," the song about the dream of love that they can never have. In the last underscoring section in the scene, the "Somewhere" motif plays in perfect counterpoint to the melody of "Tonight." In other words, what they dream of tonight is only a dream and can never be found in the real world. Under their last notes, the orchestra quotes the "Somewhere" melody and then, as it did at the end of "Maria," echoes the two notes that will soon accompany the word "Somewhere," the same notes that will end the show, over Tony's dead body.

A Dream Deferred

We see two scenes showing the gangs relaxing before the war council—the Sharks' girls to the hot-blooded, Latin flavored "America," the Jets to the jazzy "Cool." The main motif of "Cool," a twelve-tone jazz fugue, is also based on the tritone, its first three notes the same as the first three notes of the "Maria" melody and "Something's Coming." What makes the score so remarkable is that Bernstein can use this interval and this melody fragment so frequently and yet so subtly, giving the score great unity without being boring or monotonous.

In Act I, Scene 7, Tony comes to visit Maria at the bridal shop where she works and another extended musical sequence begins. Anita is there when he arrives and now knows of the illicit romance. After Anita leaves, Tony and Maria discuss how perfect their life together is going to be. The underscoring beneath their dialogue is the Cha-Cha during which they first met. They set up a pretend wedding ceremony using the mannequins in the shop. As they take their vows—which are as real to them at this moment as any vows taken in a church—the music changes to the melody of "Somewhere," the music of their doomed dream of wedded bliss. With "One Hand, One Heart," they sing their vows to each other. Even here, the "Maria" motif is hidden in the inner orchestral voices, appearing first in the instrumental break between verses, then throughout the last verse, and most obviously as it's repeated three times leading up to the final chord.

As the last chord of the song still rings, it is interrupted with the brass blast of the "Tonight" quintet. Consistent with the dance at the gym, "One Hand, One Heart" is orchestrated mostly with the woodwinds and strings, and the quintet is heavy on brass and percussion. This is another song of expectation, but one of restlessness as well, with a vocal line in duple meter and an accompaniment in triple meter, frequently dropping beats, straining at the leash. The upper register is in the key of C while the lower register is in the key of A, putting the song in harmonic as well as rhythmic conflict. Anita and the two gangs have seized Tony and Maria's song of love and twisted it so that it now describes the desire for sex and violence, intruding on the lovers' fantasy. It is ironic that both gangs sing to the same melody and, in some cases, the same lyrics. Like two countries at war, they both believe they're right and they both believe they will triumph. When Tony sings "Tonight," the strings repeat the melody a measure behind him, creating even more musical conflict and dissonance. The dream no longer sounds as pretty as it did in the Balcony Scene. His reference to an endless night is more real than he could possibly know. Finally, as Maria enters the quintet, everyone is singing at once. There is too much conflict to possibly resolve. There is no way they can all have what they want; and as we saw at the dance, the violence is stronger than the love.

The next scene is the Rumble, set to music based on the Prologue, the music of violence and hatred. Almost the entire Rumble is based on motifs established in the Prologue. And again, one of the most important scenes in the show is given to dance. As the curtain falls on Act I, Riff and Bernardo lie dead on the stage—Bernardo killed by Tony—as police sirens approach. It is clear that there cannot be a happy ending.

Meanwhile, Back at the Ranch . . .

Act II opens with the jolly "I Feel Pretty," making the already tense situation even more so, and making Maria's joy painful to watch, knowing as we do that Tony has killed Bernardo. Tony comes to her and tells her what has happened; they decide to run away together to escape all the violence and horror, but we know it's too late. The underscoring leads directly into the dream ballet, beginning with the two of them promising that they will find a place where they can be together in peace. As Tony sings, with Maria then joining him, the stage transforms to a nightmarish cityscape, filled with violence. They run, trying to break through the city walls, to escape the gangs and the violence, and as they finally break free the music changes to a transition that quotes the "Somewhere" motif. Tony and Maria have made it to the place they've dreamed about. The gangs are there too, but now happy, dressed in pastel colors, the violence and hatred gone. They dance as the music moves into the Scherzo, a term usually referring to a movement that is light, fast, with elements of surprise (the word means "joke" in Italian). Towards the end of the Scherzo, "Somewhere" is quoted again, and as the characters onstage dance together, a woman's voice is heard singing "Somewhere," heard here for the first time in its full form and with its lyrics. As the music begins to quote "I Have a Love" on top of "Somewhere," they form a processional. They all sing together that there is a place for them all, but it is only a dream. The "Somewhere" motif slows haltingly, then stops. The cityscape returns as Riff and Bernardo enter. The knife fight is reenacted to music based on the Prologue, and Tony and Maria are separated by the fighting. The nightmare gets more and more frightening until suddenly, the lovers are back in Maria's bedroom and the music returns to the unaccompanied melody of "Somewhere." Though they know it can't be, they try desperately to hold on to their dream as they sing the end of "Somewhere" again. The sequence ends with the same music that ended the Balcony Scene and that will end the show.

Tension Breaker

The next scene finds the Jets running from the cops. The show is in desperate need of a tension breaker, and it gets one in the form of an almost vaudeville flavored number, "Gee, Officer Krupke." The tritone returns again in the first two notes of the vocal line and in the sustained instrumental note before each verse against the bass. In the film, the positions of "Cool" and "Krupke" are reversed, and though "Cool" works okay in this spot, "Krupke" doesn't work in the earlier spot. Through the kids' caustic humor, we see the disdain they have for adults and the reason for that disdain—they feel that the adults only see them as a stereotype, as generic juvenile delinquents. The kids' message here is that it's no surprise they're juvenile delinquents considering the lives they've lived, that no one in their situation could've ended up any differently. Again, it is society that is to blame for all that has happened, for the violence and the hatred. Not wanting to let the audience off the emotional hook too easily, Sondheim had originally written the last line of the song as "Gee, Officer Krupke, fuck you." But he was out-voted; in 1957, you just couldn't use the F-word in a musical, no matter how progressive or gritty it might be.

Love and Death

The most difficult moment in the show to make an audience believe is Anita's conversion from hatred of Tony both as an "American" and as the killer of her boyfriend, into Maria and Tony's ally. Why would she change her mind so completely, so quickly, especially after catching Maria in bed with Bernardo's murderer? How can we believe this miraculous transformation? The fact that the man Tony kills is Maria's brother *and* the boyfriend of Maria's confidante is a complication not found in *Romeo and Juliet*. It is certainly more dramatic, but also very problematic. This change must be motivated by extreme emotion, the kind that can be conveyed only through music.

The song, "A Boy Like That," literally explodes in the brass and percussion that has represented violence throughout the show. Anita mentions killing in the very first phrase; that is all she sees in Tony. The song is in minor and full of dissonance and strange rhythmic irregularities, constantly jumping from 3/2 to 3/4 to 4/4, with the result that many phrases end up in the equivalent of 6/4 or 7/4. Maria argues back, to the same music, that Anita is wrong. Then they argue musically by singing in counterpoint. The next section, "I Have a Love," is Maria's statement that nothing matters besides love. The melody to this section is a close variant of Anita's melody from earlier in the piece, only now it's in a major key (death is in minor, love is in major). And the accompaniment is different, now in solemn, almost hymn-like chords, instead of the restless anger of the driving eighth notes at the beginning. After Maria's verse, the main "I Have a Love" motif is repeated instrumentally to prepare us for its use at the end (although it's already been used this way in the dream sequence). Finally, Anita is persuaded by Maria's conviction and they sing together at last, as the motif is repeated again under their last notes. It is significant that the song doesn't ever end—the instrumental repeat stops only halfway through the melody, leaving us hanging. This is not over yet.

While Maria is detained by Lt. Schrank, Anita goes to Doc's drugstore to tell Tony why Maria hasn't come yet. When she gets to the store, Doc isn't there, but the Jets are and they refuse to believe that Bernardo's girlfriend would help Tony. To the music of the Mambo from the dance at the gym, they throw her around savagely and almost rape her, but are interrupted by Doc, who is horrified by what he sees. The Jets have taken the sexually charged music of the Puerto Ricans and twisted it, turning it into an accompaniment for rape. In her anger and humiliation, Anita tells Doc that Chino has killed Maria. When Tony hears this he runs into the street, screaming for Chino to kill him, too. He can't live without Maria.

The Music Dies

At the moment Tony sees Maria across the playground and sees that she's actually alive, Chino also sees Tony and shoots him in the back. As Maria sobs over the dying body of Tony, another dramatic problem appears. How can the show's creators possibly express the inconsolable rage and despair that Maria feels? Arthur Laurents wrote a monologue for her with the intent that it be rewritten as a song, but after several failed attempts, Bernstein and Sondheim decided to leave the moment as spoken word. Why couldn't it work as a song? The rule of musicals is that when emotion gets too big for spoken word, that's the moment to break into song, because music can convey emotion better than words. Yet here is an instance in which some of the most brilliant minds ever to write for the musical theatre could not musicalize this moment of extreme emotion. Many writers have found it difficult to musicalize anger, but it was done two other times in *West Side Story*—in the "Tonight" quintet and in "A Boy Like That." Anger has been effectively expressed through music in other shows, including *Chess*, *Into the Woods*, *Les Misérables*, *Chicago*, and most notably, *Assassins*. It's interesting that Bernstein, Sondheim, Laurents, and Jerome Robbins couldn't figure out how to make it work. Perhaps the problem lies in the fact that Maria is dead inside; she can't sing because Tony was her music. She didn't sing until she met Tony and now he's dead. Similarly in *Carousel*, Julie can't sing after Billy's death until she feels his presence again at the end of the show; he is her music. Certainly, Maria's monologue works as it stands now, but it would be fascinating to see Bernstein and Sondheim's failed attempts.

As Tony dies, Maria begins to sing "Somewhere." Weakly, Tony joins her, but after only a few words, he dies. She sings one more word alone, but she can't finish it; the orchestra has to finish it for her. The Jets begin to advance on Chino but Maria leaps up and stops them and delivers an impassioned speech. *They* killed Tony, as well as Riff and Bernardo, with their hatred and prejudice; but we, the audience, are implicated as well. It is society that killed these kids. What kind of a world have we made in which teenagers carry guns and knives, in which they are taught by the adults around them to hate others? It is the world we live in today, even more than in 1957 Today, the weapons they carry are far more deadly, the death toll is higher, and prejudice is stronger. Maria is accusing us just as much, if not more, than the Jets and Sharks.

In the final moments of the show, Maria leans over Tony, tells him she loves him, and kisses him. Music begins; it is "I Have a Love" in the higher register over "Somewhere" below it, the two motifs that have defined both Maria and her relationship with Tony, which is now gone. But this time, the tone in the lowest instruments is not the same as it was in earlier instances. This time, that lowest tone is a tritone away from the root of the chord. The tritone is back, tainting the love motifs, making them ugly, just as the violence has tainted Maria and Tony's love. We are left with this unresolved dissonance in our ears. The problem is not resolved, the violence is not over, and love cannot triumph.

Proceed with Caution

The drama and power of *West Side Story* lies as firmly in the choreography as in the words and music. Though Bernstein's music, Sondheim's lyrics, and Laurents' dialogue are laid out carefully for anyone producing the show, Jerome Robbins' choreography is not. This is not a show that can be choreographed like *Bye Bye Birdie* or *Nunsense*. The story, the relationships, the conflict, and the subtext of the piece—hatred, destiny, death—must be expressed through the dance. The gangs must look graceful but also masculine, tough, and above all, dangerous. If the danger of these city streets is not established in the Prologue, the rest of the story loses much of its tension. It's important to find a choreographer with both ballet and jazz training, who won't be thrown by the complex rhythms and shifting meter of the score.

The creators of the show learned several valuable lessons with the original production that we can all profit from. First, they realized early on that they had to cast dancers who could act well and sing adequately. Singing was the last of the three priorities, except for Tony and Maria. Bernstein believed that using trained singers (even for Tony and Maria) would destroy the quality of youth and innocence that is so important to the piece. The songs must have a rough, gritty, realistic quality to them, exactly the opposite of a Rodgers and Hammerstein show. Certainly the actors have to be competent enough musically to handle the quintet and the other more demanding numbers, but Bernstein was adamant about not having trained voices.

Also, the gangs have to project genuine hatred toward each other and unflinching loyalty within them. Robbins wouldn't let the original Jets and Sharks eat lunch together during the rehearsal process. He forced them to form two competing camps, an attitude that was projected into their acting. He posted articles on the call board about gang violence, murders, and other news of urban brutality to remind the cast how very real the story is. It's important that the cast never forget that *West Side Story* is not set in some Never Never Land where star-crossed lovers meet; it's about the here and now. There are dozens of documentaries on videotape about urban violence that can make the show real to the actors.

Other Resources

The *West Side Story* libretto has been published in a volume with *Romeo and Juliet*. Both vocal selections and the full piano score have also been published. The original Broadway cast album is available, as well as the London cast, the film cast, and a studio recording Leonard Bernstein made in 1985 with opera singers. This last recording is the only full recording of the instrumental pieces, and they are played brilliantly. But the vocal numbers are less satisfying, due to the thick Hispanic accent of José Carreras who plays Tony, and the technically sound but bloodless singing of Maria by Kiri Te Kanawa. The other leads are strong, and though the recording is musically impressive, Bernstein made the mistake he so carefully avoided in 1957—casting trained singers instead of actors, and many of them much older than their roles—so it never achieves the fiery passion and youthful intensity of the original cast album. One of the songs cut from the show, "Like Everybody Else," was recorded by the Varèse Sarabande label for the first of its *Lost in Boston* albums, a wonderful series of albums containing songs cut from Broadway musicals.

There is a videotape called *The Best of Broadway Musicals* available, which includes Larry Kert and Carol Lawrence, of the original Broadway cast, performing the Balcony Scene on the Ed Sullivan Show. The film version of the show is also on videotape, and though it includes much of Jerome Robbins' original choreography, it's also terribly dated (made in 1961). It tampers with the material more than it should have, and the heightened realism of the dialogue and the dance often seems silly in the very realistic medium of film. PBS broadcast a documentary on the making of the 1985 recording, which offers lots of insights into how Bernstein intended his music to be performed. This has been released commercially on videotape.

Music Theatre International also offers a study guide on *West Side Story*, designed to help teachers integrate the show's issues into their curriculum. It's an excellent guide for the cast and production staff as well, with background on the show and its creators, and of particular value with this show, discussion of the social issues addressed.

Exit Music

If you followed the analyses in the preceding chapters, you should be able to use those same methods in analyzing other shows. Remember that theatre is art and is, by its nature, a subjective thing. No two people will have the same emotional response to a show. No two people will interpret a show the same way and that is part of what makes theatre so exciting. There really are no right or wrong answers. This book has referred to several productions in which the director's choices were very different from the shows' original productions—don't be afraid to do the same thing. That's what keeps the art form alive.

There is great debate these days about where a director's interpretation begins and the written word takes over. Some people believe a director should re-create as faithfully as possible the original production, which, they argue, most clearly represents what the show's creators intended. Others (myself among them) argue that what spoke to an audience in 1970 may not speak to an audience the same way in 1996, and to get the same message across, to elicit the same response, may require a wholly different approach. But how different can that approach be before it encroaches on the authors' territory? Everyone disagrees.

It's now acceptable to practice colorblind casting, but some people believe that it can change the basic nature of a show. If you're directing *Hello, Dolly!* and you cast an African American woman as Dolly Levi, does that change the show? Some people may have a problem with the logical questions such casting presents. In other words, could an African American woman own her own business and eat at the Harmonia Gardens in New York in 1897? Does that change the way we react to the show? Then again, African American audiences may find an African American Dolly lets them relate to the show more easily, perhaps for the first time. As slanted toward caucasian audiences as the musical theatre often is, African American audiences may enjoy finding themselves represented onstage, and therefore lose the outsider status they may feel at other musicals. Whether the changes are positive or negative, colorblind casting does indeed change an audience's perception of a show, sometimes in profound ways, sometimes only in very subtle ways.

There is a movement now to take nontraditional casting further, to practice gender-blind and sexuality-blind casting. Companies have cast a woman in the role of Jesus in *Godspell*, or in smaller roles like Uncle Arvide in *Guys and Dolls*, where gender has no bearing on the plot. As I write this, licensing agents are still not comfortable with this practice, but I would argue that it shouldn't be any more or less acceptable than colorblind casting. Some companies are going so far as to change the sexual orientation of characters, changing one or all of the couples in *Company* into gay and lesbian couples, making the romantic leads in *Anything Goes* into two gay men. Again, if the basic characteristics and personalities of the characters are not changed, and if the plot and dialogue are not changed (aside from the obvious pronoun corrections), is this going too far? Right now, the legal answer is yes. But many directors would argue otherwise.

So where do we draw the line between implementing a director's interpretation and rewriting material? Right now, that's a judgment call. The only advice I can give is try very hard to understand the creators' intentions—what they meant to say and how they meant to say it. If you feel you're tampering with those basic ideas, you're probably going too far. If you feel you're supporting those ideas, I would argue you're doing your job as a director. Your direction is an important part of the finished whole. As a director, you are (and should be) collaborating with Rodgers and Hammerstein, Kander and Ebb, or Stephen Sondheim. Their work is not theatre while it's still on paper; you, your actors, and designers bring it to life.

Licensing agents are there to protect writers and composers. They have to be conservative when it comes to nebulous issues like these. There's a reason they ask us to sign agreements in which we promise not to change music, lyrics, or dialogue. Writers need to know their work is being respected. But at the same time, we must always be aware that our role as artists is to be daring, to test limits, to risk making mistakes. New ideas are never discovered while following the rules. Once in a while, we need to jump off the proverbial cliff and see if we can fly.